ARISTOTLE:

ON INTERPRETATION

Commentary by
St. Thomas and Cajetan

(Peri Hermeneias)

MEDIAEVAL PHILOSOPHICAL TEXTS IN TRANSLATION

NO. 11

Marquette University Press

[iv]

ARISTOTLE:

ON INTERPRETATION

Commentary by St. Thomas and Cajetan

(Peri Hermeneias)

Translated from the Latin
With an Introduction

By

Jean T. Oesterle

MARQUETTE UNIVERSITY PRESS   MILWAUKEE, WISCONSIN

To the Memory
of My Father and Mother

CONTENTS

[ix]

FOREWORD

In the course of its development, symbolic logic has regularly been contrasted to the "traditional" logic which has come down to us through the past from the time of Aristotle; and very often the result of the comparison has been to attribute doctrines to that "traditional" logic that do not belong to it—at least to the Aristotelian part—while at the same time denying other doctrines that in point of fact have been explicitly discussed (sometimes very elaborately) by the principal logicians of the Aristotelian-medieval tradition. Consequently, it would seem beneficial for the health of the science to have some of the principal treatises of the better medieval logicians made available. And because Latin is no longer a common language, works originally done in that language must be translated.

As the title page indicates, the present publication is a translation of St. Thomas' Commentary (completed by Cajetan) on Aristotle's *Peri Hermeneias* (*De interpretatione*), which I think will be of considerable interest to modern logicians, especially those who have come to realize that there are limitations to the usefulness of symbolic representations.

This translation should also prove useful to those logicians whose convictions have never allowed them to recognize the modern symbolic apparatus as being of much benefit in ordinary philosophic considerations, but who have, perhaps subconsciously, become attached to secondary logical works that do not reflect the best efforts of the Peripatetic school. For these people Jean Oesterle's translation should prove to be a fine instrument for a more penetrating grasp of the logic of propositions.

It is also important to note, I think, that this new text contains a rendering of Aristotle's original work which corresponds in its terminology to the medieval commentary of St. Thomas. This statement should not be construed to mean, however, that Aristotle has been dealt with in an arbitrary and highhanded fashion; on the contrary, Mrs. Oesterle has been at pains to justify her rendering of Aristotle independently of the commentary so as not to distort the original meaning.

Finally, it is perhaps not unimportant to mention that by this work St. Thomas is introduced to a scientifically minded audience, on natural, scientific grounds, which should help to destroy the myth that he was interested only in theological matters, all of which were decided by appeals to authority. For this purpose, probably no one of his other writings is better proportioned to the modern disposition than a book in formal logic on propositions and their relations. Therefore, it is a great pleasure for me to have assisted in a small way in the production of Mrs. Oesterle's translation. I wish to congratulate her on what I think is a very fine piece of work.

Milwaukee, Wisconsin
November 9, 1961

Richard J. Connell

PREFACE

I owe a special debt of gratitude for assistance and encouragement in the preparation of this translation to Professor Charles De Koninck of Laval University, Quebec, Canada; and to my husband who, in using a part of it in a graduate course at Notre Dame University, discovered that its completion would contribute to knowledge of the thought of Aristotle and St. Thomas. Special acknowledgment must also be made to Professor Richard Connell of Marquette University for his painstaking examination of the manuscript and his many helpful suggestions; and to Fr. Henri DuLac, Chairman of the Department of Philosophy at the College of St. Thomas, St. Paul, Minnesota, whose doctoral dissertation "On the Modal Proposition" was very helpful in relation to Cajetan's Commentary on that subject.

South Bend, Indiana   *Jean T. Oesterle*
January, 1961

Translator's Introduction

THE TEXT OF ARISTOTLE

Aristotle's most fruitful work began about the forty-ninth year of his life (335 B.C.) when he founded his school in Athens, and lasted until he withdrew to Chalcis in 323 B.C. His departure to the seclusion of Chalcis was generated by a charge of impiety apparently brought about by a mixture of political feeling and doctrinal hostility. It goes without saying that Aristotle has undoubtedly contributed more than anyone else to the science of logic. Certainly he had no predecessors in this field and there was not much by way of additional original contribution until centuries later. His logical works, which have been known since at least the sixth century as the *Organon*, or tool, comprise eight treatises, if one includes the *Rhetoric* and the *Poetics*: the *Categories*, the *Peri Hermeneias* (*On the Enunciation*),[1] *Prior Analytics*, *Posterior Analytics*, *Topics*, and *On Sophistical Refutations*. It will be noted in this doctrinal, i.e., scientific, ordering of the logical works, that the *Peri Hermeneias* is second, but it seems to be later in date than at least three of the other logical treatises since he mentions these in this work: *On Sophistical Refutations* (at 17a 36), *Prior Analytics* (at 19b 31), and the *Topics* (at 20b 26). In fact, Father J. Isaac in his work on the *Peri Hermeneias*[2] thinks that it may even have been a last work. His argument is that the reference to the *Prior Analytics,* which presupposes the doctrine elaborated in the *Posterior Analytics* on the demonstrations of definitions also establishes the *Peri Hermeneias* as later than the *Posterior Analytics*. In addition, the elaborate doctrine on enunciations about future contingent events in Chapter 9 and on the consequents of modals in Chapter 13, and the absence of any reference to the *Peri Hermeneias* in any other work of Aristotle may indicate that it was composed at the end of his life.

---

[1] *Peri Hermeneias* means literally, "On Interpretation" or "Explanation," but these English equivalents do not quite convey what Aristotle's treatise is about. The *Greek–English Lexicon* by Henry George Liddell and Robert Scott, (rev. ed.; Oxford: The Clarendon Press, 1953) adds to the meanings of "interpretation" or "explanation," "especially of thoughts by words." Consequently, *Peri Hermeneias* might be better translated "On the Enunciation," as St. Thomas also concludes in his Commentary (Introduction, n. 3). This latter translation might be more accurate since the principle subject of the t r e a t i s e is the enunciation, i.e., speech which not only signifies something per se, as Boethius says, but which is either true or false; hence the definition of the enunciation as "speech in which there is truth or falsity." Cf. page 7, n. γ of the Leonine edition for a discussion about ancient and modern opinions about the title of this work.

[2] J. Isaac, O.P., *Le Peri Hermeneias en Occident de Boèce a Saint Thomas* (Paris: Librarie Philosophique J. Vrin, 1953).

There has been no serious question as to the authenticity of the *Peri Hermeneias*. Andronicus (early first century, B.C.) suspected its genuineness because of a reference to the *De Anima* to which he found nothing which corresponded in that treatise. Aristotle makes this reference at 16a 8 and St. Thomas in his *Commentary* (Lesson II, n. 6) answers Andronicus' objection, making reference to Book I of *De Anima*. Professor W. D. Ross, on the other hand, in his book *Aristotle*,[3] suggests that the reference at 16a 8 should be transferred to 16a 13, and relates it to *De Anima*, Book III, Chapter 6, following H. Maier, who wrote a defense of this work.[4]

There is, in fact, both external and internal evidence supporting the authenticity of the *Peri Hermeneias*. For example, Theophrastus, a fellow-academician of Aristotle's, and Aristotle's friend Eudemus, both wrote books that apparently presuppose it. Ammonius Hermiae (fifth century, A.D.), who wrote a commentary on the *Peri Hermeneias* and who doubted the genuineness of its last chapter (from 23a 27 on), mentions that Andronicus was the only critic of its genuineness as a whole. As to internal evidence, the style and grammar, though less dialectical and more didactic than in his treatises on other subjects, is typical of Aristotle's logical works. This difference can perhaps be ascribed to the fact that Aristotle was the first to write on logic and hence had no predecessors to take into account.

The Oxford edition of the Greek text, edited by L. Minio-Paluello, Praelector of Mediaeval Philosophy at Oxford, (Oxford: The University Press, 1949) has been used for the translation of Aristotle's work. Reference can be made to the Preface of that edition (p. xiv) for the codices and ancient translations used for the preparation of the Greek text, and to page 48 for the identification of the symbols used to refer to them.

II.   THE COMMENTARY OF ST. THOMAS

St. Thomas, who lived barely forty-nine years (1225?-1274) and who besides many other writings commented on twelve works of Aristotle between the years 1260 and 1273, wrote the present commentary, which is dedicated to the Provost of Louvain, between 1269 and 1272. While much learned work and research has been done to try and establish the exact dates of his commentaries by such men as Grabmann, Mandonnet, and Walz, to mention only a few, no certain and definitive conclusions have been reached.[5] It is known, however, that during the time

---

[3] W. D. Ross, *Aristotle* (New York: Meridian Book, Inc., 1959), p. 292.
[4] In *Archiv für Geschichte der Philosophie*, XIII, 23-71.
[5] For the chronology and authenticity of the works of St. Thomas, cf. P. Mandonnet, *Des écrits authentiques de s. Thomas* (2d ed., Fribourg: Imprimerie de l'oeuvre de Saint-Paul, 1910); M. Grabmann, *Die*

of the writing of this commentary he also wrote the commentaries *On the Ethics, On the Meterology* (up to Book II, Lesson 10), *On the Posterior Analytics,* the only other logical work he commented on, *On the Politics* (up to Book III, Lesson 6), and perhaps had begun the commentaries *On the Heaven and the Earth* and *On Generation and Corruption.* In addition, he wrote on many theological subjects. It is interesting to note that St. Thomas began writing his commentaries on Aristotle's works after attending a general chapter of his Order in 1259 where along with St. Albert the Great among others, he helped to organize the curriculum of studies for Dominican schools. Perhaps his experience of teaching theology had made evident its need of philosophy.

There appears to be no doubt at all about the authenticity of St. Thomas' *Commentary.* The official catalogues of his works, particularly the one by Reginald of Piperno who was St. Thomas' assistant and secretary from 1259 until his death in 1274, all list the *Commentary on the Peri Hermeneias.*

However, St. Thomas did not write a commentary on the entire work, although it seems to have been his intention to finish it. That intention is evident in the first two lessons of the second book where he states the ordering of the remainder of the text of Aristotle and in no way indicates that he does not intend to go on with his exposition of it. There seem to be differing opinions as to the reason for its being unfinished. The Piana editors (edition of St. Pius V) said that it was because of his death. This well may be the most accurate theory since this commentary was among the last writings of St. Thomas. Another view held that it was not completed because he was either too much occupied with other things or that the Provost for whom he wrote it, being a young but wise student, intended to spend more time on study before asking more of St. Thomas.

The Leonine edition of the *Commentary* has been used for the translation of this work. It is based largely on the Piana edition with the variants in texts noted. In the Preface of the Leonine edition will be found the codices and editions from which it was prepared together with their identifying symbols.

III.   THE COMMENTARY OF CARDINAL CAJETAN
Soon after the death of St. Thomas—in fact, before the end of the thirteenth century—his work on the *Peri Hermeneias* was completed by

Werke des hl. Thomas von Aquin, Beiträge, zur Geschichte der Philosophie und Theologie des Mittelalters XXII, No. 1-2 (Münster: Aschendorff, 1931); A. Walz, "Saint Thomas d'Aquin, Écrits," in *Dictionaire de théologie Catholique,* XV, No. 1, (Paris: Letouzey et Ané, 1926), 635-41; M. D. Chenu, *Introduction a l'étude de saint Thomas d'Aquin,* XI (Montreal: Institut l'Étude Médiévaux, 1950).

others, and later copies of the work usually had such a supplement. All of these were made by Dominicans or were extracts from their own commentaries. The statement made in the Venetian edition of 1496 testifies to this: "Many of the most renowned doctors of the same Order have furnished a supplement, i.e., have completed what was lacking in St. Thomas' *Commentary*."[6]

The best known of these supplements is that of Cajetan (1469-1534) which was explicitly composed with the intention of completing St. Thomas' work. Cajetan finished it in 1496 and it appeared the same year in the third Venetian edition. It was published so repeatedly after this along with the commentary of St. Thomas that it has become inseparable from it.

The text of Cajetan's commentary as it appears in the Leonine edition has been used for this translation. It is not a critical edition of his work (nor is one available at the present time). Hence, no corrections have been made nor have variants in texts been noted by the Leonine editors, but obvious difficulties with the text have been noted by the translator.

IV.   THE SIGNIFICANCE OF THE DOCTRINE

The comment often made about the *Peri Hermeneias* is that it is somewhat elementary, treating as it does such simple things as names, verbs, speech, (i.e., the verbal explicitation of reason) and the enunciation. It is indeed true that in contrast to the *Categories*, the mode of exposition in the *Peri Hermeneias* is both more elementary and elaborate. It is elementary in the sense that it is confined to the essentials of the enunciation, also called the proposition; its elaboration is made manifest in the extensive analysis of the parts of the enunciation and the enunciation itself. It should be noted in this connection that Aristotle does not expressly treat of syncategorematic terms—such as the quantifiers "all," "some," etc., and the connectives "or," "if," etc.—which in modern logic are taken to be the most basic. In fact, what Aristotle has to say about the essential parts of an enunciation, the name and the verb, most modern logicians would consider foreign to pure logic. But whatever may be said of Aristotle's development of logic, his definitions of such simple things are important for setting order in our thinking as expressed in ordinary language. Indeed, they are particularly relevant for grasping the difference between the words of common speech and the symbols of formal logic (which Albertus Magnus called *termini transcendentes*), mathematics, and theoretical physics, especially since

---

[6] The Preface of the Leonine edition can be consulted for a more detailed account of these supplements; also, Isaac, *op. cit.*, pp. 86, 111-12.

little attempt has been made in modern times to consider these elementary and basic matters carefully.

Hermann Weyl, for instance, in an essay entitled "The Mathematical Way of Thinking," remarks: "The mathematical game is played in silence, without words, like a game of chess." He then significantly adds: "Only the rules have to be explained and communicated in words, and of course any arguing about the possibilities of the game, for instance about its consistency, goes on in the medium of words and appeals to evidence."[7] This passage, as well as his whole influential essay, raises an important question: Just what is the difference between a word and a symbol? It is with respect to an answer to such a question that the *Peri Hermeneias* remains an important work and one that has special interest for the modern reader. By means of it we can see that in the phrase, "the time t," for instance, the word "time" and the symbol t do not stand for the same thing nor in the same way. The symbol has an operational value which is not true of the word. And it may be worth noting, further, that the operational value in question is a mechanical one, which is the same as to say, in modern terminology, that it is utterly formal. By this we mean that although a symbol, such as t, cannot be taken out of context, one does not have to think of what the word "time" stands for to use the symbol t operationally.

An interesting point of difference between Aristotelian and modern logic that will be found in this treatise concerns the infinite name, e.g., non-man or non-tree. Aristotle states expressly that infinite names are not names, and the reason is that while they deny a given meaning, such as *man*, they do not impose a new meaning. Name and infinite name are in fact contradictories, excluding a middle. August de Morgan, on the other hand, in his *Formal Logic*, considers both as names. In doing so, he pointedly observes that he intends to draw no distinction between contrary and contradictory names.[8] Now this distinction can be overlooked in some instances. For example, the genus "color" can be divided into "white" and "nonwhite." The mode of signification can be interpreted here as one of contrariety, for we understand "nonwhite" of any other color. But the mode of signification could also be understood as an opposition of contradiction, since "nonwhite" can be said of what is not in the genus of color at all, such as an integer, a square root, and even of what in no sense can be. The point is that if "nonwhite," understood as a contradictory term, were a name, its interpretation should be a possible one, i.e., it would have a determinate

[7] *The World of Mathematics* (New York: Simon and Schuster, 1956) III, 1848.

[8] *Formal Logic or the Calculus of Inference, Necessary and Probable* (London: Taylor and Walton, 1847), p. 37.

[5]

meaning, but the fact is that it has an infinity of possible meanings and therefore no determinate meaning at all.

A modern reader will also note that in this treatise all enunciations are predicational. He may well wonder why Aristotle did not consider what are today called relational propositions, e.g., "Peter is taller than John." The fact, however, is that relational propositions are included in predicational propositions, for a closer inspection of such a proposition will reveal that "to be taller than" expresses a relation of inequality, and it is this relation that is being predicated.

It will also be noticed that Aristotle makes no case here for conditional enunciations, e.g., "If p, then q." St. Thomas suggests the reason for this in his exposition of the text, namely, that such an enunciation signifies something that is one by hypothesis and this, unless confirmed by the truth of the simple enunciation, will not fulfill the requirements for demonstrative science to which the whole of Aristotelian logic is ordered.

A point of special significance for both Aristotelian and modern logic is that of supposition, "supposition" being taken here as the verification of the term in a proposition in relation to the copula. It has been asserted that this doctrine is a scholastic invention, now happily fallen into oblivion, as H. W. B. Joseph says in his *Introduction to Logic*.[9] But this remark seems to ignore the import of Aristotle's words in 21a 25, where he says: "Homer is something, say, a poet. Is it therefore true to say also that Homer is, or not?" And he goes on to say: "The 'is' here is predicated accidentally of Homer, for it is predicated of him with regard to 'poet,' not in itself." What is meant here should be distinguished from what Aristotle intends in the *Sophistical Refutations* where he says (165a 5): "It is impossible in a discussion to bring in the actual things discussed; we use their names as signs instead of them." The passage from the *Peri Hermeneias* is about the name in relation to the verb in a proposition, which is exactly the point at issue in the mediaeval doctrine of supposition, whereas in the *Sophistical Refutations* he is talking about names taking the place of things, i.e., that every name stands for the thing named, which refers to signification. Supposition, then, is not a later invention, nor an unimportant one, since it shows why such a statement as "Homer exists" is false whereas "Homer is a poet" is true. For to signify with time is essential to the verb as distinguished from the name, as Aristotle points out in defining the verb, but in the case of supposition, time has a new relevance: "Homer exists" is false because "to exist" is in the present tense. That time is relevant to the verb as such

9 (Oxford: The Clarendon Press, 1946), p. 14, n. 2.

will appear irrelevant to some modern logicians. But again we must bear in mind what Aristotelian logic intends. It is not formal in the modern (and quite legitimate) sense of this term "formal"—not even in the *Prior Analytics,* for it too is about second intentions.

The expressions "first intention" and "second intention" are not in Aristotle's text, but they are in no way foreign to the intent of Aristotle. The expressions are simply a convenient way of distinguishing, for example, what the predicable genus "animal" is from what an animal is. We first observe that there are animals of different kinds and that "animal" can be said of them all, and that while a horse is an animal we do not say that an animal is a horse—rather that some animal is a horse. Nor do we say that "horse" is *this* one. And so we notice that our mind has related one thing to many in a special way. This is how we come to know in a reflexive way what a predicable genus is. What animal is—however vaguely known—is a first intention, but the particular type of relation our mind conceives as we predicate it of different kinds is a second intention.

When we know an animal, whether it be a man, a horse, or an elephant, we know by means of some similitude of the known in our mind. Such is the case of first intentions. But in conceiving a second intention there is no similitude between what we conceive—the relation of reason—and that apropos of which the mental relation was formed. We can draw something like a horse, but we can sketch nothing like a predicable species. In other words, there is no resemblance between what we conceive as a man, for instance, and the relation of reason we form about man as predicable of many individuals. There is, in this respect, an analogy between words and second intentions. The word "square," for instance, is not square, and the name "house" does not look like a house. But it is only an analogy, for second intentions are not arbitrary in signification, as words are, although a sophist can use second intentions arbitrarily.

Now the verb raises a problem of its own in this connection because of the time factor. What is time as a defining element of the verb in logic? What does the word "time" stand for in the definition? Real time, of course (and not just any kind of succession): time past, present, and future. Let us return to our example of supposition. "Homer is a poet" or "Homer no longer exists" are not statements about something logical, but they do have a logical structure: they comprise name and verb, subject and predicate; they are also instances of true enunciations. The reason why "Homer exists" is false is not a logical one; it is false because Homer is dead. Logic is not concerned with Homer, nor with his kind of existence or nonexistence. But the point is that when we do talk about him, expressing our mind on the subject, we do not simply

[7]

talk about *him,* we also express our mode of thinking about him, and to examine the order among the conceptions in our mind as we think and talk about him is the business of logic. Hence we observe in this particular case that if the name "Homer" is to stand for the historical person, and "to be" is a predicate, we cannot form a true enunciation without regard to the tense of the copula. This is a rule of logic. To imply, on the other hand, that time has nothing to do with verbs, that such a consideration is purely grammatical (since different languages have different tenses and some skip the copula) would mean that logic has nothing to do with these, and therefore that the copula itself is foreign to logic, since it too signifies with time. If this were true, the *Peri Hermeneias* would not be a logical treatise.

In this work Aristotle also takes up the question of enunciations about future contingent events, and this matter deserves extended comment. This is a recurrent problem in our time because the symbolic reconstruction of time is sometimes believed to be a substitute for the time we experience and express in ordinary language. The symbolic reconstruction of time in relativity theory, for instance, when interpreted as an adequate substitute for time as we name it, can only lead to determinism—a determinism of a baffling kind, since, from this point of view, time has no direction. Thus, according to this interpretation we would have to say not only that what happened later was entirely determined in what happened before, but also that what happened before was equally determined in what happened thereafter. The determinism of Laplace, often equated with the principle of causality, left no room for contingency, nor would the symbolic reconstruction of time as interpreted by some philosophers of science. If 'the principle of causality' so understood were true, a considerable part of the *Peri Hermeneias,* including the treatise on modal propositions, would be irrelevant. But if some measure of indeterminism (not necessarily of the kind called fortune or chance) is to be considered in physics, as in thermodynamics and quantum theory, it will require an importation foreign to this principle of causality, such as Aristotle's *potentia,* which is Heisenberg's expressly stated view, one not unlike that of Max Born. But this *potentia*[10] implies time as we know it before its symbolic reconstruction, which shows that 'time' is not quite the same as *t* after all.

There are two questions that arise regarding Aristotle's treatment of enunciations about future contingent events. First, why should he mention contingency at all in logic?[11] The purpose of logic, the order-

---

[10] Actually: δύναμις ἅμα τῆς ἀντιφασεώς. See *Metaphysics,* Θ, 8, 1050b 10.

[11] The prima facie explanation of this

apparent digression on contingency might be found in what seems to be a similar case. In *Physics* I, Aristotle points out that it is not for the

[8]

ing of second intentions, which are nothing outside of the mind, seems to rule out such a consideration; and again, as Aristotle himself says later on in the *Posterior Analytics,* there can be no science of the contingent; hence why consider enunciations about future contingent events? The second question concerns the adequacy of his treatment of such enunciations, for it seems to ignore what lies between what shall be or what shall not be, i.e., what might be.

Aristotle's discussion of contingency in the *Peri Hermeneias* brings out forcefully the idea that although the primary concern of his logic is to set order in our mind, it is nonetheless remotely based upon reality, and in the end is no more than a tool *(organon)* in the service of the other sciences. Now it should be pointed out first of all that contingency in one way or another enters into all of the logical works of Aristotle. Even prior to them—prior in a doctrinal sense—Porphyry's *Isagoge* introduces contingency in the definition of predicable accident —"that which can be present or absent without destroying the subject." In the *Categories,* accident means something quite different: that which is present in and is predicable of a subject; and while some such accidents are necessarily present in a subject, others can be present or absent, and in this respect they are also predicable accidents, e.g., to blush.

In the *Prior Analytics* (Book I, Chapter 13) contingency is discussed as affecting the form of the syllogism. It is here that Aristotle first points out the distinction between the possible as opposed to the impossible and the possible as opposed to the necessary. In the *Posterior Analytics* he shows that there can be demonstration only in necessary matter, excluding thereby the extreme cases of possibility opposed to the necessary, namely, fortune and chance. On the other hand, he notes that demonstration in necessary matter does not exclude natural probability, i.e., what happens for the most part. The *Topics* introduces a new type of contingency, i.e., one that in argumentation does not lead to a necessary conclusion. This possibility is the same as likelihood or verisimilitude, as distinguished from truth. In the *Rhetoric* the enthy-

---

natural scientist to argue against those (such as Parmenides a n d Melissus) who deny the very subject and principles of his science; he then proceeds, without explicit justification, to do so nonetheless. His discussion is actually logical and metaphysical, as he himself points out. Why then could one not say the same of his procedure in the *Peri Hermeneias?* Actually, the difference is a considerable one. In the *Physics* he proceeds as he does to relieve our minds, for if Parmenides were right, there could be no natural science. But in the *Peri Hermeneias,* the treatment of contingency is not a digression: it is intrinsically necessary to a certain division of propositions, namely, into those which are determinately true or determinately false and those which are neither.

meme persuades in contingent matters, largely from singulars, by an appeal to appetite. In the *Sophistical Refutations* Aristotle shows that it is the infinity of *ens per accidens* that is exploited by the sophist, such exploitation being rooted in his own desires. Finally, in the *Poetics*, contingency is shown to be necessary for tragedy.

We must now bring out the proper reason why contingency is discussed in the present work, and how it shows that logic, as Aristotle conceived it, is necessarily, though only remotely, based upon reality. We have already pointed out the time factor in the definition of the verb. But time appears in a new guise in the discussion of enunciations about the future. If a statement such as "Socrates will be in the forum tonight" is true, it implies that it is impossible for him not to be there tonight. But common experience tells us that though this may be his firm resolve, he may not get there after all, for any number of reasons, e.g., his wife, lack of transportation, being dissuaded by friends, threatened by enemies, etc. Now if it is true that such a statement cannot be determinately true, it means that we are here faced with a possibility to be *and* not to be: Socrates now at home, or on his way to the forum, *can* reach the forum *and* not reach it. The fact of being at home, or on his way, coincides exactly, in time, with ability to be in the forum thereafter.

The foregoing is an instance of what Aristotle calls "simultaneous potency of contradiction." Potency, so understood, implies temporal succession, yet a temporal succession of a special kind. Even while at home, Socrates' remaining there for as long as he does implies time, but not quite the time this kind of potency demands. If he could not possibly leave home, time would go on all the same, but there would, for that time, be no simultaneous potency of contradiction. Where there is no such potency, every proposition will be either determinately true or determinately false. Now there is no such potency in the past, i.e., what has been can no longer not have been; and what is present cannot fail to be present so long as it *is* present. Any proposition stating where Socrates was or is now will be either determinately true or determinately false. Let us notice that all this is explained by merely pointing out particular instances which are familiar enough. All of which goes to show that the division between propositions about past and present, and propositions about non-necessary future things or events cannot be made without reference to the uncertain temporal succession that simultaneous potency of contradiction implies—whether this potency be active, as Socrates' will and resolve to leave his home or not to leave it, or passive, as when he is prevented from leaving his home. We must note, then, that the time factor in the definition of the verb does not take care of the time factor as it appears in propositions about future contingents.

Now if there is this kind of potency in the real world, in the world of first intentions, does this entail that we will find its counterpart in logic as well? The matter is not that simple. The potency we have been talking about is real. But we have also been talking about the way we talk about it, and this reflects our way of thinking. All we aim to do in logic is to set order in our thinking, and one way of achieving it at this juncture is to notice in an explicit way that not all propositions are either determinately true or determinately false; if they were, this would assume, contrary to common experience, that everything is or occurs of necessity.

Further, it may be opportune to recall Aristotle's warning that when we use the word *dynamis*—possible or potency—apropos of mathematical subjects, it stands as a metaphor, which simply means that it is applied, without change or extension of meaning, to something that the word does not properly signify. His specific example is geometry;[12] but the same will be true of logic where some conversions, for instance, are "possible" and others not. The "power" of a number or the very name "predicable" are instances of possibility or potency taken as a metaphor. The reason is that the denomination is taken from something extrinsic to that of which the word "potency" is said. A number, for instance, has a power because of what our mind can do with it operationally; the potency of a predicable genus will be greater than that of a species because of its wider predicability—predication being an act of the mind. But even an apt metaphor requires some foundation. In the present case, the basis is none other than reason itself as applied to numbers or second intentions, but which are not the power that reason is.

By way of fully answering the question as to why Aristotle considers contingency in logic, then, we should say first of all that his purpose in considering contingency in the *Peri Hermeneias* as well as in the rest of the *Organon* is, of course, strictly logical. But a logic of second intentions cannot treat of these *in vacuo;* there must always be some reference to first intentions, as was clear from the outset in the *Categories,* which points to instances in nature or in mathematics. Hence in the *Peri Hermeneias,* Aristotle cannot establish or analyze the special type of proposition which is neither determinately true nor determinately false without reference to the extra-logical. Or to put the matter in another way, if there were no contingency in human actions or in nature, the question of propositions that are neither determinately true nor determinately false would never arise.

It should perhaps also be pointed out that the whole question of modal propositions, which is taken up later in this work, would have to be ruled out of logic if we prescinded from contingency, for we mani-

12 *Metaph.* Δ, 12, 1019b 34.

fest necessity by opposing it to contingency and vice versa; otherwise contingency would be opposed only to the impossible and therefore might be reducible to the necessary since the necessary is not impossible, else it would not be.

With respect to the adequacy of Aristotle's treatment of propositions about future contingent events in view of a possible middle ground between what will be or will not be (the second question we raised above), we should point out that from the viewpoint of the opposition of contradiction there is no intermediary: there is going to be a naval battle tomorrow or there is not going to be; hence, someone who reasons in such a way as to think the event is *likely* would have to make a distinction in his own mind if he is to be in conformity with reality, i.e., if his knowledge is to be true. For while he may have every reason to believe that it is likely that there will be a naval battle, and in this he may be quite right, he must know that it is only likely; and whether likely or not, there will in fact be or not be a naval battle tomorrow.

The distinctive way in which contingency is treated in a logical context, namely, that it is a consideration of second intentions as relative to first, can be pointed up by considering the treatment of contingency in other works of Aristotle. In the *Physics*, for example, he is concerned with the ancient philosophical opinions that the whole universe was formed by chance (Democritus) and that even all the natural species are originally the work of chance mutations (Empedocles), which is another way of saying that contingent causality lies at the root of all things. Aristotle approaches this problem in an entirely different way. He begins by *analyzing* fortune, the extreme kind of contingency, which is well known because it occurs in human action, although his aim is to manifest chance in nature, more obscure to us, and recognizable only in familiar living things. In contrast to this, in the *Peri Hermeneias* he merely mentions our deliberation as a principle of future events by way of manifesting the fact of contingency.

In *On the Heavens* (Book II, Chapter 12) he shows that whatever can cease to exist will at sometime actually cease to be (a conclusion that becomes a basic proposition in the *Tertia Via* of St. Thomas). This contingency is quite different from the kind treated in the *Physics*; it is not opposed to the necessary in the way chance and fortune are, as can be seen in *On Generation and Corruption* (Book II, Chapter 11).

In the *Ethics*, which deals with human actions, contingency is treated in still a different way. Contingency is the very reason why it is so difficult to reach the proper principles of moral science, all of which are uncertain when it comes to applying them here and now—whereas the general principles hold in all circumstances, e.g., good must be done and evil avoided.

[12]

In the *Metaphysics,* as in the *Posterior Analytics,* Aristotle treats accidental being only in order to exclude it (except as to what it is in general) from the subject of science. In this connection he shows in the *Metaphysics* that the true and the accidental (in the sense of contingent) are comparable: both are extrinsic to what is primarily called "being," namely, to what is per se and outside the mind. The consideration of being as true is logical. The *Posterior Analytics* showed that there can be no necessary discourse about any particular contingent thing or event, whereas there can be true statements about these, e.g., "Socrates is walking." But the subject of *Metaphysics* is "being," and "being" is divided into necessary and contingent. It seems, therefore, that this science should treat of the contingent as well as of the necessary. Actually, although metaphysics does define what the contingent is and what its cause is, being a science, it cannot extend to what is purely accidental, as was shown in the *Posterior Analytics.* But the *Metaphysics* makes the same point. Is this process not circular? It would be if we divorced the logical entirely from the real—second intentions from first intentions. The logician shows that there is contingency on the basis of common experience, but he is not concerned to analyze the nature of contingency; the metaphysician proves that not everything that happens in the world has a per se cause, and that a sufficient cause, once posited, does not necessarily entail its effect. Both the logician and the metaphysician start from common knowledge, but the one examines the logical conditions of demonstration whereas the other examines directly the very nature of real contingency, to show in a distinct and definitive way the reason why there can be no science of the contingent.

We have dwelt at some length on the role of time and contingency because it is so basic to a large part of the *Peri Hermeneias* and needs to be particularly stressed nowadays for three reasons: (a) traditional logic takes it all too much for granted; (b) it provides a fine occasion to point out, in a particular instance, how Aristotelian logic is founded, however remotely, on reality without presupposing any distinct knowledge of the subjects of other sciences, and (c) how it differs from without replacing purely symbolic logic.

What has just been said conveys that we would distinguish between Aristotelian and so-called traditional logic. Indeed, the difference between these two is perhaps greater than that which can be seen between the *Organon* and logic in the modern sense. For traditional logic, at least as it is usually taught, presupposes distinctly articulated knowledge of reality and, as formulated in textbooks, is seen to be in the end utterly dependent upon metaphysics,[13] which entails that to be under-

---

[13] The logical treatises of the late fif-
teenth, sixteenth, and seventeenth centuries contain far more metaphysics than logic.

stood logic should be the last course in philosophy—a position which St. Thomas declares absurd.[14] Aristotle's logic, on the other hand, requires no such distinct knowledge of real things. All we need to start with is things as commonly named and nominally defined. In fact, if we do not begin in this way the student will never see that in the first operation of the intellect, for instance, to go from "man" to "rational animal" is to go from confused to more distinct knowledge,[15] or to put it another way, from what is known to what was unknown apropos of the same thing. Because it supposes no more than a common confused knowledge, logic, however difficult it may be[16] since it is about second intentions, can and

[14] "And because it is not easy for a man to grasp two things at once, for when he attends to two things he can grasp neither, it is absurd that a man should seek simultaneously to acquire scientific knowledge and the method which belongs to this science. This is the reason one must learn logic before the other sciences, for logic provides the common method of procedure in all the other sciences. But the method proper to any given science must be taught at the beginning of that science." *In II Metaph.* lect. 5, (Cathala edit.) n. 335.

[15] On this score even the more outstanding late Scholastics are more Cartesian than Aristotelian for they believed that whatever we understand first is distinctly and infallibly grasped once and for all. If such were indeed the case, divisions and definitions would not display new knowledge. How, then, could we account for the necessity of these? Such a position is patently contrary to experience and to what Aristotle records in the *Physics* (Book I, Chapter 1, 184b 10): "For names signify a kind of whole indistinctly, such as 'circle'; whereas the definition analyzes this into its [defining] parts." Seeing that a definition is in itself neither true nor false, such a passage from *definiendum* to *definitum* occurs within the first operation of the mind (*Metaph. θ*, 10, 1051b 18 ff.). In fact, St. Thomas calls this going from one to another a composition (*Summa Theologiae* I, q. 85, a. 6), a discourse (*Scripta super libros Sententiarum* III, d. 35, q. 2, a. 2, sol. 1), and a reasoning process (*In Joannem*, Chapter 1, Lesson 1, [Marietta] n. 26). A complete Aristotelian logic should therefore include—as Boethius held—special treatises which, after a treatise on the predicables and one on the categories, aim to set further order within the very first operation of the mind—a section on division and one on definition. The decadence of late Scholasticism can be traced to this failure: confused knowledge is taken for distinct because of its certitude and, consequently, the relevance and sufficiency of confused knowledge for logic is not realized. Little wonder, then, that logic should eventually degenerate into a pseudo-metaphysics.

[16] Although on the one hand purely symbolic logic, sometimes called logistics, can be taught to the young like arithmetic—understood as an art of computation—Aristotelian logic, on the other hand, is extremely difficult. This logic, then, is somewhat anomalous, for it must be taught first, after computation, and has at the same time *maxima difficultas*, as St. Thomas observes: ". . . In learning we start from what is easier, unless necessity requires otherwise. For sometimes, in learning, it is necessary to begin, not with

should nevertheless be the first course in philosophy and taught prefer-
ably to freshmen, for the development of reasoned knowledge about
reality depends upon the student's possession of logical processes of
thought.

what is easier, but with the knowledge upon which further knowledge
depends. This is the reason in learning that we must begin with logic,
not because it is easier than the
other sciences, for it has the greatest
difficulty seeing that it is about
things secondarily understood, but
rather because the other sciences
depend upon it inasmuch as logic
teaches the method of procedure in
all the other sciences. Hence we
must first know the method of a
science before the science itself, as
is said in *Metaph.* II" (995a 12-14).
*Exposito super librum Boethii De
Trinitate* q. 6, a. 1, ad 2 am q., ad 3.

[15]

BOOK I
Introduction

1.   There is a twofold operation of the intellect, as the Philosopher says in III *De anima*.[1] One is the understanding of simple objects, that is, the operation by which the intellect apprehends just the essence of a thing alone; the other is the operation of composing and dividing. There is also a third operation, that of reasoning, by which reason proceeds from what is known to the investigation of things that are unknown. The first of these operations is ordered to the second, for there cannot be composition and division unless things have already been apprehended simply. The second, in turn, is ordered to the third, for clearly we must proceed from some known truth to which the intellect assents in order to have certitude about something not yet known.

2.   Since logic is called rational science it must direct its consideration to the things that belong to the three operations of reason we have mentioned. Accordingly, Aristotle treats those belonging to the first operation of the intellect, i.e., those conceived by simple understanding, in the book *Praedicamentorum;* those belonging to the second operation, i.e., affirmative and negative enunciation, in the book *Perihermeneias;* those belonging to the third operation in the book *Priorum* and the books following it in which he treats the syllogism absolutely, the different kinds of syllogism, and the species of argumentation by which reason proceeds from one thing to another. And since the three operations of reason are ordered to each other so are the books: the *Praedicamenta* to the *Perihermeneias* and the *Perihermeneias* to the *Priora* and the books following it.

3.   The one we are now examining is named *Perihermeneias*, that is, *On Interpretation*. Interpretation, according to Boethius, is *significant vocal sound—whether complex or incomplex—which signifies something by itself.* Conjunctions, then, and prepositions and other words of this kind are not called interpretations since they do not signify anything by themselves. Nor can sounds signifying naturally but not from purpose or in connection with a mental image of signifying something[2]—such as the sounds of brute animals—be called interpretations, for one who interprets intends to explain something. Therefore only names and verbs and speech are called interpretations and these Aristotle treats in this book.

---

[1] *De Anima* III, 6, 430a 26 ff.
[2] "In connection with the mental image of signifying something," see

ibid., II, 8, 420b 30-34; St. Thomas, Lesson XVII, n. 477; also, *Summa Theologiae* I, q. 34, a. 1.

The name and verb, however, seem to be principles of interpretation rather than interpretations, for one who interprets seems to explain something as either true or false. Therefore, only enunciative speech in which truth or falsity is found is called interpretation. Other kinds of speech, such as optatives and imperatives, are ordered rather to expressing volition than to interpreting what is in the intellect. This book, then, is entitled *On Interpretation,* that is to say, *On Enunciative Speech* in which truth or falsity is found. The name and verb are treated only insofar as they are parts of the enunciation; for it is proper to a science to treat the parts of its subject as well as its properties.

It is clear, then, to which part of philosophy this book belongs, what its necessity is, and what its place is among the books on logic.

Lesson I

16a 1   First we must establish what a name[3] is and what a verb is; then what negation is and affirmation, and the enunciation[4] and speech.[5]

---

[3] This treatise of Aristotle's has as its subject logic, not grammar, and therefore he is treating here—and will define later (16a 19)—the name, not the noun. One indication of this is his use of "name" to cover both the noun and the adjective. Another is his statement (16b 19) that verbs in themselves are names. To translate this as "verbs in themselves are nouns" confuses what he has said up to this point (for he does not mean the infinitive form of the verb). "Name," on the other hand, clarifies what he is saying, for "name" is taken here as a genus which includes names (i.e., nouns and adjectives) and verbs (cf. St. Thomas, Lesson V, n. 15). This reading is again confirmed in Book II, 19b 20, where Aristotle speaks of "is" as a name or a verb. "Name" is therefore used generally at first to cover the substantive name, the adjectival name, and the verb; then it is taken more determinately (16a 19) to include only the first two when it is defined as opposed to the verb, i.e., where the species of the genus *name* are defined.

[4] Modern usage has substituted "proposition" for "enunciation" and "premise" for "proposition." In the present work ἀπόφανσις has been translated as "enunciation" which is its literal meaning, rather than as "proposition," the Greek word for which is πρότασις. ("Declaration" and "statement," which are also meanings of ἀπόφανσις and which at first sight might seem to clarify Aristotle's thought, are quite ambiguous in English because of their generality and their lack of logical significance and hence the literal meaning has been used here.) Now while it is true that an enunciation and a proposition may be materially the same, there is a formal difference between them. "Enunciation" denotes either part of a contradiction indifferently, whether affirmative or negative, universal, particular, or even singular, true or false, one or many. "Proposition" originally meant the conclusion of a syllogism, i.e., what had to be proved. Its meaning was extended to the enunciation assumed as part of a syllogism in order to prove something. The point is that the enunciation taken as part of a syllogism constitutes a second intention quite distinct from an enunciation taken absolutely. The former would deserve the name "proposition" in the strict sense of the term, and so taken immediately conveys a universal enunciation.

[5] The Greek word λόγος, which is translated here as "speech," means any connection of words to express thought. It is used for anything from a phrase to an epic poem (cf. *Categories* 4b 23 and 4b 31; *Posterior Analytics* II, 93b 36 ff.). It has usually been translated as "sentence," but this is a word imposed to signify a grammatical construction rather than a logical construction, and hence is too narrow in meaning for what Aristotle intends. Signs of this can be found within this work. One would not ask whether a sentence is true or false, because grammar only deals with the order of words among themselves. Logic, on

[19]

4.   The Philosopher begins this work with an introduction in which he points out one by one the things that are to be treated. For, since every science begins with a treatment of the principles, and the principles of composite things are their parts, one who intends to treat enunciation must begin with its parts. Therefore Aristotle begins by saying: *First we must determine,*[6] i.e., define, *what a name is and what a verb is.* In the Greek text it is *First we must posit,* which signifies the same thing, for demonstrations presuppose definitions, from which they conclude, and hence definitions are rightly called "positions." This is the reason he only points out here the definitions of the things to be treated; for from definitions other things are known.

5.   It might be asked why it is necessary to treat simple things again, i.e., the name and the verb, for they were treated in the book *Praedicamentorum.* In answer to this we should say that simple words can be considered in three ways: first, as they signify simple intellection absolutely, which is the consideration proper to the book *Praedicamentorum;* secondly, according to their function as parts of the enunciation, which is the way they are considered in this book. Hence, they are treated here under the formality of the name and the verb, and under this formality they signify something with time or without time and other things of the kind that belong to the formality of words as they are components of an enunciation. Finally, simple words may be considered as they are components of a syllogistic ordering. They are treated then under the formality of terms and this Aristotle does in the book *Priorum.*

6.   It might be asked why he treats only the name and verb and omits the other parts of speech. The reason could be that Aristotle in-

16a1

---

the other hand, deals with speech as expressing conceptions of the intellect and therefore is concerned about such a question. Again, in Lesson VI (Aristotle, 16b 34; St. Thomas, nn. 7 and 8) there is a question as to whether speech is significant by convention or as an instrument, i.e., as an instrument of a natural power such as throat, lungs, etc., and therefore significant naturally. Such a question would not arise with respect to the sentence as a grammatical construction.

[6] The Greek text reads: "πρῶτον δεῖ θέσθαι. . . ." "Establish," which is used in the translation of Aristotle, seemed the best English word to use

in this context, but the *Commentary* at this point required the more literal word "posit," which is being related here to "position" to bring out, at least implicitly, that logic proceeds scientifically, (in accordance with the Aristotelian meaning of science).

[7] The editors of the Leonine edition suggest this alternate reading: ". . . in treating the simple enunciation it is sufficient to treat only those parts of speech from which the simple enunciation is necessarily formed." Cf. note ζ, Lesson I, p. 6 in the Leonine edition for the variations in the manuscripts.

tends to establish rules about the simple enunciation and for this it is sufficient to consider only the parts of the enunciation[7] that are necessary for simple speech. A simple enunciation can be formed from just a name and a verb, but it cannot be formed from other parts of speech without these. Therefore, it is sufficient to treat these two.

On the other hand, the reason could be that names and verbs are the principal parts of speech. Pronouns, which do not name a nature but determine a person—and therefore are put in place of names—are comprehended under names. The participle—although it has similarities with the name—signifies with time and is therefore comprehended under the verb. The others are things that unite the parts of speech. They signify relations of one part to another rather than as parts of speech; as nails and other parts of this kind are not parts of a ship, but connect the parts of a ship.

7.   After he has proposed these parts [the name and the verb] as principles, Aristotle states what he principally intends to establish: . . . *then what negation is and affirmation.* These, too, are parts of the enunciation, not integral parts however, as are the name and verb—otherwise every enunciation would have to be formed from an affirmation and negation—but subjective parts, i.e., species. This is supposed here but will be proved later.

8.   Since enunciation is divided into categorical and hypothetical, it might be asked why he does not list these as well as affirmation and negation. In reply to this we could say that Aristotle has not added these because the hypothetical enunciation is composed of many categorical propositions and hence categorical and hypothetical only differ according to the difference of one and many.

Or we could say—and this would be a better reason—that the hypothetical enunciation does not contain absolute truth, the knowledge of which is required in demonstration, to which this book is principally ordered; rather, it signifies something as true by supposition, which does not suffice for demonstrative sciences unless it is confirmed by the absolute truth of the simple enunciation. This is the reason Aristotle does not treat either hypothetical enunciations or syllogisms.

He adds, *and the enunciation,* which is the genus of negation and affirmation; *and speech,* which is the genus of enunciation.

9.   If it should be asked why, besides these, he does not mention vocal sound, it is because vocal sound is something natural and therefore belongs to the consideration of natural philosophy, as is evident in II *De anima* and at the end of *De generatio animalium.*[8] Also, since it is

[8] *De Anima* II, 8, 420b 5-421a 6; De *Generatio Animalium,* chapter 8.

something natural, vocal sound is not properly the genus of speech but is presupposed for the forming of speech, as natural things are presupposed for the formation of artificial things.

10. In this introduction, however, Aristotle seems to have inverted the order of the enunciation,[9] for affirmation is naturally prior to negation and enunciation prior to these as a genus; and consequently, speech to enunciation. We could say in reply to this that he began to enumerate from the parts and consequently he proceeds from the parts to the whole. He puts negation, which contains division, before affirmation, which consists of composition, for the same reason: division is closer to the parts, composition closer to the whole.

Or we could say, as some do, that he puts negation first because in those things that can be and not be, nonbeing, which negation signifies, is prior to being, which affirmation signifies.

Aristotle, however, does not refer to the fact that one of them is placed before the other, for they are species equally dividing a genus and are therefore simultaneous according to nature.

[9] Suggested reading by the editors of the Leonine: ". . . order of enumeration."

Lesson II

The Signification of Vocal Sound

16a 3   Now those that are in vocal sound are signs[10] of passions in the soul, and those that are written are signs of those in vocal sound.

16a 5   And just as letters are not the same for all men so neither are vocal sounds the same;

16a 6   but the passions[11] of the soul, of which vocal sounds are the first signs,[12] are the same for all; and the things of which passions of the soul are likenesses are also the same.

16a 8   This has been discussed, however, in our study of the soul for it belongs to another subject of inquiry.

---

1.   After his introduction the Philosopher begins to investigate the things he has proposed. Since the things he promised to speak of are either complex or incomplex significant vocal sounds, he prefaces this with a treatment of the signification of vocal sounds; then he takes up the significant vocal sounds he proposed in the introduction where he says, *A name, then, is a vocal sound significant by convention,* 16a19
without time, etc.[13] In regard to the signification of vocal sounds he first determines what kind of signification vocal sound has and then shows the difference between the signification of complex and incomplex vocal sounds where he says, *As sometimes there is thought in the soul,* etc.[14] 16a9
With respect to the first point, he presents the order of the signification

10 The Greek word σύμβολον means "token" and the Latin word *nota* used by William of Moerbeke is an exact translation of this. "Sign" and "symbol" are later meanings which have become technical and therefore less directly convey what Aristotle intends here. "Sign" has nevertheless been used in the present translation because "token" is now an uncommon word, and "sign" is at least closer to the first imposition, which was related more directly to sense experience.

11 The Greek word πάθημα, translated here as "passions," in its verb form meant being subject to or affected by something. "Being acted upon" would be a good translation of the verb form, but since there is no equivalent noun except "affections," which is too narrow in meaning as commonly used, and since the commentary on this passage is made in terms of "passions," this literal word has been kept.

12 The Latin text adds another "first" and consequently reads: ". . . but the passions of the soul, of which *first* passions these a r e t h e first signs . . .," etc. (Italics added.)

13 St. Thomas, Lesson IV.

14 St. Thomas, Lesson III.

of vocal sounds and then shows what kind of signification vocal sound has, i.e., whether it is from nature or by imposition. This he does where he says, *And just as letters are not the same for all men,* etc.

16a5

2.   Apropos of the order of signification of vocal sounds he proposes three things, from one of which a fourth is understood. He proposes *writing, vocal sounds,* and *passions of the soul; things* is understood from the latter, for passion is from the impression of something acting, and hence passions of the soul have their origin from things.

Now if man were by nature a solitary animal the passions of the soul by which he was conformed to things so as to have knowledge of them would be sufficient for him; but since he is by nature a political and social animal it was necessary that his conceptions be made known to others. This he does through vocal sound. Therefore there had to be significant vocal sounds in order that men might live together. Whence those who speak different languages find it difficult to live together in social unity.

Again, if man had only sensitive cognition, which is of the here and now, such significant vocal sounds as the other animals use to manifest their conceptions to each other would be sufficient for him to live with others. But man also has the advantage of intellectual cognition, which abstracts from the here and now, and as a consequence, is concerned with things distant in place and future in time as well as things present according to time and place. Hence the use of writing was necessary so that he might manifest his conceptions to those who are distant according to place and to those who will come in future time.

3.   However, since logic is ordered to obtaining knowledge about things, the signification of vocal sounds, which is immediate to the conceptions of the intellect, is its principal consideration. The signification of written signs, being more remote, belongs to the consideration of the grammarian rather than the logician. Aristotle therefore begins his explanation of the order of signification from vocal sounds, not written

16a3

signs. First he explains the signification of vocal sounds: *Therefore*[15] *those that are in vocal sound are signs of passions in the soul.* He says "therefore" as if concluding from premises, because he has already said that we must establish what a name is, and a verb and the other things he mentioned; but these are significant vocal sounds; therefore, signification of vocal sounds must be explained.

[15] The οὖν in the Greek text is very rarely used by Aristotle to mean "therefore" and has been omitted from the translation of the Aristotelian text, since it probably only indicates a continuation of his discussion. It is put in the text here only because St. Thomas immediately comments on it.

4.   When he says "Those that are in vocal sound," and not "vocal sounds," his mode of speaking implies a continuity with what he has just been saying, namely, we must define the name and the verb, etc. Now these have being in three ways: in the conception of the intellect, in the utterance of the voice, and in the writing of letters. He could therefore mean when he says "Those that are in vocal sound," etc., names and verbs and the other things we are going to define, insofar as they are in vocal sound, are signs.

On the other hand, he may be speaking in this way because not all vocal sounds are significant, and of those that are, some are significant naturally and hence are different in nature from the name and the verb and the other things to be defined. Therefore, to adapt what he has said to the things of which he intends to speak he says, "Those that are in vocal sound," i.e., that are contained under vocal sound as parts under a whole.

There could be still another reason for his mode of speaking. Vocal sound is something natural. The name and verb, on the other hand, signify by human institution, that is, the signification is added to the natural thing as a form to matter, as the form of a bed is added to wood. Therefore, to designate names and verbs and the other things he is going to define he says, "Those that are in vocal sound," in the same way he would say of a bed, "that which is in wood."

5.   When he speaks of passions in the soul we are apt to think of the affections of the sensitive appetite, such as anger, joy, and the other passions that are customarily and commonly called passions of the soul, as is the case in II *Ethicorum*.[16] It is true that some of the vocal sounds man makes signify passions of this kind naturally, such as the groans of the sick and the sounds of other animals, as is said in I *Politicae*.[17] But here Aristotle is speaking of vocal sounds that are significant by human institution. Therefore "passions in the soul" must be understood here as conceptions of the intellect, and names, verbs, and speech, signify these conceptions of the intellect immediately according to the teaching of Aristotle. They cannot immediately signify things, as is clear from the mode of signifying, for the name "man" signifies human nature in abstraction from singulars; hence it is impossible that it immediately signify a singular man. The Platonists for this reason held that it signified the separated idea of man. But because in Aristotle's teaching man in the abstract does not really subsist, but is only in the mind, it was necessary for Aristotle to say that vocal sounds signify the conceptions of the intellect immediately and things by means of them.

[16] *Nichomachean Ethics* II, 5, 1105b 21.   [17] *Politics* I, 2, 1253a 10-14.

6.   Since Aristotle did not customarily speak of conceptions of the intellect as passions, Andronicus took the position that this book was not Aristotle's. In I *De anima*, however, it is obvious that he calls all of the operations of the soul "passions" of the soul.[18] Whence even the conception of the intellect can be called a passion and this either because we do not understand without a phantasm, which requires corporeal passion (for which reason the Philosopher calls the imaginative power the passive intellect);[19] or because by extending the name "passion" to every reception, the understanding of the possible intellect is also a kind of undergoing, as is said in III *De anima*.[20]

Aristotle uses the name "passion," rather than "understanding," however, for two reasons: first, because man wills to signify an interior conception to another through vocal sound as a result of some passion of the soul, such as love or hate; secondly, because the signification of vocal sound is referred to the conception of the intellect inasmuch as the conception arises from things by way of a kind of impression or passion.

7.   When he says, *and those that are written are signs of those in vocal sound,* he treats of the signification of writing.

According to Alexander he introduces this to make the preceding clause evident by means of a similitude; and the meaning is: those that are in vocal sound are signs of the passions of the soul in the way in which letters are of vocal sound; then he goes on to manifest this point—

16a5   where he says, *And just as letters are not the same for all men so neither are vocal sounds the same*—by introducing this as a sign of the preceding. For when he says in effect, just as there are diverse vocal sounds among diverse peoples so there are diverse letters, he is signifying that letters signify vocal sounds. And according to this exposition Aristotle said *those that are written are signs* . . . and not, *letters are signs of those that are in vocal sound,* because they are called letters in both speech and writing, although they are more properly called letters in writing; in speech they are called elements of vocal sound.

Aristotle, however, does not say, *just as* those that are written, but continues with his account. Therefore it is better to say as Porphyry does, that Aristotle adds this to complete the order of signification; for after he says that names and verbs in vocal sound are signs of those in the soul, he adds—in continuity with this—that names and verbs that are written are signs of the names and verbs that are in vocal sound.

16a5   8.   Then where he says, *And just as letters are not the same for all men so neither are vocal sounds the same,* he shows that the foresaid

[18] *De Anima* I, 1, 403a 3 ff; cf. also, ibid., II, 5, 416b 32 ff. and II, 8, 420b 5 ff.; *ibid.*, III, 4 and 5.   [19] *De Anima* III, 5, 430a 25.   [20] *De Anima* III, 4, 429b 29 ff.

things differ as signified and signifying inasmuch as they are either according to nature or not. He makes three points here. He first posits a sign to show that neither vocal sounds nor letters signify naturally; things that signify naturally are the same among all men; but the signification of letters and vocal sounds, which is the point at issue here, is not the same among all men. There has never been any question about this in regard to letters, for their character of signifying is from imposition and their very formation is through art. Vocal sounds, however, are formed naturally and hence there is a question as to whether they signify naturally. Aristotle determines this by comparison with letters: these are not the same among all men, and so neither are vocal sounds the same. Consequently, like letters, vocal sounds do not signify naturally but by human institution. The vocal sounds that do signify naturally, such as groans of the sick and others of this kind, are the same among all men.

9.   Secondly, when he says, *but the passions of the soul, of which*   16a6
vocal sounds are the first signs, are the same for all, he shows that passions of the soul exist naturally, just as things exist naturally, for they are the same among all men. For, he says, *but the passions of the soul,* i.e., just as the passions of the soul are the same for all men; *of which first,* i.e., of which passions, being first, *these,* namely, vocal sounds, are tokens,[21] i.e., signs[22] (for passions of the soul are compared to vocal sounds as first to second since vocal sounds are produced only to express interior passions of the soul), *so also the things . . . are the same, i.e.,* are the same among all, *of which,* i.e., of which things, *passions of the soul are likenesses.*

     Notice he says here that letters are signs, i.e., signs of vocal sounds, and similarly vocal sounds are signs of passions of the soul, but that passions of the soul are *likenesses* of things. This is because a thing is not known by the soul unless there is some likeness of the thing existing either in the sense or in the intellect. Now letters are signs of vocal sounds and vocal sounds of passions in such a way that we do not attend to any idea of likeness in regard to them but only one of institution, as is the case in regard to many other signs, for example, the trumpet as a sign of war."[23] But in the passions of the soul we have to take into account the idea of a likeness to the things represented, since passions of the soul designate things naturally, not by institution.

10.   There are some who object to Aristotle's position that passions

---

[21] *Supra,* note 10.

[22] In the Greek text this reads: ". . . but the passions of the soul, of which these [vocal sounds] are the

first signs . . ." *Supra,* note 12.

[23] The Latin word translated as "idea" here is *ratio.*

[27]

of the soul, which vocal sounds signify, are the same for all men.[24] Their argument against it is as follows: different men have different opinions about things; therefore, passions of the soul do not seem to be the same among all men.

Boethius in reply to this objection says that here Aristotle is using "passions of the soul" to denote conceptions of the intellect, and since the intellect is never deceived, conceptions of the intellect must be the same among all men; for if someone is at variance with what is true, in this instance he does not understand.

However, since what is false can also be in the intellect, not as it knows what a thing is, i.e., the essence of a thing, but as it composes and divides, as is said in III *De anima*,[25] Aristotle's statement should be referred to the simple conceptions of the intellect—that are signified by the incomplex vocal sounds—which are the same among all men; for if someone truly understands what man is, whatever else than man he apprehends he does not understand as man. Simple conceptions of the intellect, which vocal sounds first signify, are of this kind. This is why Aristotle says in IV *Metaphysicae* that the notion which the name signifies is the definition.[26] And this is the reason he expressly says, "of which *first* [passions] these are signs,"[27] i.e., so that this will be referred to the first conceptions first signified by vocal sounds.

11.   The equivocal name is given as another objection to this position, for in the case of an equivocal name the same vocal sound does not signify the same passion among all men. Porphyry answers this by pointing out that a man who utters a vocal sound intends it to signify one conception of the intellect. If the person to whom he is speaking understands something else by it, the one who is speaking, by explaining himself, will make the one to whom he is speaking refer his understanding to the same thing.

However it is better to say that it is not Aristotle's intention to maintain an identity of the conception of the soul in relation to a vocal sound such that there is one conception in relation to one vocal sound, for vocal sounds are different among different peoples; rather, he intends to maintain an identity of the conceptions of the soul in relation to things, which things he also says are the same.

16a8   12.   Thirdly when he says, *This has been discussed, however, in our study of the soul*, etc., he excuses himself from a further consideration of these things, for the nature of the passions of the soul and the way in

---

[24] In Boethius' Preface of *Commentarii in librum Aristotelis* Περὶ ἑρμηνείας, 2nd ed., p. 303, (cited in the Leonine edition, n. o, p. 14).

[25] *De Anima* III, 6, 430a 26 ff.

[26] *Metaphysicae*, Γ, 4, 1006b 4 ff.

[27] *Supra*, note 22.

which they are likenesses of things does not pertain to logic but to philosophy of nature and has already been treated in the book *De anima.*[28]

---

[28] *De Anima* III, 4-8.

LESSON III

The Diverse Signification of Vocal Sound

16a 9   As sometimes there is thought in the soul without its being true or false, but sometimes it must be one or the other, so it is in vocal sound;

16a 12   for in composition and division there is truth and falsity.

16a 13   Names and verbs, then, are like thought without composition or division, for example, "man" and "white" when nothing is added; for neither is yet true or false.

16a 16   A sign of this is that "goatstag" signifies something but is neither true nor false unless "to be" or "not to be" is added either absolutely or according to time.

---

1.   After the Philosopher has treated the order of the signification of vocal sounds, he goes on to discuss a diversity in the signification of vocal sounds, i.e., some of them signify the true or the false, others do
16a12   not. He first states the difference and then manifests it where he says, *for in composition and division there is truth and falsity.* Now because in the order of nature conceptions of the intellect precede vocal sounds, which are uttered to express them, he assigns the difference in respect to the significations of vocal sounds from a likeness to the difference in intellection. Thus the manifestation is from a likeness and at the same time from the cause which the effects imitate.

2.   The operation of the intellect is twofold, as was said in the beginning, and as is explained in III *De anima.*[29] Now truth and falsity is found in one of these operations but not in the other. This is what Aristotle says at the beginning of this portion of the text, i.e., that in the soul sometimes there is thought without truth and falsity, but sometimes of necessity it has one or the other of these. And since significant vocal sounds are formed to express these conceptions of the intellect, it is necessary that some significant vocal sounds signify without truth and falsity, others with truth and falsity—in order that the sign be conformed to what is signified.

16a12   3.   Then when he says, *for in composition and division there is truth and falsity,* he manifests what he has just said: first with respect to what he has said about thought; secondly, with respect to what he

[29] *De Anima* III, 6, 430a 26 ff.

[30]

has said about the likeness of vocal sounds to thought, where he says 16a13 *Names and verbs, then are like understanding without composition or division,* etc.

To show that sometimes there is thought without truth or falsity and sometimes it is accompanied by one of these, he says first that truth and falsity concern composition and division. To understand this we must note again that one of the two operations of the intellect is the understanding of what is indivisible. This the intellect does when it understands the *quiddity* or essence of a thing absolutely, for instance, *what* man is or *what* white is or what something else of this kind is. The other operation is the one in which it composes and divides simple concepts of this kind. He says that in this second operation of the intellect, i.e., composing and dividing, truth and falsity is found; the conclusion being that it is not found in the first, as he also says in III *De anima.*[30]

4.   There seems to be a difficulty about this point, for division is made by resolution to what is indivisible, or simple, and therefore it seems that just as truth and falsity is not in simple things, so neither is it in division.

To answer this it should be pointed out that the conceptions of the intellect are likenesses of things and therefore the things that are in the intellect can be considered and named in two ways: according to themselves, and according to the nature of the things of which they are the likenesses. For just as a statue—say of Hercules—in itself is called and is *bronze* but as it is a likeness of Hercules is named *man,* so if we consider the things that are in the intellect in themselves, there is always composition where there is truth and falsity, for they are never found in the intellect except as it compares one simple concept with another. But if the composition is referred to reality, it is sometimes called composition, sometimes division: composition when the intellect compares one concept to another as though apprehending a conjunction or identity of the things of which they are conceptions; division, when it so compares one concept with another that it apprehends the things to be diverse. In vocal sound, therefore, affirmation is called composition inasmuch as it signifies a conjunction on the part of the thing and negation is called division inasmuch as it signifies the separation of things.

5.   There is still another objection in relation to this point. It seems that truth is not in composition and division alone, for a thing is also said to be true or false. For instance, gold is said to be true gold or false gold.

Furthermore, *being* and *true* are said to be convertible. It seems,

---

[30] *De Anima* III, 6, 430a 26 ff.

therefore, that the simple conception of the intellect, which is a likeness of the thing, also has truth and falsity.

Again, the Philosopher says in his book *De anima,* that the sensation of proper sensibles is always true.[31] But the sense does not compose or divide. Therefore, truth is not in composition and division exclusively.

Moreover, in the divine intellect there is no composition, as is proved in XII *Metaphysicae.*[32] But the first and highest truth is in the divine intellect. Therefore, truth is not in composition and division exclusively.

6.   To answer these difficulties the following considerations are necessary. Truth is found in something in two ways: as it is in that which is true, and as it is in the one speaking or knowing truth. Truth as it is in that which is true is found in both simple things and composite things, but truth in the one speaking or knowing truth is found only according to composition and division. This will become clear in what follows.

7.   Truth, as the Philosopher says in VI *Ethicorum,* is the good of the intellect.[33] Hence, anything that is said to be true is such by reference to intellect. Now vocal sounds are related to thought as signs, but things are related to thought as that of which thoughts are likenesses. It must be noted, however, that a thing is related to thought in two ways: in one way as the measure to the measured, and this is the way natural things are related to the human speculative intellect. Whence thought is said to be true insofar as it is conformed to the thing, but false insofar as it is not in conformity with the thing.

However, a natural thing is not said to be true in relation to our thought in the way it was taught by certain ancient natural philosophers who supposed the truth of things to be only in what they seemed to be. According to this view it would follow that contradictories could be at once true, since the opinions of different men can be contradictory. Nevertheless, some things are said to be true or false in relation to our thought—not essentially or formally, but effectively—insofar as they are so constituted naturally as to cause a true or false estimation of themselves. It is in this way that gold is said to be true or false.

In another way, things are compared to thought as measured to the measure, as is evident in the practical intellect, which is a cause of things. In this way, the work of an artisan is said to be true insofar as it achieves the conception in the mind of the artist, and false insofar as it falls short of that conception.

---

[31] *De Anima* II, 6, 418a 15.
[32] *Metaph.,* Λ, 9, 1074b 15 - 1075a 11, especially 1075a 5-11.
[33] *Nic. Eth.* VI, 2, 1139a 28-30.

8.　　Now all natural things are related to the divine intellect as arti-facts to art and therefore a thing is said to be true insofar as it has its own form, according to which it represents divine art; false gold, for example, is true copper. It is in terms of this that *being* and *true* are converted, since any natural thing is conformed to divine art through its form. For this reason the Philosopher in I *Physicae* says that form is something divine.[34]

9.　　And just as a thing is said to be true by comparison to its meas-ure, so also is sensation or thought, whose measure is the thing outside of the soul. Accordingly, sensation is said to be true when the sense through its form is in conformity with the thing existing outside of the soul. It is in this way that the sensation of proper sensibles is true, and the intellect apprehending what a thing is apart from composition and division is always true, as is said in III *De anima*.[35]

It should be noted, however, that although the sensation of the proper object is true the sense does not perceive the sensation to be true, for it cannot know its relationship of conformity with the thing but only apprehends the thing. The intellect, on the other hand, can know its relationship of conformity and therefore only the intellect can know truth. This is the reason the Philosopher says in VI *Metaphysicae* that truth is only in the mind, that is to say, in one knowing truth.[36]

To know this relationship of conformity is to judge that a thing is such or is not, which is to compose and divide; therefore, the intellect does not know truth except by composing and dividing through its judg-ment. If the judgment is in accordance with things it will be true, i.e., when the intellect judges a thing to be what it is or not to be what it is not. The judgment will be false when it is not in accordance with the thing, i.e., when it judges that what is, is not, or that what is not, is. It is evident from this that truth and falsity as it is in the one knowing and speaking is had only in composition and division.

This is what the Philosopher is speaking of here. And since vocal sounds are signs of thought, that vocal sound will be true which signifies true thought, false which signifies false thought, although vocal sound insofar as it is a real thing is said to be true in the same way other things are. Thus the vocal sound "Man is an ass" is truly vocal sound and truly a sign, but because it is a sign of something false it is said to be false.

10.　　It should be noted that the Philosopher is speaking of truth here as it relates to the human intellect, which judges of the conformity of things and thought by composing and dividing. However, the judgment

[34] *Physics* I, 9, 192a 17.
[35] *De Anima* III, 3, 427b 12 and 428a 11 in relation to the senses; 6, 430a 26 in relation to the intellect.
[36] *Metaph.* E, 4, 1027b 26 ff.

of the divine intellect concerning this is without composition and division, for just as our intellect understands material things immaterially, so the divine intellect knows composition and division simply.[37]

16a13   11.   When he says, *Names and verbs, then, are like thought without composition or division,* he manifests what he has said about the likeness of vocal sounds to thought. Next he proves it by a sign when he says,
16a16   *A sign of this is that "goatstag" signifies something but is neither true nor false,* etc.

     Here he concludes from what has been said that since there is truth and falsity in the intellect only when there is composition or division, it follows that names and verbs, taken separately, are like thought which is without composition and division; as when we say "man" or "white," and nothing else is added. For these are neither true nor false at this point, but when "to be" or "not to be" is added they become true or false.

     12.   Although one might think so, the case of someone giving a single name as a true response to a question is not an instance that can be raised against this position; for example, suppose someone asks, "What swims in the sea?" and the answer is "Fish"; this is not opposed to the position Aristotle is taking here, for the verb that was posited in the question is understood.

     And just as the name said by itself does not signify truth or falsity, so neither does the verb said by itself. The verbs of the first and second person and the intransitive verb[38] are not instances opposed to this position either, for in these a particular and determined nominative is understood. Consequently there is implicit composition, though not explicit.

16a16   13.   Then he says, *A sign of this is that "goatstag" signifies something but is neither true nor false unless "to be" or "not to be" is added either absolutely or according to time.* Here he introduces as a sign the composite name "goatstag," from "goat" and "stag." In Greek the word is "tragelaphos," from "tragos" meaning goat and "elaphos" meaning stag. Now names of this kind signify something, namely, certain simple concepts (although the things they signify are composite), and therefore are not true or false unless "to be" or "not to be" is added, by which a judgment of the intellect is expressed. The "to be" or "not to be" can be added either according to present time, which is to be or not to be *in act* and for this reason is to be *simply;* or according to past or future

---

[37] Cf. *Sum. Theol.* I, q. 14, a. 14.
[38] E.g. "It is raining" or "It snows," although these of course have more than one word in English. The point made here is relevant only in an inflected language.

time, which is to be *relatively,* not simply; as when we say that something has been or will be.

Notice that Aristotle expressly uses as an example here a name signifying something that does not exist in reality, in which fictiveness is immediately evident, and which cannot be true or false without composition and division.[39]

---

[39] The editors of the Leonine suggest this reading: ". . . in which the falsity would appear immediately if it could be true or false without composition and division." However, the reading as it is in the text seems better, for with a name such as "goatstag" it is immediately evident that a name alone is neither true nor false, and in addition, only becomes true or false when used in composition or division. These points would not be as evident if a name of something really existing were used.

The Name

16a 19 A name, then, is a vocal sound significant by convention, without time, no part of which is significant separately;

16 a21 for in the name "Campbell"[40] the part "bell," as such signifies nothing, although in the expression "camp bell" it does.

16a 22 However the case is not exactly the same in simple names and composite names; for in the former the part is in no way significant, but in the latter the part has meaning but of nothing apart from the word, as "fast" in "breakfast."[41]

16a 26 "By convention" is added because nothing is by nature a name, but it is a name when it is made a sign; for unlettered sounds, such as those of the brutes, designate but none of them is a name.

16a 29 "Non-man," however, is not a name. No name has been imposed to designate this—for it is neither speech nor a negation—but let us call it an infinite name.

16a 32 "Of Philo" and "to Philo" and all such expressions are not names but modes[42] of names.

---

[40] The Greek name used here is κάλλιππος, the Latin, *equiferus*. The Greek word seems to be a proper name and in the Oxford edition is translated as "Fairsteed," in the Loeb as "Goodsteed," which are literal translations of the Greek. "Campbell" has been substituted for the Greek name in the present translation as a more evident example of a proper name. It is interesting to note that St. Thomas uses a name that is only compound and makes no comment on the fact that Aristotle uses a name that is both proper and compound. Actually Aristotle's point is made more evident by the use of a proper compound name, and hence in giving such an example first he is following his principle of going from what is more known to what is less known.

[41] The Greek word here is κέλης in the word ἐπακτροκέλης. κέλης means a courser, riding horse or fast sailing yacht with one bank of oars; when compounded with ἐπακτρίς (a skiff), the whole word has the meaning of a light piratical skiff. The Latin uses *equiferus* again. The Oxford edition translates this as "pirate-boat," the Loeb, as "pirate-vessel," which are literal translations of the Greek example. In order to duplicate more closely Aristotle's use of a compound name imposed to signify a simple concept (which is obscured by the hyphenated word) "fast" in the word "breakfast" has been used in the present translation.

[42] In Greek the word, πτῶσις, is used for cases of names and tenses of verbs. In Latin *casus*, or cases has been used for both. The Greek word seems to signify a more general and logical notion than our "cases" and "tenses," which were introduced

[36]

16b 1   The definition of these is the same in all other respects as that of the name itself, but in conjunction with "is" or "has been" or "will be" they are not true or false, whereas if one of these is added to a name there is always truth or falsity; for example, "of Philo is," or "of Philo is not" are neither true nor false.

---

1.   Having determined the order of the signification of vocal sounds, the Philosopher begins here to establish the definitions of the significant vocal sounds. His principal intention is to establish what an enunciation is—which is the subject of this book—but since in any science the principles of the subject must be known first, he begins with the principles of the enunciation and then establishes what an enunciation is where he says, *All speech is not enunciative,* etc.[43] With respect to the principles   17b2 of the enunciation he first determines the nature of the quasi material principles, i.e., its integral parts, and secondly the formal principle, i.e., speech, which is the genus of the enunciation, where he says, *Speech is*   16b26 *significant vocal sound,* etc.[44] Apropos of the quasi material principles of the enunciation he first establishes that a name signifies the substance of a thing and then that the verb signifies action or passion proceeding from a thing, where he says *The verb is that which signifies with time,*   16b5 etc.[45] In relation to this first point, he first defines the name, and then explains the definition where he says, *for in the name "Campbell" the part*   16a21 *"bell," as such, signifies nothing,* etc., and finally excludes certain things— those that do not have the definition of the name perfectly—where he   16a29 says, *"Non-man," however, is not a name,* etc.

2.   It should be noted in relation to defining the name, that a definition is said to be a limit because it includes a thing totally, i.e., such that nothing of the thing is outside of the definition, that is, there is nothing

later by grammarians. The first meaning of πτῶσις, as also of *casus,* is "a falling away from," or a kind of "diminishing" or "declining." In order, then, to preserve the more general logical notion, the πτῶσις has been translated as "modes;" but the *casus* in the commentary kept as "cases" since the commentary is made in terms of this. In relation to this point, see R. H. Robins, *Ancient and Medieval Grammatical Theory in Europe* (London: Bell, 1951), especially pp. 19-25, 31-32.

I disagree, however, with Mr. Robins' position that Aristotle is defining grammatical notions in the *Peri Hermeneias.* See also, *The Oxford Classical Dictionary,* ed. by M. Cary and others, (Oxford: The Clarendon Press, 1949), under Grammar, (Greek). The latter reference, in my opinion, is not exact with respect to the meaning of λόγος in Aristotle (cf. *supra* note 2.)

[43] St. Thomas, Lesson VII.
[44] St. Thomas, Lesson VI.
[45] St. Thomas, Lesson V.

of the thing to which the definition does not belong; nor is any other thing under the definition, that is, the definition belongs to no other thing.

3.   Aristotle posits five parts in the definition of the name.[46] *Vocal sound* is given first, as the genus. This distinguishes the name from all sounds that are not vocal; for vocal sound is sound produced from the mouth of an animal and involves a certain kind of mental image, as is said in II *De anima*.[47] The second part is the first difference, i.e., *significant*, which differentiates the name from any nonsignificant vocal sound, whether lettered and articulated, such as "biltris," or nonlettered and nonarticulated, as a hissing for no reason. Now since he has already determined the signification of vocal sounds, he concludes from what has been established that a name is a significant vocal sound.

4.   But vocal sound is a natural thing, whereas a name is not natural but instituted by men; it seems, therefore, that Aristotle should have taken *sign*, which is from institution, as the genus of the name, rather than vocal sound, which is from nature. Then the definition would be: a name is a vocal *sign*, etc., just as a salver would be more suitably defined as a wooden dish than as wood formed into a dish.

5.   It should be noted, however, that while it is true that artificial things are in the genus of substance on the part of matter, they are in the genus of accident on the part of form, since the forms of artificial things are accidents. A name, therefore, signifies an accidental form made concrete in a subject. Now the subject must be posited in the definition of every accident; hence, when names signify an accident in the abstract the accident has to be posited directly (i.e., in the nominative case) as a quasi-genus in their definition and the subject posited obliquely (i.e., in an oblique case such as the genitive, dative, or accusative) as a quasi-difference; as for example, when we define snubness as curvedness of the nose. But when names signify an accident in the concrete, the matter or subject has to be posited in their definition as a quasi-genus and the accident as a quasi-difference, as when we say that a snub nose is a curved nose. Accordingly, if the names of artificial things signify accidental forms as made concrete in natural subjects, then it is more appropriate to posit the natural thing in their definition as a quasi-genus. We would say, therefore, that a salver is shaped wood, and likewise, that a name is a significant vocal sound. It would be another matter if names of artificial things were taken as signifying artificial forms in the abstract.

[46] "Name" is taken here as a species under the genus *name* and is therefore opposed to the verb; it includes both the substantive and adjective name. A parallel case of this usage is *animal* taken as a species under the genus animal.

[47] *De Anima* II, 8, 420b 30-34.

6.   The third part is the second difference, i.e., *by convention*, namely, according to human institution deriving from the will of man. This differentiates names from vocal sounds signifying naturally, such as the groans of the sick and the vocal sounds of brute animals.

7.   The fourth part is the third difference, i.e., *without time*, which differentiates the name from the verb.

This, however, seems to be false, for the name "day" or "year" signifies time.

But there are three things that can be considered with respect to time; first, time itself, as it is a certain kind of thing or reality, and then it can be signified by a name just like any other thing; secondly, that which is measured by time, insofar as it is measured by time. Motion, which consists of action and passion, is what is measured first and principally by time, and therefore the verb, which signifies action and passion, signifies with time. Substance considered in itself, which a name or a pronoun signify, is not as such measured by time, but only insofar as it is subjected to motion, and this the participle signifies. The verb and the participle, therefore, signify with time, but not the name and pronoun. The third thing that can be considered is the very relationship of time as it measures. This is signified by adverbs of time such as "tomorrow," "yesterday," and others of this kind.

8.   The fifth part is the fourth difference, *no part of which is significant separately*, that is, separated from the whole name; but it is related to the signification of the name according as it is in the whole. The reason for this is that signification is a quasi-form of the name. But no separated part has the form of the whole; just as the hand separated from the man does not have the human form. This difference distinguishes the name from speech, some parts of which signify separately, as for example in "just man."

9.   When he says, *for in the name "Campbell"*[48] *the part "bell" as such signifies nothing*, etc., he explains the definition. First he explains the last part of the definition; secondly, the third part, *by convention*. The first two parts were explained in what preceded, and the fourth part, *without time*, will be explained later in the section on the verb. And first he explains the last part by means of a composite name; then he shows what the difference is between simple and composite names where he says, *However the case is not exactly the same in simple names and composite names*, etc.   16a21

16a22

First, then, he shows that a part separated from a name signifies nothing. To do this he uses a composite name because the point is more

[48] *Supra*, note 40.

[39]

striking there. For in the name "Campbell" the part "bell" per se signifies nothing, although it does signify something in the phrase "camp bell." The reason for this is that one name is imposed to signify one simple conception; but that from which a name is imposed to signify is different from that which a name signifies. For example, the name "pedigree"[49] is imposed from *pedis* and *grus* [crane's foot] which it does not signify, to signify the concept of a certain thing. Hence, a part of the composite name—which composite name is imposed to signify a simple concept—does not signify a part of the composite conception from which the name is imposed to signify. Speech, on the other hand, does signify a composite conception. Hence, a part of speech signifies a part of the composite conception.

16a22   10.   When he says, *However, the case is not exactly the same in simple names and composite names,* etc., he shows that there is a difference between simple and composite names in regard to their parts not signifying separately. Simple names are not the same as composite names in this respect because in simple names a part is in no way significant, either according to truth or according to appearance, but in composite names the part has meaning, i.e., has the appearance of signifying; yet a part of it signifies nothing, as is said of the name "breakfast."[50] The reason for this difference is that the simple name is imposed to signify a simple concept and is also imposed from a simple concept; but the composite name is imposed from a composite conception, and hence has the appearance that a part of it signifies.

16a27   11.   Then he says, *"By convention" is added because nothing is by nature a name,* etc. Here Aristotle explains the third part of the definition. The reason it is said that the name signifies by convention, he says, is that no name exists naturally. For it is a name because it signifies; it does not signify naturally however, but by institution. This he adds when he says, *but it is a name when it is made a sign,* i.e., when it is imposed to signify. For that which signifies naturally is not made a sign, but is a sign naturally. He explains this when he says: *for unlettered sounds, such as those of the brutes designate,* etc., i.e., since they cannot be signified by letters. He says *sounds* rather than *vocal sounds* because some animals—those without lungs—do not have vocal sounds. Such animals signify proper passions by some kind of nonvocal sound which signifies naturally. But none of these sounds of the brutes is a name. We are given to understand from this that a name does not signify naturally.

---

[49] The Latin here is *lapis,* from *laesione pedis.* To bring out the point St. Thomas is making here an equivalent English word of Latin derivation, i.e., "pedigree," has been used.

[50] The Latin word used here is again *equiferus.*

[40]

12.   However, there were diverse opinions about this. Some men said that names in no way signify naturally and that it makes no difference which things are signified by which names. Others said that names signify naturally in every way, as if names were natural likenesses of things. Still others said names do not signify naturally, i.e., insofar as their signification is not from nature, as Aristotle maintains here, but that names do signify naturally in the sense that their signification corresponds to the natures of things, as Plato held.[51]

The fact that one thing is signified by many names is not in opposition to Aristotle's position here, for there can be many likenesses of one thing; and similarly, from diverse properties many diverse names can be imposed on one thing.

When Aristotle says, *but none of them is a name,* he does not mean that the sounds of animals are not named, for we do have names for them; "roaring," for example, is said of the sound made by a lion, and "lowing" of that of a cow. What he means is that no such *sound* is a name.

13.   When he says, *"Non-man," however, is not a name,* etc., he points out that certain things do not have the nature of a name. First he excludes the infinite name; then the cases of the name where he says, *"Of Philo" and "to Philo,"* etc.   16a29

16a32

He says that "non-man" is not a name because every name signifies some determinate nature, for example, "man," or a determinate person in the case of the pronoun, or both determinately, as in "Socrates." But when we say "non-man" it signifies neither a determinate nature nor a determinate person, because it is imposed from the negation of man, which negation is predicated equally of *being* and *nonbeing.* Consequently, "non-man" can be said indifferently both of that which does not exist in reality, as in "A chimera is non-man," and of that which does exist in reality, as in "A horse is non-man."

Now if the infinite name were imposed from a privation it would require at least an existing subject, but since it is imposed from a negation, it can be predicated of being and nonbeing, as Boethius and Ammonius say.[52] However, since it signifies in the mode of a name, and can therefore be subjected and predicated, a suppositum is required at least in apprehension.

In the time of Aristotle there was no name for words of this kind. They are not speech since a part of such a word does not signify something separately, just as a part of a composite name does not sig-

[51] Cf. Plato's *Cratylus.*
[52] Boethius', *Commentarii in librus Aristotelis* Περὶ ἑρμηνείας, 2nd ed.,   Bk. I, De nomine: Ammonius, *In Aristotelis De interpretatione Commentarius,* sect. I, 7.

[41]

nify separately; and they are not negations, i.e., negative speech, for speech of this kind adds negation to affirmation, which is not the case here. Therefore he imposes a new name for words of this kind, the "infinite name," because of the indetermination of signification, as has been said.

16a32 14. When he says, *"Of Philo" and "to Philo" and all such expressions are not names but modes of names,* he excludes the cases of names from the nature of the name. The nominative is the one that is said to be a name principally, for the imposition of the name to signify something was made through it. Oblique expressions of the kind cited are called cases of the name because they fall away from the nominative as a kind of source of their declension. On the other hand, the nominative, because it does not fall away, is said to be erect. The Stoics held that even the nominatives were cases (with which the grammarians agree), because they fall, i.e., proceed from the interior conception of the mind; and they said they were also called erect because nothing prevents a thing from falling in such a way that it stands erect, as when a pen falls and is fixed in wood.

16b1 15. Then he says, *The definition of these is the same in all other respects as that of the name itself,* etc. Here Aristotle shows how oblique cases are related to the name. The definition, as it signifies the name, is the same *in the others,* namely, in the cases of the name.[53] But they differ in this respect: the name joined to the verb "is" or "will be" or "has been" always signifies the true or false; in oblique cases this is not so. It is significant that the substantive verb is the one he uses as an example, for there are other verbs, i.e., impersonal verbs, that do signify the true or false when joined with a name in an oblique case, as in "It grieves Socrates," because the act of the verb is understood to be carried over to the oblique cases, as though what were said were, "Grief possesses Socrates."

[53] According to the Greek text Aristotle seems to be saying here that the definition of the name, i.e., vocal sound significant by convention, without time, no part of which is significant separately, applies also to the modes, that is, to what we would call cases of the name. There might appear to be a difficulty in relation to this point apropos of the last part of the definition, i.e., no part of which is significant separately, as far as English is concerned, because we sometimes have to use a preposition with a name to express cases. The preposition, however, is a "syncategorematic" word, i.e., it is, used with names, as a connecter; it does not have meaning by itself. This difficulty does not arise in an inflected language since oblique cases of names are like names in that they are one word, i.e., the name with an inflected ending. This is the very reason that Aristotle discusses them.

[42]

16.   However, an objection could be made against Aristotle's position in this portion of his text. If the infinite name and the cases of the name are not names, then the definition of the name (which belongs to these) is not consistently presented.

There are two ways of answering this objection. We could say, as Ammonius does, that Aristotle defines the name broadly, and afterward limits the signification of the name by subtracting these from it. Or, we could say that the definition Aristotle has given does not belong to these absolutely, since the infinite name signifies nothing determinate, and the cases of the name do not signify according to the first intent of the one instituting the name, as has been said.

On the Nature of the Verb and Its Conformity with the Name

16b 5   The verb is that which signifies with time; no part of it signifies separately, and it is a sign of something said of something else.

16b 8   I mean by "signifies with time" that "maturity," for example, is a name, but "matures" is a verb, for it connotes the present existence of maturity.[54]

16b 10   Moreover, a verb is always a sign of something that belongs to something, i.e., of something present in a subject.

16b 12   "Non-matures" and "non-declines" I do not call verbs. They signify with time and always belong to something but they differ from the verb and no name has been established for the difference. Let us call them infinite verbs, since they belong equally to anything whatever, to both what is and what is not.

16b 16   Likewise, "has matured" and "will mature" are not verbs but modes of the verb.[55] They differ from the verb in that the verb signifies with present time, whereas the modes signify time outside of the present.

16b 19   Verbs in themselves, said alone, are names, and signify something

16b 20   — for in uttering a verb the one speaking informs the mind of the one hearing it and sets it at rest—but they do not yet signify whether a thing is or is not, for the verb is not a sign of the being or nonbeing of a thing. Nor would it be a sign of the being or nonbeing of a thing if you were to say "being"[56] alone, for it is nothing; it signifies with a composition which cannot be conceived apart from the things composing it.

---

1.   After determining the nature of the name the Philosopher now determines the nature of the verb. First he defines the verb; secondly,

[54] The Greek name used here is ὑγίεια and the verb ὑγιαίνει. The Latin uses *cursus* and *currit*. The ὑγιαίνει cannot be translated into English as a verb since it becomes a predicate adjective with the verb "is," i.e., "is healthy." This would not fulfill Aristotle's purpose here, for he is defining the verb, not a predicate adjective; nor would the "is" serve the purpose here for there are

special difficulties about it which will be taken up later (Aristotle, 16b 20, St. Thomas, n. 18 of this lesson).

[55] *Supra*, note 42.

[56] The Latin text of Aristotle has *est* for τὸ ὄν. St. Thomas points out this difference when he comments on this part of the text in n. 19 of this lesson.

he excludes certain forms of verbs from the definition, where he says, "*Non-matures*" *and* "*non-declines*" *I do not call verbs,* etc.; finally, he shows in what the verb and name agree where he says, *Verbs in themselves, said alone, are names,* etc. First, then, he defines the verb and immediately begins to explain the definition where he says, *I mean by* "*signifies with time,*" etc.

16b12
16b19

16b8

2.   In order to be brief, Aristotle does not give what is common to the name and the verb in the definition of the verb, but leaves this for the reader to understand from the definition of the name.

He posits three elements in the definition of the verb. The first of these distinguishes the verb from the name, for the verb *signifies with time,* the name without time, as was stated in its definition. The second element, *no part of which signifies separately,* distinguishes the verb from speech.

3.   This second element was also given in the definition of the name and therefore it seems that this second element along with *vocal sound significant by convention,* should have been omitted.

Ammonius says in reply to this that Aristotle posited this in the definition of the name to distinguish it from speech which is composed of names, as in "Man is an animal"; but speech may also be composed of verbs, as in "To walk is to move"; therefore, this also had to be repeated in the definition of the verb to distinguish it from speech.

We might also say that since the verb introduces the composition which brings about speech signifying truth or falsity, the verb seems to be more like speech (being a certain formal part of it) than the name which is a material and subjective part of it; therefore this had to be repeated.

4.   The third element distinguishes the verb not only from the name, but also from the participle, which also signifies with time. He makes this distinction when he says, *and it is a sign of something said of something else,* i.e., names and participles can be posited on the part of the subject and the predicate, but the verb is always posited on the part of the predicate.

5.   But it seems that verbs are used as subjects. The verb in the infinitive mode is an instance of this, as in the example, "To walk is to be moving."

Verbs of the infinitive mode, however, have the force of names when they are used as subjects. (Hence in both Greek and ordinary Latin usage articles are added to them as in the case of names.) The reason for this is that it is proper to the name to signify something as existing per se, but proper to the verb to signify action or passion. Now

[45]

there are three ways of signifying action or passion. It can be signified per se, as a certain thing in the abstract and is thus signified by a name such as "action," "passion," "walking," "running," and so on. It can also be signified in the mode of an action, i.e., as proceeding from a substance and inhering in it as in a subject; in this way action or passion is signified by the verbs of the different modes attributed to predicates.[57] Finally—and this is the third way in which action or passion can be signified—the very process or inherence of action can be apprehended by the intellect and signified as a thing. Verbs of the infinitive mode signify such inherence of action in a subject and hence can be taken as verbs by reason of concretion, and as names inasmuch as they signify as things.

6.   On this point the objection may also be raised that verbs of other modes sometimes seem to be posited as subjects; for example when we say, " 'Matures' is a verb."

In such a statement, however, the verb "matures" is not taken formally according as its signification is referred to a thing, but as it signifies the vocal sound itself materially, which vocal sound is taken as a thing. When posited in this way, i.e., materially, verbs and all parts of speech are taken with the force of names.

16b8   7.   Then he says, *I mean by "signifies with time" that "maturity," for example, is a name, but "matures" is a verb*, etc.[58] With this he begins to explain the definition of the verb: first in regard to *signifies with time;* secondly, in regard to the verb being *a sign of something said of something else*. He does not explain the second part, *no part of which signifies separately*, because an explanation of it has already been made in connection with the name.

First, he shows by an example that the verb signifies with time. "Maturity," for example, because it signifies action, not in the mode of action but in the mode of a thing existing per se, does not signify with time, for it is a name. But "matures," since it is a verb signifying action, signifies with time, because to be measured by time is proper to motion; moreover, actions are known by us in time. We have already mentioned that to signify with time is to signify something measured in time.[59]

---

[57] Four of the manuscripts of St. Thomas' *Commentary* have "to persons" *(personis)* rather than "to predicates."

[58] See note 54. "Maturity" and "matures" have been substituted for the examples used in the Greek and Latin texts here and throughout the rest of the text, except in n. 15 of Lesson III where "runs" seemed to fit the case better. These examples are more equivalent to the Greek examples and in addition remove some of the ambiguity of the Latin examples when translated into English, i.e., " 'runs' is a verb" would be ambiguous since "runs" is also a noun.

[59] Lesson IV, n. 7.

Hence it is one thing to signify time principally, as a thing, which is appropriate to the name; however, it is another thing to signify with time, which is not proper to the name but to the verb.

8.   Then he says, *Moreover, a verb is always a sign of something* 16b8 *that belongs to something, i.e., of something present in a subject.*[60] Here he explains the last part of the definition of the verb. It should be noted first that the subject of an enunciation signifies as *that in which something inheres.* Hence, when the verb signifies action through the mode of action (the nature of which is to inhere) it is always posited on the part of the predicate and never on the part of the subject—unless it is taken with the force of a name, as was said. The verb, therefore, is always said to be a sign of something said of another, and this not only because the verb always signifies that which is predicated but also because there must be a verb in every predication, for the verb introduces the composition by which the predicate is united with the subject.

9.   The last phrase of this portion of the text presents a difficulty, namely, "of something belonging to [i.e., *of*] a subject or in a subject."[61] For it seems that something is said *of* a subject when it is predicated essentially, as in "Man is an animal"; but *in* a subject, when it is an accident that is predicated of a subject, as in "Man is white." But if verbs signify action or passion (which are accidents), it follows that they always signify what is *in* a subject. It is useless, therefore, to say "belonging to [i.e., *of*] a subject or in a subject."

In answer to this Boethius says that both pertain to the same thing, for an accident is predicated of a subject and is also in a subject.[62]

Aristotle, however, uses a disjunction, which seems to indicate that he means something different by each. Therefore it could be said in reply to this that when Aristotle says the verb is always a sign of those things that are predicated of another[63] it is not to be understood as though the things signified by verbs are predicated. For predication seems to

---

[60] The Oxford Greek text of this sentence reads: ". . . καὶ ἀεὶ τῶν ὑπαρχόντων σημεῖόν ἐστιν, οἷον τῶν καθ᾽ ὑποκειμένου." The L e o n i n e Greek text (and several other manuscripts) read: ". . . καὶ ἀεί τῶν καθ᾽ ἑτέρου λεγομένων σημεῖόν ἐστιν, οἷον τῶν καθ᾽ ὑποκειμένου, ἤ ἐν ὑποκειμένῳ." St. Thomas comments on the text as having the phrase "said [i.e., belonging to] a subject *or in a subject*" (n. 9; italics added).

[61] See note 60 for this variation in the text.

[62] Boethius, *Comment. in librum Aristotelis* Περὶ ἑρμηνείας, I, De verbo, p. 314.

[63] ". . . predicated of another" is not in the Greek text, as can be noted in the quotation of the text in note 60, but it is implied in "of something that belongs to something" and is in the definition of the verb (16b 5) in the sense that "said of something else" could be translated as "predicated of another."

[47]

pertain more properly to composition; therefore, the verbs themselves are what are predicated, rather than signify predicates.[64] The verb, then, is always a sign that something is being predicated because all predication is made through the verb by reason of the composition introduced, whether what is being predicated is predicated essentially or accidentally.

16b12 10.   When he says, *"Non-matures" and "non-declines" I do not call verbs*, etc., he excludes certain forms of verbs from the definition of the verb. And first he excludes the infinite verb, then the verbs of past and future time.

"Non-matures" and "non-declines" cannot strictly speaking be called verbs for it is proper to the verb to signify something in the mode of action or passion. But these words remove action or passion rather than signify a determinate action or passion. Now while they cannot properly be called verbs, all the parts of the definition of the verb apply to them. First of all the verb signifies time[65] because it signifies to act or to be acted upon; and since these are in time so are their privations; whence rest, too, is measured by time, as is said in VI *Physicorum*.[66] Again, the infinite verb is always posited on the part of the predicate just as the verb is; the reason is that negation is reduced to the genus of affirmation. Hence, just as the verb, which signifies action or passion, signifies something as existing in another, so the foresaid words signify the remotion of action or passion.

11.   Now someone might object that if the definition of the verb applies to the above words, then they are verbs. In answer to this it should be pointed out that the definition which has been given of the verb is the definition of it taken commonly. Insofar as these words fall short of the perfect notion of the verb, they are not called verbs.

Before Aristotle's time a name had not been imposed for a word that differs from verbs as these do. He calls them infinite verbs because such words agree in some things with verbs and yet fall short of the determinate notion of the verb. The reason for the name, he says, is that an infinite verb can be said indifferently of what is or what is not;

[64] For a further discussion of this point see p. 24, n. β of the Leonine edition of the *Peri Hermeneias*, where the distinction is made between the predicate as formal and material.

[65] This might seem inaccurate as it stands. One would expect "signifies with time," for it is of the nature of the verb to signify action or passion and by reason of this to signify time,

i.e., as a consequence it signifies time. One manuscript of St. Thomas' *Commentary* (Codex B, ed. 1526) does have *consignificat tempus* (see p. 25, n. ζ of the Leonine) but St. Thomas could be using "signifies" here in a broader sense.

[66] *Phys.* VI, 3, 234a 24-234b 9; and 8, 238a 23-239b 41.

[48]

for the adjoined negation is taken, not with the force of privation, but with the force of simple negation since privation supposes a determinate subject. Infinite verbs do differ from negative verbs, however, for infinite verbs are taken with the force of one word, negative verbs with the force of two.

12.　　　When he says, *Likewise, "has matured" and "will mature" are* *not verbs, but modes of verbs,* etc.,[67] he excludes verbs of past and future time from the definition. For just as infinite verbs are not verbs absolutely, so "will mature," which is of future time, and "has matured," of past time, are not verbs. They are cases of the verb and differ from the verb—which signifies with present time—by signifying time before and after the present. Aristotle expressly says "present time" and not just "present" because he does not mean here the indivisible present which is the instant; for in the instant there is neither movement, nor action, nor passion. Present time is to be taken as the time that measures action which has begun and has not yet been terminated in act. Accordingly, verbs that signify with past or future time are not verbs in the proper sense of the term, for the verb is that which signifies to act or to be acted upon and therefore strictly speaking signifies to act or to be acted upon in act, which is to act or to be acted upon simply, whereas to act or to be acted upon in past or future time is relative.

13.　　　It is with reason that verbs of past or future time are called cases of the verb signifying with present time, for past or future are said with respect to the present, the past being that which was present, the future, that which will be present.

14.　　　Although the inflection of the verb is varied by mode, time, number, and person, the variations that are made in number and person do not constitute cases of the verb, the reason being that such variation is on the part of the subject, not on the part of the action. But variation in mode and time refers to the action itself and hence both of these constitute cases of the verb. For verbs of the imperative or optative modes are called cases as well as verbs of past or future time. Verbs of the indicative mode in present time, however, are not called cases, whatever their person and number.

15.　　　He points out the conformity between verbs and names where he says, *Verbs in themselves, said alone, are names.* He proposes this first and then manifests it.

　　　He says then, first, that verbs said by themselves are names. Some have taken this to mean the verbs that are taken with the force

---

[67] *Supra,* note 42.

of names, either verbs of the infinitive mode, as in "To run is to be moving," or verbs of another mode, as in " 'Matures' is a verb."

But this does not seem to be what Aristotle means, for it does not correspond to what he says next. Therefore "name" must be taken in another way here, i.e., as it commonly signifies any word whatever that is imposed to signify a thing. Now, since to act or to be acted upon is also a certain thing, verbs themselves as they name, i.e., as they signify to act or to be acted upon, are comprehended under names taken commonly. The name as distinguished from the verb signifies the thing under a determinate mode, i.e., according as the thing can be understood as existing per se. This is the reason names can be subjected and predicated.

16b20   16.   He proves the point he has just made when he says, *and signify something*, etc., first by showing that verbs, like names, signify some-
16b22   thing; then by showing that, like names, they do not signify truth or falsity when he says, *for the verb is not a sign of the being or nonbeing of a thing*.

He says first that verbs have been said to be names only insofar as they signify a thing. Then he proves this: it has already been said that significant vocal sound signifies thought; hence it is proper to significant vocal sound to produce something understood in the mind of the one who hears it. To show, then, that a verb is significant vocal sound he assumes that the one who utters a verb brings about understanding in the mind of the one who hears it. The evidence he introduces for this is that the mind of the one who hears it is set at rest.

17.   But what Aristotle says here seems to be false, for it is only perfect speech that makes the intellect rest. The name or the verb, if said by themselves, do not do this. For example, if I say "man," the mind of the hearer is left in suspense as to what I wish to say about man; and if I say "runs," the hearer's mind is left in suspense as to whom I am speaking of.

It should be said in answer to this objection that the operation of the intellect is twofold, as was said above, and therefore the one who utters a name or a verb by itself, determines the intellect with respect to the first operation, which is the simple conception of something. It is in relation to this that the one hearing, whose mind was undetermined before the name or the verb was being uttered and its utterance terminated, is set at rest. Neither the name nor the verb said by itself, however, determines the intellect in respect to the second operation, which is the operation of the intellect composing and dividing; nor do the verb or the name said alone set the hearer's mind at rest in respect to this operation.

[50]

18.   Aristotle therefore immediately adds, *but they do not yet signify*   16b21
whether a thing is or is not, i.e., they do not yet signify something by
way of composition and division, or by way of truth or falsity. This is
the second thing he intends to prove,[68] and he proves it by the verbs
that especially seem to signify truth or falsity, namely the verb *to be*
and the infinite verb *to non-be,* neither of which, said by itself, signifies
real truth or falsity; much less so any other verbs.

This could also be understood in a more general way, i.e., that
here he is speaking of all verbs; for he says that the verb does not signify
whether a thing is or is not; he manifests this further, therefore, by
saying that no verb is significative of a thing's being or non-being, i.e.,
that a thing is or is not. For although every finite verb implies *being,* for
"to run" is "to be running," and every infinite verb implies nonbeing,
for "to non-run" is "to be non-running," nevertheless no verb signifies
the whole, i.e., *a thing is* or *a thing is not.*

19.   He proves this point from something in which it will be clearer
when he adds, *Nor would it be a sign of the being or nonbeing of a*   16b23
thing if you were to say "is" alone,[69] *for it is nothing.* It should be noted
that the Greek text has the word "being" in place of "is" here.

In order to prove that verbs do not signify that a thing is or is
not, he takes the source and origin of *to be [esse],* i.e., *being [ens]* itself,
of which he says, *it is nothing.* Alexander explains this passage in the
following way: Aristotle says being itself is nothing because "being"
[ens] is said equivocally of the ten predicaments; now an equivocal
name used by itself signifies nothing unless something is added to determine its signification; hence, "is" *[est]* said by itself does not signify
what is or *is not.*

But this explanation is not appropriate for this text. In the first
place "being" is not, strictly speaking, said equivocally but according to
the prior and posterior. Consequently, said absolutely, it is understood
of that of which it is said primarily. Secondly, an equivocal word does
not signify nothing, but many things, sometimes being taken for one,
sometimes for another. Thirdly, such an explanation does not have much
application here.

Porphyry explains this passage in another way. He says that
"being" *[ens]* itself does not signify the nature of a thing as the name
"man" or "wise" do, but only designates a certain conjunction and this
is why Aristotle adds, *it signifies with a composition, which cannot be
conceived apart from the things composing it.*

[68] Cf. n. 16 of St. Thomas's *Commen-*   [69] The Greek text has τὸ ὄν here; the
tary for this division.   Latin, *est.*

[51]

This explanation does not seem to be consistent with the text either, for if "being" itself does not signify a thing, but only a conjunction, it, like prepositions and conjunctions, is neither a name nor a verb.

Therefore Ammonius thought this should be explained in another way. He says "being itself is nothing" means that it does not signify truth or falsity. And the reason for this is given when Aristotle says, *it signifies with a composition.* The "signifies with," according to Ammonius, does not mean what it does when it is said that the verb *signifies with time;* "signifies with" means here *signifies with something,* i.e., joined to another it signifies composition, which cannot be understood without the extremes of the composition. But this explanation does not seem to be in accordance with the intention of Aristotle, for it is common to all names and verbs not to signify truth or falsity, whereas Aristotle takes "being" here as though it were something special.

20.   Therefore in order to understand what Aristotle is saying we should note that he has just said that the verb does not signify that a thing exists or does not exist *[rem esse vel non esse];* nor does "being" *[ens]* signify that a thing exists or does not exist. This is what he means when he says, *it is nothing,* i.e., it does not signify that a thing exists. This is indeed most clearly seen in saying "being" *[ens],* because *being* is nothing other than *that which is.* And thus we see that it signifies both a thing, when I say "that which," and existence *[esse]* when I say "is" *[est].* If the word "being" *[ens]* as signifying *a thing* having existence were to signify existence *[esse]* principally, without a doubt it would signify that a thing exists. But the word "being" *[ens]* does not principally signify the composition that is implied in saying "is" *[est];* rather, it signifies with composition inasmuch as it signifies *the thing* having existence. Such signifying with composition is not sufficent for truth or falsity; for the composition in which truth and falsity consists cannot be understood unless it connects the extremes of a composition.

21.   If in place of what Aristotle says we say *nor would "to be" itself [nec ipsum esse],* as it is in our texts, the meaning is clearer.[70] For Aristotle proves through the verb "is" *[est]* that no verb signifies that a thing exists or does not exist, since "is" said by itself does not signify that a thing exists, although it signifies existence. And because *to be* itself seems to be a kind of composition, so also the verb "is" *[est],* which signifies *to be,* can seem to signify the composition in which there is truth or falsity. To exclude this Aristotle adds that the composition which the verb "is" signifies cannot be understood without the compos-

[70] The Greek τὸ ὄν is closer to this reading.

ing things. The reason for this is that an understanding of the composition which "is" signifies depends on the extremes, and unless they are added, understanding of the composition is not complete and hence cannot be true or false.

22.   Therefore he says that the verb "is" signifies with composition; for it does not signify composition principally but consequently. It primarily signifies that which is perceived in the mode of actuality absolutely; for "is" said simply, signifies *to be in act,* and therefore signifies in the mode of a verb. However, the actuality which the verb "is" principally signifies is the actuality of every form commonly, whether substantial or accidental. Hence, when we wish to signify that any form or act is actually in some subject we signify it through the verb "is," either absolutely or relatively; absolutely, according to present time, relatively, according to other times; and for this reason the verb "is" signifies composition, not principally, but consequently.

On Speech, the Formal Principle of the Enunciation

16b 26   Speech[71] is significant vocal sound, some parts of which are significant separately, i.e., as words but not as an affirmation.

16b 28   Let me explain. The word "animal"[72] signifies something, but it does not signify that it is or that it is not; it will be an affirmation or negation, however, if something is added.

16b 30   But one syllable of "animal" does not signify anything; similarly, in the word "fowl," "owl" does not signify anything in itself, but is only a vocal sound.[73] In composite names, however, the part does signify something, but not in itself, as has been said.

16b 34   But all speech [i.e., words put together to express thought] is significant—not just as an instrument, however, but by convention, as has been said.

---

1.   Having established and explained the definition of the name and the verb, which are the material principles of the enunciation inasmuch as they are its parts, the Philosopher now determines and explains what speech is, which is the formal principle of the enunciation inasmuch as it is its genus. First he proposes the definition of speech; then he explains
16b28   it where he says, *Let me explain. The word "animal" signifies something*, etc.; finally, he excludes an error where he says, *But all speech is significant—not just as an instrument, however*, etc.

2.   In defining speech the Philosopher first states what it has in
16b26   common with the name and verb where he says, *Speech is significant vocal sound.* This was posited in the definition of the name but not re-

---

[71] *Supra*, note 5.

[72] The Greek word Aristotle uses for this illustration is ἄνθρωπος (the Latin, *homo*), which because of its two syllables he can use in the next sentence (16b 30) to make a point in relation to his definition of speech. To preserve the value of the example the word "animal" has been used in the present translation. "Man" would not do this; nor would "human" or "mortal" which are closer to the Greek word in mean-

ing and do have more than one syllable, since "is" or "is not" cannot be meaningfully added to them in English.

[73] Another example has also been substituted for Aristotle's here. He uses ὗς from μῦς (mouse) because ὗς appears to have a meaning since there is a Greek word ὗς, which means "the wild swine." To preserve the value of this example, "owl" from the word "fowl" has been used.

[54]

peated in the case of the verb, because it was supposed from the definition of the name. This was done for the sake of brevity and to avoid repetition; but subsequently he did prove that the verb signifies something. He repeats this, however, in the definition of speech because the signification of speech differs from that of the name and the verb; for the name and the verb signify simple thought, whereas speech signifies composite thought.

3.　　　Secondly, he posits what differentiates speech from the name and verb when he says, *of which some of the parts are significant separately;* for a part of a name taken separately does not signify anything per se, except in the case of a name composed of two parts, as he said above.[74] Note that he says, *of which some of the parts are significant,* and not, *a part of which is significant separately;* this is to exclude negations and the other words used to unite categorical words, which do not in themselves signify something absolutely, but only the relationship of one thing to another.

Then because the signification of vocal sound is twofold, one being referred to composite thought, the other to simple thought (the first belonging to speech, the second, not to speech but to a part of speech), he adds, *as words but not as an affirmation.* What he means is that a part of speech signifies in the way a word signifies, a name or a verb, for instance; it does not signify in the way an affirmation signifies, which is composed of a name and a verb. He only mentions affirmation because negation adds something to affirmation as far as vocal sound is concerned for if a part of speech, since it is simple, does not signify as an affirmation, it will not signify as a negation.

4.　　　Aspasius objects to this definition because it does not seem to belong to all parts of speech. There is a kind of speech he says, in which some of the parts signify as an affirmation; for instance, "If the sun shines over the earth, it is day," and so in many other examples.

Porphyry says in reply to this objection that in whatever genus there is something prior and posterior, it is the prior thing that has to be defined.[75] For example, when we give the definition of a species— say, of man—the definition is understood of that which is *in act,* not of that which is *in potency.* Since, then, in the genus of speech, simple speech is prior, Aristotle defines it first.

---

[74] Cf. 16a 22.

[75] There is a question as to whether this is Alexander's or Porphyry's answer to the objection; and in relation to St. Thomas' statement later on that Porphyry's solution reduces to the same thing, etc., whether this solution is Porphyry's or Alexander's. Boethius attributes it to Alexander. Cf. p. 30, n. η of the Leonine, where there is also a discussion of Porphyry's and Alexander's opinions.

[55]

Or, we can answer the objection in the way Alexander and Ammonious do. They say that speech is defined here commonly. Hence what is common to simple and composite speech ought to be stated in the definition. Now to have parts signifying something as an affirmation belongs only to composite speech, but to have parts signifying something in the mode of a word and not in the mode of an affirmation is common to simple and composite speech. Therefore this had to be posited in the definition of speech. We should not conclude, however, that it is of the nature of speech that its part not be an affirmation, but rather that it is of the nature of speech that its parts be something that signify in the manner of words and not in the manner of an affirmation.

Porphyry's solution reduces to the same thing as far as meaning is concerned, although it is a little different verbally. Aristotle frequently uses "to say" for "to affirm," and hence to prevent "word" from being taken as "affirmation" when he says that a part of speech signifies as a word, he immediately adds, *not as an affirmation,* meaning—according to Porphyry's view—"word" is not taken here in the sense in which it is the same as "affirmation."[76]

A philosopher called John the Grammarian thought that this definition could only apply to perfect speech because there only seem to be parts in the case of something perfect, or complete; for example, a house to which all of the parts are referred. Therefore only perfect speech has significant parts.

He was in error on this point, however, for while it is true that all the parts are referred principally to the perfect, or complete whole, some parts are referred to it immediately, for example, the walls and roof to a house and organic members to an animal; others, however, are referred to it through the principal parts of which they are parts; stones, for example, to the house by the mediate wall, and nerves and bones to the animal by the mediate organic members like the hand and the foot, etc. In the case of speech, therefore, all of the parts are principally referred to perfect speech, a part of which is imperfect speech, which also has significant parts. Hence this definition belongs both to perfect and to imperfect speech.

16b28   5.   When he says, *Let me explain. The word "animal" signifies something,* etc., he elucidates the definition. First he shows that what

---

[76] This point is difficult to see when translated into English. The Latin word for "to say" is *dicere* and for "word" *dictio,* in Greek κατάφασις and φάσις. Actually the Greek φάσις which has been translated as "word" means an utterance or a saying, and could easily be confused with "affirmation." Cf. St. Thomas', *Commentary on De Anima* II, Lesson 18 n. 469 for the meaning of *dictio* as word.

he says is true; secondly, he excludes a false understanding of it where he says, *But one syllable of "animal" does not signify anything,* etc.

He explains that when he says *some parts* of speech are significant, he means that some of the parts signify something in the way the name "animal," which is a part of speech, signifies something and yet does not signify as an affirmation or negation, because it does not signify *to be* or *not to be.* By this I mean it does not signify affirmation or negation in act, but only in potency; for it is possible to add something that will make it an affirmation or negation, i.e., a verb.

6.   He excludes a false understanding of what has been said by his next statement. *But one syllable of "animal" does not signify anything.* This could be referred to what has just been said and the meaning would be that the name will be an affirmation or negation if something is added to it, but not if what is added is one syllable of a name. However, what he says next is not compatible with this meaning and therefore these words should be referred to what was stated earlier in defining speech, namely, to *some parts* of which are significant separately. Now, since what is properly called a part of a whole is that which contributes immediately to the formation of the whole, and not that which is a part of a part, "some parts" should be understood as the parts from which speech is immediately formed, i.e., the name and verb, and not as parts of the name or verb, which are syllables or letters. Hence, what is being said here is that a part of speech is significant separately but not such a part as the syllable of a name.

He manifests this by means of syllables that sometimes can be words signifying per se. "Owl," for example, is sometimes one word signifying per se.[77] When taken as a syllable of the name "fowl," however, it does not signify something per se but is only a vocal sound. For a word is composed of many vocal sounds, but it has simplicity in signifying insofar as it signifies simple thought. Hence, a word inasmuch as it is a composite vocal sound can have a part which is a vocal sound,[78] but inasmuch as it is simple in signifying it cannot have a signifying part. Whence syllables are indeed vocal sounds, but they are not vocal sounds signifying per se.

---

[77] The Latin uses *rex* and *sorex* here in place of the Greek example μῦς (mouse), a word of two syllables rather than one as in the example used by Aristotle.

[78] This is the reading of codices. C, D, and E; A has "it can have a part which is a non-significant vocal sound." The Piana edition adds to this "and which is 'rex.'" Edition b (Veneta, 1495), has "it [a word] can have a part which will signify." The editors of the Leonine suggest that "significative" should either be added or understood here. Cf. p. 31 n. ξ, of the Leonine edition for the variations in the texts and the Preface for identification of the manuscripts.

[57]

In contrast to this it should be noted that in composite names, which are imposed to signify a simple thing from some composite understanding, the parts appear to signify something, although according to truth they do not. For this reason he adds that in compound words, i.e., composite names, the syllables may be words contributing to the composition of a name, and therefore signify something, namely, in the composite, and according as they are words; but as parts of this kind of name they do not signify something per se, but in the way that has already been explained.[79]

16b34 7.   Then he says, *But all speech is significant—not just as an instrument, however,* etc. Here he excludes the error of those who said that speech and its parts signify naturally rather than by convention. To prove their point they used the following argument. The instruments of a natural power must themselves be natural, for nature does not fail in regard to what is necessary; but the interpretive power is natural to man; therefore, its instruments are natural. Now the instrument of the interpretive power is speech since it is through speech that expression is given to the conception of the mind; for we mean by an instrument that by which an agent operates. Therefore, speech is something natural, signifying, not from human institution, but naturally.

8.   Aristotle refutes this argument, which is said to be that of Plato in the *Cratylus*, when he says that all speech is significant, but not as an instrument of a power, that is, of a natural power; for the natural instruments of the interpretive power are the throat and lungs, by which vocal sound is formed, and the tongue, teeth and lips by which letters and articulate sounds are formulated. Rather, speech and its parts are effects of the interpretative power through the aforesaid instruments. For just as the motive power uses natural instruments such as arms and hands to make an artificial work, so the interpretative power uses the throat and other natural instruments to make speech. Hence, speech and its parts are not natural things, but certain artificial effects. This is the reason Aristotle adds here that speech signifies by convention, i.e., according to the ordinance of human will and reason.

It should be noted, however, that if we do not attribute the interpretative power to a motive power, but to reason, then it is not a natural power but is beyond every corporeal nature, since thought is not an act of the body, as is proved in III *De anima.*[80] Moreover, it is reason itself that moves the corporeal motive power to make artificial works, which reason then uses as instruments; and thus artificial works

[79] Cf. 16a 21-16a 25; St. Thomas, Lesson IV, nn. 9-10.   [80] *De Anima* III, 4, 429a 10 ff.

are not instruments of a corporeal power. Reason can also use speech and its parts in this way, i.e., as instruments, although they do not signify naturally.

The Definition of Enunciation

17a 2   Yet not all speech is enunciative; but only speech in which there is truth or falsity.

17a 4   Truth and falsity is not present in all speech, however; a prayer, for example, is speech but it is neither true nor false.

17a 5   Let us therefore consider enunciative speech, which belongs to our present inquiry, and omit the other kinds, for the study of these belongs rather to rhetoric and poetics.

————————————

1.   Having defined the principles of the enunciation, the Philosopher now begins to treat the enunciation itself. This is divided into two parts. In the first he examines the enunciation absolutely; in the second the diversity of enunciations resulting from an addition to the simple enunciation. The latter is treated in the second book, where he 19b5   says, *Since an affirmation signifies something about a subject,* etc.[81] The first part, on the enunciation absolutely, is divided into three parts. In the first he defines enunciation; in the second he divides it where he 17a8   says, *First affirmation, then negation, is enunciative speech that is one,* etc.;[82] in the third he treats of the opposition of its parts to each other, 17a26   where he says, *Since it is possible to enunciate that what belongs to a subject does not belong to it,* etc.[83] In the portion of the text treated in this lesson, which is concerned with the definition of enunciation, he first states the definition, then shows that this definition differentiates the 17a4   enunciation from other species of speech, where he says, *Truth and falsity is not present in all speech however,* etc., and finally indicates that only 17a5   the enunciation is to be treated in this book where he says, *Let us therefore consider enunciative speech,* etc.

2.   The point has just been made that speech, although it is not an instrument of a power operating naturally, is nevertheless an instrument of reason. Now every instrument is defined by its end, which is the use of the instrument. The use of speech, as of every significant vocal sound, is to signify a conception of the intellect.[84] But there are two operations of the intellect. In one truth and falsity is found, in the other not. Aristotle therefore defines enunciative speech by the signification of the true

[81] Book II, Lesson I.
[82] In Book I, Lesson VIII.

[83] In Book I, Lesson IX.
[84] Cf. Book I, Lesson II, n. 5.

and false: *Yet not all speech is enunciative; but only speech in which* 17b2
there is truth or falsity. Note with what remarkable brevity he signifies
the division of speech by *Yet not all speech is enunciative,* and the definition by, *but only speech in which there is truth or falsity.* This, then, is
to be understood as the definition of the enunciation: *speech in which*
there is truth and falsity.

3.   True or false is said to be in the enunciation as in a sign of true
or false thought; but true or false is in the mind as in a subject (as is said
in VI *Metaphysicae*),[85] and in the thing as in a cause (as is said in the
book *Predicamentorum*)[86]—for it is from the facts of the case, i.e., from
a thing's being so or not being so, that speech is true or false.

4.   Next he shows that this definition differentiates the enunciation
from other speech, when he says, *Truth or falsity is not present in all* 17a4
speech however, etc. In the case of imperfect or incomplete speech it is
clear that it does not signify the true or false, since it does not make complete sense to the mind of the hearer and therefore does not completely
express a judgment of reason in which the true or false consists. Having
made this point, however, it must be noted that there are five species of
perfect speech that are complete in meaning: enunciative, deprecative,
imperative, interrogative, and vocative. (Apropos of the latter it should
be noted that a name alone in the vocative case is not vocative speech,
for some of the parts must signify something separately, as was said
above. So, although the mind of the hearer is provoked or aroused to attention by a name in the vocative case, there is not vocative speech,
unless many words are joined together, as in "O good Peter!") Of these
species of speech the enunciative is the only one in which there is truth
or falsity, for it alone signifies the conception of the intellect absolutely
and it is in this that there is truth or falsity.

5.   But the intellect, or reason, does not just conceive the truth of
a thing. It also belongs to its office to direct and order others in accordance with what it conceives. Therefore, besides enunciative speech,
which signifies the concept of the mind, there had to be other kinds of
speech to signify the order of reason by which others are directed. Now,
one man is directed by the reason of another in regard to three things:
first, to attend with his mind, and vocative speech relates to this; second,
to respond with his voice, and interrogative speech relates to this; third,
to execute a work, and in relation to this, imperative speech is used with
regard to inferiors, deprecative with regard to superiors. Optative speech
is reduced to the latter, for a man does not have the power to move a
superior except by the expression of his desire.

[85] *Metaph.* E, 4, 1027b 17-1028a 5.   [86] *Categ.* 5, 4a 35-4b 9.

These four species of speech do not signify the conception of the intellect in which there is truth or falsity, but a certain order following upon this. Consequently truth or falsity is not found in any of them, but only in enunciative speech, which signifies what the mind conceives from things. It follows that all the modes of speech in which the true or false is found are contained under the enunciation, which some call *indicative* or *suppositive*. The dubitative, it should be noted, is reduced to the interrogative, as the optative is to the deprecative.

17a5 6.   Then Aristotle says, *Let us therefore consider enunciative speech,* etc. Here he points out that only enunciative speech is to be treated; the other four species must be omitted as far as the present intention is concerned, because their investigation belongs rather to the sciences of rhetoric or poetics. Enunciative speech belongs to the present consideration and for the following reason: this book is ordered directly to demonstrative science, in which the mind of man is led by an act of reasoning to assent to truth from those things that are proper to the thing; to this end the demonstrator uses only enunciative speech, which signifies things according as truth about them is in the mind. The rhetorician and the poet, on the other hand, induce assent to what they intend not only through what is proper to the thing but also through the dispositions of the hearer. Hence, rhetoricians and poets for the most part strive to move their auditors by arousing certain passions in them, as the Philosopher says in his *Rhetorica*.[87] This kind of speech, therefore, which is concerned with the ordination of the hearer toward something, belongs to the consideration of rhetoric or poetics by reason of its intent, but to the consideration of the grammarian as regards a suitable construction of the vocal sounds.

[87] *Rhetoric* I, 2, 1356a 2, 1356a 14;
    III, 1, 1403b 12.

[62]

LESSON VIII

The Division of Enunciation into Simple and Composite, Affirmative and Negative

17a 8   First affirmation, then negation, is enunciative speech that is one; the others are one by conjunction.

17a 9   Every enunciative speech, however, must contain a verb or a mode of the verb; for the definition of man, if "is" or "was" or "will be" or something of the kind is not added, is not yet enunciative speech;

17a 13   (but then the question arises as to why the definition "terrestrial biped animal" is something one and not many—for clearly it will not be one by reason of the words being said in juxtaposition—but this belongs to another subject of inquiry).[88]

17a 15   Enunciative speech is one when it signifies one thing or is one by conjunction; but it is many when it signifies many things and not one, or many things not joined together.

17a 17   Let us call the name or the verb a word only, since to speak in this way is not to signify something with the voice so as to enunciate, either in reply to someone asking a question or by one's own choice.

17a 20   Of enunciations that are one, simple enunciation is one kind, i.e., something affirmed of something or something denied of something; the other kind is composite, i.e., speech composed of these simple enunciations.

17a 23   A simple enunciation is vocal sound signifying that something belongs or does not belong to a subject according to the divisions of time.

17a 25   Affirmation is the enunciation of something about something; negation the enunciation of something separated from something.

---

1.   Having defined the enunciation the Philosopher now divides it. First he gives the division, and then manifests it where he says, *Every* 17a9 *enunciative speech however, must contain a verb*, etc.

2.   It should be noted that Aristotle in his concise way gives two divisions of the enunciation. The first is the division into one simply and one by conjunction. This parallels things outside of the soul where there is also something one simply, for instance the indivisible or the con-

[88] Cf. *Metaph.* Z, 12, 1037b 7 ff.

tinuum, and something one either by aggregation or composition or order. In fact, since being and one are convertible, every enunciation must in some way be *one*, just as every thing is.

3.　　The other is a subdivision of the enunciation: the division of it as it is one into affirmative and negative.

The affirmative enunciation is prior to the negative for three reasons, which are related to three things already stated. It was said that vocal sound is a sign of thought and thought a sign of the thing. Accordingly, with respect to vocal sound, affirmative enunciation is prior to negative because it is simpler, for the negative enunciation adds a negative particle to the affirmative. With respect to thought, the affirmative enunciation, which signifies composition by the intellect, is prior to the negative, which signifies division, for division is posterior by nature to composition since division is only of composite things—just as corruption is only of generated things. With respect to the thing, the affirmative enunciation, which signifies *to be* is prior to the negative, which signifies *not to be,* as the having of something is naturally prior to the privation of it.

17a8　4.　　What he says, then, is this: *Affirmation,* i.e., affirmative enunciation, *is one and the first enunciative speech.*[89] And in opposition to first he adds, *then negation,* i.e., negative speech, for it is posterior to affirmative, as we have said. In opposition to one, i.e., one simply, he adds, *certain others are one,* not simply, but *one by conjunction.*

5.　　From what Aristotle says here Alexander argues that the division of enunciation into affirmation and negation is not a division of a genus into species, but a division of a multiple name into its meanings; for a genus is not predicated according to the prior and posterior, but is predicated univocally of its species; this is the reason Aristotle would not grant that *being* is a common genus of all things, for it is predicated first of substance, and then of the nine genera of accidents.

6.　　However, in the division of that which is common, one of the dividing members can be prior to another in two ways: according to the proper notions[90] or natures of the dividing members, or according to the

---

[89] The Greek text here is: "ἔστι δὲ εἷς πρῶτος λόγος ἀποφαντικὸς κατάφασις εἶτα ἀπόφασις. οἱ δὲ ἄλλοι συνδέσμῳ εἷς." This could have been translated as "Affirmation is the first *kind,* negation the second of enunciative speech that is one; the other kinds are only one by conjunction." However, Aristotle seems to be speaking more generally here, as the balance of the text bears out, for he goes on to elucidate what he means by "one" (17a 15) and to divide enunciations that are one into kinds (17a 20).

[90] The Latin word *ratio,* translated here as "notion," means that which the intellect conceives from the sig-

participation of that common notion that is divided in them. The first of these does not destroy the univocity of a genus, as is evident in numbers. Twoness, according to its proper notion, is naturally prior to threeness, yet they equally participate in the notion of their genus, i.e., number; for both a multitude consisting of three and a multitude consisting of two is measured by one. The second, however, does impede the univocity of a genus. This is why *being* cannot be the genus of substance and accident, for in the very notion of *being,* substance, which is being per se, has priority in respect to accident, which is being through another and in another.

Applying this distinction to the matter at hand, we see that affirmation is prior to negation in the first way, i.e., according to its notion, yet they equally participate in the definition Aristotle has given of the enunciation, i.e., speech in which there is truth or falsity.

7.   Where he says, *Every enunciative speech, however, must contain a verb or a mode of the verb,* etc., he explains the divisions. He gives 17a9
two explanations, one of the division of enunciation into one simply and one by conjunction, the second of the division of the enunciation which is one simply into affirmative or negative. The latter explanation begins where he says, *A simple enunciation is vocal sound signifying that some-* 17a23
thing belongs or does not belong to a subject, etc. Before he explains the first division, i.e., into one simply and one by conjunction, he states certain things that are necessary for the evidence of the explanation, and then explains the division where he says, *Enunciative speech is one when* 17a15
it signifies one thing, etc.

8.   He states the first thing that is necessary for his explanation when he says that every enunciative speech must contain a verb in present time, or a case of the verb, i.e., in past or future time. (The infinite verb is not mentioned because it has the same function in the enunciation as the negative verb.) To manifest this he shows that one name, without a verb, does not even constitute imperfect enunciative speech, let alone perfect speech. Definition, he points out, is a certain kind of speech, and yet if the verb "is" or modes of the verb such as "was" or "has been" or something of the kind, is not added to the notion of man, i.e., to the definition, it is not enunciative speech.

9.   But, one might ask, why mention the verb and not the name, for the enunciation consists of a name and a verb?

nification of a name, even though it may not have a definition. *Ratio* does not signify the conception itself but the intention of the conception. Cf. St. Thomas, *Commentary on the* *Sentences of Peter Lombard* I, d. 2. 1, 3. He also points out here that there is something corresponding to this intention in things.

This can be answered in three ways. First of all because enunciative speech is not attained without a verb or a mode of the verb, but it is without a name, for instance, when infinitive forms of the verb are used in place of names, as in "To run is to be moving."

A second and better reason for speaking only of the verb is that the verb is a sign of what is predicated of another.[91] Now the predicate is the principal part of the enunciation because it is the formal part and completes it. This is the reason the Greeks called the enunciation a categorical, i.e., predicative, proposition. It should also be noted that denomination is made from the form which gives species to the thing. He speaks of the verb, then, but not the name, because it is the more principal and formal part of the enunciation. A sign of this is that the categorical enunciation is said to be affirmative or negative solely by reason of the verb being affirmed or denied, and the conditional enunciation is said to be affirmative or negative by reason of the conjunction by which it is denominated being affirmed or denied.

A third and even better reason is that Aristotle did not intend to show that the name or verb is not sufficient for a complete enunciation, for he explained this earlier. Rather, he is excluding a misunderstanding that might arise from his saying that one kind of enunciation is one simply and another kind is one by conjunction. Some might think this means that the kind that is one simply, lacks all composition. But he excludes this by saying that there must be a verb in every enunciation; for the verb implies composition and composition cannot be understood apart from the things composed, as he said earlier.[92] The name, on the other hand, does not imply composition and therefore did not have to be mentioned.

10.   The other point necessary for the evidence of the first division
17a13 is made where he says, *but then the question arises as to why the definition "terrestial biped animal" is something one,* etc. He indicates by this that "terrestial biped animal," which is a definition of man, is one and not many. The reason it is one is the same as in the case of all definitions but, he says, to assign the reason belongs to another subject of inquiry. It belongs, in fact, to metaphysics and he assigns the reason in VII and VIII *Metaphysicae,* which is this: the difference does not accrue to the genus accidentally but per se and is determinative of it in the way in which form determines matter; for the genus is taken from matter, the difference from form. Whence, just as one thing—not many—comes to be from form and matter, so one thing comes to be from the genus and difference.[93]

[91] 16b 7; St. Thomas, Lesson V, n. 4.   [93] *Metaph.* z, 12, 1037b 7 ff.; H, 6,
[92] 16b 25; St. Thomas, Lesson V, n. 21.   1045a 6 ff.

11.   The reason for the unity of this definition might be supposed by some to be only that of juxtaposition of the parts, i.e., that "terrestial biped animal" is said to be one only because the parts are side by side without conjunction or pause. But he excludes such a notion of its unity.

Now it is true that noninterruption of locution is necessary for the unity of a definition, for if a conjunction were put between the parts the second part would not determine the first immediately and the many in locution would consequently signify many in act. The pause used by rhetoricians in place of a conjunction would do the same thing. Whence it is a requirement for the unity of a definition that its parts be uttered without conjunction and interpolation, the reason being that in the natural thing, whose definition it is, nothing mediates between matter and form.

However, noninterruption of locution is not the only thing that is needed for unity of the definition, for there can be continuity of utterance in regard to things that are not one simply, but are accidentally, as in "white musical man." Aristotle has therefore manifested very subtly that absolute unity of the enunciation is not impeded either by the composition which the verb implies or by the multitude of names from which a definition is established. And the reason is the same in both cases, i.e., the predicate is related to the subject as form to matter, as is the difference to a genus; but from form and matter a thing that is one simply comes into existence.

12.   He begins to explain the division when he says, *Enunciative*   17a15
speech is one when it signifies one thing, etc. First he makes the common thing that is divided evident, i.e., the enunciation as it is one; secondly, he makes the parts of the division evident according to their own proper notions, where he says, *Of enunciations that are one, simple enunciation*   17a20
is one kind, etc. After he has made the division of the common thing evident, i.e., enunciation, he then concludes that the name and the verb are excluded from each member of the division where he says, *Let us*   17a17
call the name or the verb a word only, etc.

Now plurality is opposed to unity. Therefore he is going to manifest the unity of the enunciation through the modes[94] of plurality.

13.   He begins his explanation by saying that enunciation is either one absolutely, i.e., it signifies one thing said of one thing, or one relatively, i.e., it is one by conjunction. In opposition to these are the enunciations that are many, either because they signify not one but many things, which is opposed to the first mode of unity or because they are

[94] In the Piana edition this is "mode" rather than "modes."

uttered without a connecting particle, which is opposed to the second mode of unity.

14.   Boethius interprets this passage in the following way. "Unity" and "plurality" of speech refers to what is signified, whereas "simple" and "composite" is related to the vocal sounds.[95] Accordingly, an enunciation is sometimes one and simple, namely, when one thing is signified by the composition of name and verb, as in "Man is white." Sometimes it is one and composite. In this case it signifies one thing, but is composed either from many terms, as in "A mortal rational animal is running," or from many enunciations, as in conditionals that signify one thing and not many. On the other hand, sometimes there is plurality along with simplicity, namely, when a name signifying many things is used, as in "The dog barks," in which case the enunciation is many because it signifies many things [i.e., it signifies equivocally], but it is simple as far as vocal sound is concerned. But sometimes there is plurality and composition, namely, when many things are posited on the part of the subject or predicate from which one thing does not result, whether a conjunction intervenes or not, as in "The musical white man is arguing." This is also the case if there are many enunciations joined together, with or without connecting particles as in "Socrates runs, Plato discusses."

According to this exposition the meaning of the passage in question is this: an enunciation is one when it signifies one thing said of one thing, and this is the case whether the enunciation is one simply or is one by conjunction; an enunciation is many when it signifies not one but many things, and this not only when a conjunction is inserted between either the names or verbs or between the enunciations themselves, but even if there are many things that are not conjoined. In the latter case they signify many things either because an equivocal name is used or because many names signifying many things from which one thing does not result are used without conjunctions, as in "The white grammatical logical man is running."

15.   However, this exposition does not seem to be what Aristotle had in mind. First of all the disjunction he inserts seems to indicate that he is distinguishing between speech signifying one thing and speech which

[95] Boethius (*Comment. in librum Aristotelis* Περὶ ἑρμηνείας, 2nd ed., I, p. 328, quoted in the Leonine, note φ, p. 38) says: "Speech is understood as one or many if it signifies one or many; and they are always judged with respect to the proper significa- tion. But simple and composite is not with respect to the signification but is known from the plurality of words and names, for if a proposi- tion has more than two terms it is composite; if it has only two it is simple."

is one by conjunction. In the second place, he has just said that terrestial biped animal is something one and not many. Moreover, what is one by conjunction is not one, and not many, but one from many. Hence it seems better to say that since he has already said that one kind of enunciation is one simply and another kind is one by conjunction he is showing here what *one* enunciation is.

Having said, then, that many names joined together are something one as in the example "terrestial biped animal," he goes on to say that an enunciation is to be judged as *one,* not from the unity of the name but from the unity of what is signified, even if there are many names signifying the one thing; and if an enunciation which signifies many things is one, it will not be one simply, but one by conjunction. Hence, the enunciation "A terrestial biped animal is risible," is not one in the sense of one by conjunction as the first exposition would have it, but because it signifies one thing.

16.   Then—because an opposite is manifested through an opposite— he goes on to show which enunciations are many, and he posits two modes of plurality. Enunciations are said to be many which signify many things. Many things may be signified in some one common thing however; when I say, for example, "An animal is a sentient being," many things are contained under the one common thing, *animal,* but such an enunciation is still one, not many. Therefore Aristotle adds, *and not one.* It would be better to say, however, that the *and not one* is added because of definition, which signifies many things that are one.

The mode of plurality he has spoken of thus far is opposed to the first mode of unity. The second mode of plurality covers enunciations that not only signify many things but many that are in no way joined together. This mode is opposed to the second mode of unity. Thus it is evident that the second mode of unity is not opposed to the first mode of plurality. Now those things that are not opposed can be together. Therefore, the enunciation that is one by conjunction is also many— many insofar as it signifies many and not one.

According to this understanding of the text there are three modes of the enunciation: the enunciation that is one simply inasmuch as it signifies one thing; the enunciation that is many simply inasmuch as it signifies many things, but is one relatively inasmuch as it is one by conjunction; finally, the enunciations that are many simply—those that do not signify one thing and are not united by any conjunction.

Aristotle posits four kinds of enunciation rather than three, for an enunciation is sometimes many because it signifies many things, and yet is not one by conjunction; a case in point would be an enunciation in which a name signifying many things is used.

[69]

17. Where he says, *Let us call the name or the verb a word only,* etc., he excludes the name and the verb from the unity of speech. His reason for making this point is that his statement, "an enunciation is one inasmuch as it signifies one thing," might be taken to mean that an enunciation signifies one thing in the same way the name or verb signify one thing. To prevent such a misunderstanding he says, *Let us call the name or the verb a word only,* i.e., a locution which is not an enunciation. From his mode of speaking it would seem that Aristotle himself imposed the name "phasis" [word] to signify such parts of the enunciation.

Then he shows that a name or verb is only a word by pointing out that we do not say that a person is enunciating when he signifies something in vocal sound in the way in which a name or verb signifies. To manifest this he suggests two ways of using the enunciation. Sometimes we use it to reply to questions; for example if someone asks "Who is it who discusses," we answer "The teacher."[96] At other times we use the enunciation, not in reply to a question, but of our own accord, as when we say "Peter is running."

What Aristotle is saying, then, is that the person who signifies something one by a name or a verb is not enunciating in the way in which either the person who replies to a question or who utters an enunciation of his own accord is enunciating. He introduces this point because the simple name or verb, when used in reply to a question seems to signify truth or falsity and truth or falsity is what is proper to the enunciation. Truth and falsity is not proper, however, to the name or verb unless it is understood as joined to another part proposed in a question; if someone should ask, for example, "Who reads in the schools," we would answer, "The teacher," understanding also, "reads there." If, then, something expressed by a name or verb is not an enunciation, it is evident that the enunciation does not signify one thing in the same way as the name or verb signify one thing. Aristotle draws this by way of a

conclusion from, *Every enunciative speech must contain a verb or a mode of the verb,* which was stated earlier.

18. Then when he says, *Of enunciations that are one,*[97] *simple enunciation is one kind,* etc., he manifests the division of enunciation by the natures of the parts. He has said that the enunciation is one when it signifies one thing or is one by conjunction. The basis of this division

---

[96] All the editions of Veneta of the fifteenth century and of 1526 have here *Quid* sit in scholis" for "*Quis* sit in scholis" (italics added) and the answer, "Magester disputat." This answer, however, supposes the question "Quid fit in scholis." Cf. p. 40, n. $\eta\eta$ of the Leonine edition.

[97] The Greek text and the Latin translation of it read here: "Of these," but what is intended, of course, is, "Of enunciations that are one."

is the nature of *one*, which is such that it can be divided into simple and composite. Hence, Aristotle says, *Of these*, i.e., enunciations into which one is divided, which are said to be one either because the enunciation signifies one thing simply or because it is one by conjunction, *simple enunciation is one kind*, i.e., the enunciation that signifies one thing. And to exclude the understanding of this as signifying one thing in the same way as the name or the verb signifies one thing he adds, *something affirmed of something*, i.e., by way of composition, *or something denied of something*, i.e., by way of division. *The other kind*—the enunciation that is said to be one by conjunction—*is composite*, i.e., *speech composed of these simple enunciations.* In other words, he is saying that the unity of the enunciation is divided into simple and composite, just as one is divided into simple and composite.

19.   He manifests the second division of the enunciation where he says, *A simple enunciation is vocal sound signifying that something belongs or does not belong to a subject*, i.e., the division of enunciation into affirmation and negation. This is a division that belongs primarily to the simple enunciation and consequently to the composite enunciation; therefore, in order to suggest the basis of the division he says that a simple enunciation is *vocal sound signifying that something belongs to a subject*, which pertains to affirmation, *or does not belong to a subject*,[98] which pertains to negation. And to make it clear that this is not to be understood only of present time he adds, *according to the divisions of time*, i.e., this holds for other times as well as the present.

20.   Alexander thought that Aristotle was defining the enunciation here and because he seems to put affirmation and negation in the "definition" he took this to mean that enunciation is not the genus of affirmation and negation, for the species is never posited in the definition of the genus. Now what is not predicated univocally of many (namely, because it does not signify something one that is common to many) cannot be made known except through the many that are signified. "*One*" is not said equivocally[99] of the simple and composite, but primarily and consequently, and hence Aristotle always used both "simple" and "composite" in the preceding reasoning to make the unity of the enunciation known. Now, here he seems to use affirmation and negation to make the enunciation known; therefore, Alexander took this to mean that enunciation is not said of affirmation and negation univocally as a genus of its species.

---

[98] The Greek text reads here: "... φωνὴ σημαντικὴ περὶ τοῦ εἰ ὑπάρχει τι ἤ μὴ ὑπάρχει . . ." The εἰ is omitted in some manuscripts. The Latin reads: ". . . vox significativa de eo quod est aliquid, vel non est . . ."

[99] The editors of the Leonine suggest that this should perhaps be "univocally."

21.   But the contrary appears to be the case, for the Philosopher subsequently uses the name "enunciation" as a genus when in defining

17a25 affirmation and negation he says, *Affirmation is the enunciation of something about something,* i.e., by way of composition; *negation is the enunciation of something separated from something,* i.e., by way of division.

Moreover, it is not customary to use an equivocal name to make known the things it signifies. Boethius for this reason says that Aristotle with his customary brevity is using both the definition and its division at once. Therefore when he says *that something belongs or does not belong to a subject* he is not referring to the definition of enunciation but to its division.

However, since the differences dividing a genus do not fall in its definition and since *vocal sound signifying* is not a sufficient definition of the enunciation, Porphyry thought it would be better to say that the whole expression, *vocal sound signifying that something belongs or does not belong to a subject,* is the definition of the enunciation. According to his exposition this is not affirmation and negation that is posited in the definition[100] but capacity for affirmation and negation, i.e., what the enunciation is a sign of, which is *to be* or *not to be,* which is prior in nature to the enunciation. Then immediately following this he defines affirmation and negation in terms of themselves when he says, *Affirmation is the enunciation of something about something; negation the enunciation of something separated from something.*

But just as the species should not be stated in the definition of the genus, so neither should the properties of the species. Now to signify *to be* is the property of the affirmation, and to signify *not to be* the property of the negation. Therefore Ammonius thought it would be better to say that the enunciation was not defined here, but only divided. For the definition was posited above when it was said that the enunciation is speech in which there is truth or falsity[101]—in which definition no mention is made of either affirmation or negation.

It should be noticed, however, that Aristotle proceeds very skillfully here, for he divides the genus, not into species, but into specific differences. He does not say that the enunciation is an affirmation or negation, but *vocal sound signifying that something belongs to a subject,* which is the specific difference of affirmation, *or does not belong to a subject,* which is the specific difference of negation. Then when he adds, *Affirmation is the enunciation of something about something* which signifies *to be,* and *negation is the enunciation of something separated from something,* which signifies *not to be,* he establishes the definition of the species by joining the differences to the genus.

---

[100] I.e., the definition of enunciation does not have affirmation and nega- tion as a difference.

[101] *Supra,* 17a 2.

[72]

The Opposition of Affirmation and Negation Absolutely

17a 26 Since it is possible to enunciate that what belongs to a subject does not belong to it and what does not, does, and that what does belong to it, does, and what does not, does not, and to enunciate these in regard to those times outside of the present as well as of the present, it would be possible to deny whatever someone affirms and to affirm what he denies. It is evident, therefore, that there is a negation opposed to every affirmation and an affirmation opposed to every negation.

17a 33 We will call this opposed affirmation and negation "contradiction."

17a 34 I mean by "opposed" the enunciation of the same thing of the same subject—not equivocally however, nor in any of the other ways that we have distinguished in reference to the specious difficulties of the sophists.

---

1. Having made the division of the enunciation, Aristotle now deals with the opposition of the parts of the enunciation, i.e., the opposition of affirmation and negation. He has already said that the enunciation is speech in which there is truth or falsity; therefore, he first shows how enunciations are opposed to each other; secondly, he raises a doubt about some things previously determined and then resolves it where he says, *In enunciations about that which is or has taken place,* 18a28 etc.[102] He not only shows how one enunciation is opposed to another, but that only one is opposed to one, where he says, *It is evident also* 17b37 *that there is one negation of one affirmation.*[103] In showing how one enunciation is opposed to another, he first treats of the opposition of affirmation and negation absolutely, and then shows in what way opposition of this kind is diversified on the part of the subject where he says, *Since some of the things we are concerned with are universal and* 17a38 *others singular,* etc.[104] With respect to the opposition of affirmation and negation absolutely, he first shows that there is a negation opposed to every affirmation and vice versa, and then where he says, *We will* 17a33 *call this opposed affirmation and negation "contradiction,"* he explains the opposition of affirmation and negation absolutely.

2. In relation to the first point, that there is a negation opposed to every affirmation and vice versa, the Philosopher assumes a twofold

---

[102] St. Thomas, Lesson XIII.
[104] St. Thomas, Lesson X.
[103] St. Thomas, Lesson XII.

[73]

diversity of enunciation. The first arises from the very form or mode of enunciating. According to this diversity, enunciation is either affirmative—in which it is enunciated that something is—or negative—in which it is signified that something is not.[105]

The second is the diversity that arises by comparison to reality. Truth and falsity of thought and of the enunciation depend upon this comparison, for when it is enunciated that something is or is not, if there is agreement with reality, there is true speech; otherwise there is false speech.

3.   The enunciation can therefore be varied in four ways according to a combination of these two divisions: in the first way, what is in reality is enunciated to be as it is in reality. This is characteristic of true affirmation. For example, when Socrates runs, we say, "Socrates is running." In the second way, it is enunciated that something is not what in reality it is not. This is characteristic of true negation, as when we say, "An Ethiopian is not white." In the third way, it is enunciated that something is what in reality it is not. This is characteristic of a false affirmation, as in "The raven is white." In the fourth way, it is enunciated that something is not what it is in reality. This is characteristic of a false negation, as in "Snow is not white."

In order to proceed from the weaker to the stronger the Philosopher puts the false before the true, and among these he states the nega-
17a26   tive before the affirmative. He begins, then, with the false negative; *it is possible to enunciate, that what is,*[106] namely, in reality, *is not.* Secondly, he posits the false affirmative, *and that what is not,* namely, in reality, *is.* Thirdly, he posits the true affirmative—which is opposed to the false negative he gave first—*and that what is,* namely, in reality, *is.* Fourthly, he posits the true negative—which is opposed to the false affirmative—*and that what is not,* namely, in reality, *is not.*

4.   In saying *what is* and *what is not,* Aristotle is not referring only to the existence or nonexistence of a subject. What he is saying is that the reality signified by the predicate is in or is not in the reality signified by the subject. For what is signified in saying, "The raven is white," is that what is not, is, although the raven itself is an existing thing.

5.   These four differences of enunciations are found in propositions in which there is a verb of present time and also in enunciations

[105] Cf. 17a 23; St. Thomas, Lesson VII, n. 19.
[106] The Greek text here reads: "ἐπεὶ δὲ ἔστι καὶ τὸ ὑπάρχον ἀποφαίνεσθαι ὡς μὴ ὑπάρχον . . ." The forms of ὑπάρχω in this context have the meaning of "belong to" or "present in," but "is" is also one of its meanings.

[74]

in which there are verbs of past or future time.[107] He said earlier that every enunciative speech must contain a verb or a mode of the verb.[108] Here he makes this point in relation to the four differences of enunciations: *similarly it is possible to enunciate these,* i.e., that the enunciation be varied in diverse ways *in regard to those times outside of the present,* i.e., with respect to the past or future, which are in a certain way extrinsic in respect to the present, since the present is between the past and the future.

17a30
17a29

6.   Since there are these four differences of enunciation in past and future time as well as in present time, it is possible to deny everything that is affirmed and to affirm everything that is denied. This is evident from the premises, for it is only possible to affirm either that which is in reality according to past, present, or future time, or that which is not; and it is possible to deny all of this. It is clear, then, that everything that is affirmed can be denied or vice versa.

Now, since affirmation and negation are per se opposed, i.e., in an opposition of contradiction, it follows that any affirmation would have a negation opposed to it, and conversely. The contrary of this could happen only if an affirmation could affirm something that the negation could not deny.

7.   When he says, *We will call this opposed affirmation and negation "contradiction,"* he explains what *absolute* opposition of affirmation and negation is. He does this first through the name; secondly, through the definition where he says, *I mean by "opposed" the enunciation of the same thing of the same subject,* etc.

17a33

17a34

"Contradiction," he says, is the name imposed for the kind of opposition in which a negation is opposed to an affirmation and conversely. By saying *We will call this "contradiction,"* we are given to understand—as Ammonius points out—that he has himself imposed the name "contradiction" for the opposition of affirmation and negation.

8.   Then he defines contradiction when he says, *I mean by "opposed" the enunciation of the same thing of the same subject,* etc. Since contradiction is the opposition of affirmation and negation, as he has said, whatever is required for the opposition of affirmation and negation

17a34

---

[107] "In propositions" has been added by by the editors of the Leonine because it is contained in all of the manuscripts except the Piana, and the latter appeared to them obscure. It reads: "Et sicut quatuor differentiae enunciationum inveniuntur, in quibus ponitur verbum praesentis temporis, ita etiam inveniuntur in enunciationibus in quibus ponuntur verba praeteriti vel futui temporis." That is, it is not clear to what the "in quibus" refers.

[108] Cf. 17a 9; St. Thomas, Lesson VIII, n. 8.

is required for contradiction. Now, opposites must be about the same thing and since the enunciation is made up of a subject and predicate the first requirement for contradiction is affirmation and negation of the same predicate, for if we say "Plato runs" and "Plato does not discuss," there is no contradiction. The second is that the affirmation and negation be of the same subject, for if we say "Socrates runs" and "Plato does not run," there is no contradiction. The third requirement is identity of subject and predicate not only according to name but according to the thing and the name at once; for clearly, if the same name is not used there is not one and the same enunciation; similarly there must be identity of the thing, for as was said above, the enunciation is one when it signifies one thing said of one thing.[109] This is why he adds, *not equivocally however*, for identity of name with diversity of the thing—which is equivocation—is not sufficient for contradiction.

9.   There are also certain other things that must be observed with respect to contradiction in order that all diversity be destroyed except the diversity of affirmation and negation, for if the negation does not deny in every way the same thing that the affirmation affirms there will not be opposition. Inquiry can be made about this diversity in respect to four things: first, are there diverse parts of the subject, for if we say "An Ethiopian is white as to teeth" and "An Ethiopian is not white as to foot," there is no contradiction; secondly, is there a diverse mode on the part of the predicate, for there is no contradiction if we say "Socrates runs slowly" and "Socrates is not moving swiftly," or "An egg is an animal in potency" and "An egg is not an animal in act"; thirdly, is there diversity on the part of measure, for instance, of place or time, for there is no contradiction if we say "It is raining in Gaul" and "It is not raining in Italy," or "It rained yesterday" and "It did not rain today"; fourthly, is there diversity from a relationship to something extrinsic, as when we say "Ten men are many in respect to a house, but not in respect to a court house."

Aristotle designates all of these when he adds, *nor in any of the other ways that we have distinguished*, i.e., that it is usual to determine in disputations against the *specious difficulties of the sophists*, i.e., against the fallacious and quarrelsome objections of the sophists, which he mentions more fully in I *Elenchorum*.[110]

[109] This statement does not appear in exactly this form in the Greek text or in Moerbeke's Latin translation of it. It is actually St. Thomas' statement in his commentary on 17a 15 of Aristotle (cf. Lesson VIII, n. 13).
[110] *De Sophisticis Elenchis* 5, 166b 28-167a 36.

The Division of the Proposition on the Part of the Subject and the Opposition of Affirmation and Negation in Universal and in Indefinite Propositions

17a 38   Since some of the things we are concerned with are universal and others singular[111]—by "universal" I mean that which is of such a nature as to be predicated of many, and by "singular" that which is not; for example "man" is universal, "Callias" singular—

17b 1   we have to enunciate either of a universal or of a singular that something belongs or does not belong to it.

17b 3   If, then, it is universally enunciated of a universal that something belongs or does not belong to it, the enunciations will be contraries. By "universally enunciated of a universal" I mean such enunciations as "Every man is white," "No man is white."

17b 7   On the other hand, when the enunciations are of a universal but not universally enunciated, they are not contraries, although it is possible for the things signified to be contraries.

17b 8   I mean by "enunciated of a universal but not universally" such enunciations as "Man is white," "Man is not white." For, while "man" is a universal, it is not used as universal in the enunciation; for "every" does not signify the universal but signifies that it is taken universally.

17b 12   But as regards the predicate the universal universally predicated is not true; for no affirmation will be true in which a universal predicate is predicated universally, for example, "Every man is every animal."

---

1.   The Philosopher has just said that contradiction is the opposition of the affirmation and negation of the same thing of the same subject. Following upon this he distinguishes the diverse oppositions of affirmation and negation, the purpose being to know what true contra-

---

[111] The Greek text is: " Ἐπεὶ δὲ ἔστι τὰ μὲν καθόλου τῶν πραγμάτων τὰ δὲ καθ' ἕκαστον . . ." The πραγμάτων undoubtedly means "of the things we are concerned with," i.e., things from the point of view of logic are either universal or singular. In the phrase following this Aristotle makes it perfectly clear that he is speaking of things in this way. This passage is usually translated as: "Some *things* are universal and others singular (italics added). In n. 2 St. Thomas seems to take this as "things"; but in n. 3 he takes this up as a possible misinterpretation of the text.

diction is. He first states a division of enunciation which is necessary in order to assign the difference of these oppositions; then he begins to
17b3 manifest the different oppositions where he says, *If, then, it is universally enunciated of a universal that something belongs or does not belong to it,* etc. The division he gives is taken from the difference of the subject and therefore he divides the subject of enunciations first; then
17b1 he concludes with the division of enunciation, where he says, *we have to enunciate either of a universal or of a singular,* etc.

2.   Now the subject of an enunciation is a name or something taken in place of a name. A name is a vocal sound significant by convention of simple thought, which, in turn, is a likeness of the thing. Hence, Aristotle distinguishes the subject of enunciation by a division of things; and he says that of things, some are universals, others singulars. He then explains the members of this division in two ways. First he defines them. Then he manifests them by example when he says, *"man" is universal, "Plato" singular.*

3.   There is a difficulty about this division, for the Philosopher proves in VII *Metaphysicae*[112] that the universal is not something existing outside of the thing; and in the *Predicamenta*[113] he says that second substances are only in first substances, i.e., singulars. Therefore, the division of things into universals and singulars does not seem to be consistent, since according to him there are no things that are universal; on the contrary, all things are singular.

4.   The things divided here, however, are things as signified by names—which names are subjects of enunciations. Now, Aristotle has already said that names signify things only through the mediation of the intellect;[114] therefore, this division must be taken as a division of things as apprehended by the intellect. Now in fact, whatever is joined together in things can be distinguished by the intellect when one of them does not belong to the notion of the other. In any singular thing, we can consider what is proper to the thing insofar as it is this thing, for instance, what is proper to Socrates or to Plato insofar as he is this man. We can also consider that in which it agrees with certain other things, as, that Socrates is an animal, or man, or rational, or risible, or white. Accordingly, when a thing is denominated from what belongs only to this thing insofar as it is this thing, the name is said to signify a singular. When a thing is denominated from what is common to it and to many others, the name is said to signify a universal since it signifies a nature or some disposition which is common to many.

[112] *Metaph.* Z, 14, 1039a 23 ff.   [114] 16a 3; St. Thomas, Lesson II, n. 5.
[113] *Categ.* 5, 2a 11 ff.

[78]

Immediately after giving this division of things, then—not of things absolutely as they are outside of the soul, but as they are referred to the intellect—Aristotle defines the universal and the singular through the act of the intellective soul, as that which is such as to be predicated of many or of only one, and not according to anything that pertains to the thing, that is, as if he were affirming such a universal outside of the soul, an opinion relating to Plato's teaching.

5.   There is a further point we should consider in relation to this portion of the text. The intellect apprehends the thing-understood according to the thing's essence or definition. This is the reason Aristotle says in III *De anima* that the proper object of the intellect is what the thing essentially is.[115] Now, sometimes the proper nature of some understood form is not repugnant to being in many but is impeded by something else, either by something occurring accidentally (for instance if all men but one were to die) or because of the condition of matter; the sun, for instance, is only one, not because it is repugnant to the notion of the sun to be in many according to the condition of its form, but because there is no other matter capable of receiving such a form. This is the reason Aristotle did not say that the universal is that which is predicated of many, but *that which is of such a nature as to be predicated of many.*

6.   Now, since every form which is so constituted as to be received in matter is communicable to many matters, there are two ways in which what is signified by a name may not be of such a nature as to be predicated of many: in one way, because a name signifies a form as terminated in this matter, as in the case of the name "Socrates" or "Plato," which signifies human nature as it is in this matter; in another way, because a name signifies a form which is not constituted to be received in matter and consequently must remain per se one and singular. *Whiteness,* for example, would be only one if it were a form not existing in matter, and consequently singular. This is the reason the Philosopher says in VII *Metaphysicae* that if there were separated species of things, as Plato held, they would be individuals.[116]

7.   It could be objected that the name "Socrates" or "Plato" is of such a kind as to be predicated of many, since there is nothing to prevent their being applied to many. The response to this objection is evident if we consider Aristotle's words. Notice that he divides things into universal and particular, not names. It should be understood from this that what is said to be universal not only has a name that can be predicated

---

[115] *De Anima* III, 4, 429b 10 ff.   see also I, 10, 1059a 12-14.
[116] *Metaph.* H, 6, 1045a 36-1045b 7;

[79]

of many but what is signified by the name is of such a nature as to be found in many. Now this is not the case in the above-mentioned names, for the name "Socrates" or "Plato" signifies human nature as it is in this matter. If one of these names is imposed on another man it will signify human nature in other matter and thus another signification of it. Consequently, it will be equivocal, not universal.

17b1 8.   When he says, *we have to enunciate either of a universal or of a singular that something belongs or does not belong to it,* he infers the division of the enunciation. Since something is always enunciated of some thing, and of things some are universals and some singulars, it follows that sometimes it will be enunciated that something belongs or does not belong to something universal, sometimes to something singular.

The construction of the sentence was interrupted by the explanation of universal and singular but now we can see the meaning: *Since some of the things we are concerned with are universal and others singular . . . we have to enunciate either of a universal or of a singular that something belongs or does not belong to it.*

9.   In relation to the point being made here we have to consider the four ways in which something is enunciated of the universal. On the one hand, the universal can be considered as though separated from singulars, whether subsisting per se as Plato held or according to the being it has in the intellect as Aristotle held; considered thus, something can be attributed to it in two ways. Sometimes we attribute something to it which pertains only to the operation of the intellect; for example when we say, *"Man,"* whether the universal or the species, "is predicable" of many. For the intellect forms intentions of this kind, attributing them to the nature understood according as it compares the nature to the things outside of the mind. But sometimes we attribute something to the universal thus considered (i.e., as it is apprehended by the intellect as one) which does not belong to the act of the intellect but to the being that the nature apprehended has in things outside of the soul; for example, when we say "Man is the noblest of creatures." For this truly belongs to human nature as it is in singulars, since any single man is more noble than all irrational creatures; yet all singular men are not one man outside of the mind, but only in the apprehension of the intellect; and the predicate is attributed to it in this way, i.e., as to one thing.

On the other hand, we attribute something to the universal as in singulars in another way, and this is twofold: sometimes it is in view of the universal nature itself; for instance, when we attribute something to it that belongs to its essence, or follows upon the essential

[80]

principles, as in "Man is an animal," or "Man is risible." Sometimes it is in view of the singular in which the universal is found; for instance, when we attribute something to the universal that pertains to the action of the individual, as in "Man walks."[117]

Moreover, something is attributed to the singular in three ways: in one way, as it is subject to the intellect, as when we say "*Socrates* is a singular," or "Predicable of only one"; in another way, by reason of the common nature, as when we say "Socrates is an animal"; in the third way, by reason of itself, as when we say "Socrates is walking."

The negations are varied in the same number of ways, since everything that can be affirmed can also be denied, as was said above.[118]

10.   This is the third division the Philosopher has given of the enunciation. The first was the division of the enunciation into one simply and one by conjunction.[119] This is an analogous division into those things of which one is predicated primarily and consequently, for *one* is divided according to the prior and posterior into simple and composite.

The second was the division of enunciation into affirmation and negation.[120] This is a division of genus into species, for it is taken from the difference of the predicate to which a negation is added. The predicate is the formal part of the enunciation and hence such a division is said to pertain to the quality of the enunciation. By "quality" I mean essential quality, for in this case the difference signifies the quality of the essence.[121]

The third division is based upon the difference of the subject as predicated of many or of only one, and is therefore a division that per-

---

[117] The word *ratione* translated here as "in view of" or "by reason of" indicates that predication is made in reference to the nature or the singular. The point St. Thomas is making throughout this lesson is this: the reason why we say something of a universal may be found in the singulars, as when we say "Man walks," or it may be found in the universal nature considered absolutely, as when we say "Man is an animal," or again, in the indeterminate singular, as in "Some man is wise."

[118] 17b 30; St. Thomas, Lesson IX, n. 6.

[119] Cf. Lesson VIII, n. 2. For the fourth and fifth divisions see Lesson XIII, n. 3 *infra*.

[120] Cf. Lesson VIII, n. 3.

[121] *Quale quid* (quality of the essence): when a predicate is attributed to something essentially it is said to be predicated *in quid*, since to ask what the essence of a thing is is to ask what (*quid*) the thing is. When a predicate is attributed to something *in quale quid* it is predicated essentially (hence, the *in quid*), but the way in which the predicate is attributed to the subject is as an adjective, i.e., in the mode of a quality. St. Thomas' point here is that affirmation and negation are species of enunciation that are specifically different because of the difference of the predicate, i.e., of the form of the enunciation.

tains to the quantity of the enunciation, for quantity follows upon matter.

11.   Aristotle shows next how enunciations are opposed in diverse ways according to the diversity of the subject when he says, *If, then, it is universally enunciated of a universal that something belongs or does not belong to it,* etc. He first distinguishes the diverse modes of opposition in enunciations; secondly, he shows how these diverse oppositions are related in different ways to truth and falsity where he says, *Hence in the case of the latter it is impossible that both be at once true,* etc.[122]

17b3

17b22

12.   First, then, he distinguishes the diverse modes of opposition and since these depend upon a diversity in the subject we must first consider the latter diversity. Now the universal can be considered either in abstraction from singulars or as it is in singulars, and by reason of this something is attributed in diverse modes to the universal, as we have already said. To designate diverse modes of attribution certain words have been conceived which may be called determinations or signs and which designate that something is predicated in this or that mode.

But first we should note that since it is not commonly apprehended by all men that universals subsist outside of singulars there is no word in common speech to designate the mode of predicating in which something is said of a universal thus in abstraction from singulars. Plato, who held that universals subsist outside of singulars, did, however, invent certain determinations to designate the way in which something is attributed to the universal as it is outside of singulars. With respect to the species *man* he called the separated universal subsisting outside of singulars "man per se" or "man itself," and he designated other such universals in like manner.

The universal as it is in singulars, however, does fall within the common apprehension of men and accordingly certain words have been conceived to signify the mode of attributing something to the universal taken in this way.

13.   As was said above, sometimes something is attributed to the universal in view of the universal nature itself; for this reason it is said to be predicated of the universal universally, i.e., that it belongs to the universal according to the whole multitude in which it is found. The word "every" has been devised to designate this in affirmative predications. It designates that the predicate is attributed to the universal subject with respect to the whole of what is contained under the subject. In negative predications the word "no" has been devised to signify

[122] St. Thomas, Lesson XI.

[82]

that the predicate is removed from the universal subject according to the whole of what is contained under it. Hence, saying *nullus* in Latin is like saying *non ullus* [not any] and in Greek οὐδείς [none] is like οὐδὲ εἷς [not one], for not a single one is understood under the universal subject from which the predicate is not removed.

Sometimes something is either attributed to or removed from the universal in view of the particular. To designate this in affirmative enunciations, the word "some," or "a certain one," has been devised.[123] We designate by this that the predicate is attributed to the universal subject by reason of the particular. "Some," or "a certain one," however, does not signify the form of any singular determinately, rather, it designates the singular under a certain indetermination. The singular so designated is therefore called the vague individual. In negative enunciations there is no designated word, but "not all" can be used. Just as "no," then, removes universally, for it signifies the same thing as if we were to say "not any," (i.e., "not some") so also "not all" removes particularly inasmuch as it excludes universal affirmation.

14.   There are, therefore, three kinds of affirmations in which something is predicated of a universal: in one, something is predicated of the universal universally, as in "Every man is an animal"; in another, something is predicated of the universal particularly, as in "Some man is white." The third is the affirmation in which something is predicated of the universal without a determination of universality or particularity. Enunciations of this kind are customarily called indefinite. There are the same number of opposed negations.

15.   In the case of the singular, although something is predicated of it in a different respect, as was said above, nevertheless the whole is referred to its singularity because the universal nature is individuated in the singular; therefore it makes no difference as far as the nature of singularity is concerned whether something is predicated of the singular by reason of the universal nature, as in "Socrates is a man," or belongs to it by reason of its singularity.

16.   If we add the singular to the three already mentioned there will be four modes of enunciation pertaining to quantity: universal, singular, indefinite, and particular.

17.   Aristotle assigns the diverse oppositions of enunciations according to these differences. The first opposition is based on the difference of universals and indefinites; the second on the difference of universals and particulars, the latter being treated where he says,

[123] "A certain one" is one word in Latin.

[83]

17b16   *Affirmation is opposed to negation in the way I call contradictory,* *etc.*[124] With respect to the first opposition, the one between universals and indefinites, the opposition of universal propositions to each other is treated first, and then the opposition of indefinite enunciations where

17b7   he says, *On the other hand, when the enunciations are of a universal but* *not universally enunciated,* etc. Finally he precludes a possible ques-

17b12   tion where he says, *In the predicate, however, the universal universally* *predicated is not true,* etc.

18.   He says first, then, that if someone enunciates universally of a universal subject, i.e., according to the content of its universality, *that* *it is,* i.e., affirmatively, *or is not,*[125] i.e., negatively, these enunciations will be contrary; as when we say, "Every man is white," "No man is white." And the reason is that the things that are most distant from each other are said to be contraries.[126] For a thing is not said to be black only because it is not white but because over and beyond not being white— which signifies the remotion of white commonly—it is, in addition, black, the extreme in distance from white. What is affirmed by the enunciation "Every man is white" then, is removed by the negation "Not every man is white"; the negation, therefore, removes the *mode* in which the predi- cate is said of the subject which the word "every" designates. But over and beyond this remotion, the enunciation "No man is white" which is most distant from "Every man is white," adds total remotion, and this belongs to the notion of contrariety. He therefore appropriately calls this opposition *contrariety.*

17b7   19.   When he says, *On the other hand, when the enunciations are* *of a universal but not universally enunciated,* etc., he shows what kind of opposition there is between affirmation and negation in indefinite enunciations. First he states the point; he then manifests it by an ex-

17b8   ample when he says, *I mean by "enunciated of a universal but not uni-*

17b10   *versally,"* etc. Finally he gives the reason for this when he says, *For* *while "man" is a universal, it is not used as universal,* etc.

He says first, then, that when something is affirmed or denied of a universal subject, but not universally, the enunciations are not con- trary but the things that are signified may be contraries. He clarifies

17b18   this with examples where he says, *I mean by "enunciated of a universal* *but not universally,"* etc. Note in relation to this that what he said just before this was "when . . . of universals but not universally enunciated"

---

[124] See Lesson XI *infra.*
[125] The Greek again uses the verb ὑπάρχω and τι is understood ("some- thing belongs to or is present in"); the Latin translation has *est.*

[126] St. Thomas, *In octo libros physi-* *corum exposito,* V, Lesson 3, n. 5; Aristotle, *Metaph.* Δ 10, 1018a 25- 31.

and not, "when . . . of universals particularly," the reason being that he only intends to speak of indefinite enunciations, not of particulars. This he manifests by the examples he gives. When we say *"Man is white"* and *"Man is not white,"* the universal subjects do not make them universal enunciations. He gives as the reason for this, that although *man,* which stands as the subject, is universal, the predicate is not predicated of it universally because the word "every" is not added, which does not itself signify the universal, but the mode of universality, i.e., that the predicate is said universally of the subject. Therefore when "every" is added to the universal subject it always signifies that something is said of it universally.

This whole exposition relates to his saying, *On the other hand, when the enunciations are of a universal but not universally enunciated, they are not contraries.*

20.   Immediately after this he adds, *although it is possible for the things signified to be contraries,* and in spite of the fact that this is obscure he does not explain it. It has therefore been interpreted in different ways.

Some related it to the contrariety of truth and falsity proper to enunciations of this kind. For such enunciations may be simultaneously true, as in "Man is white" and "Man is not white," and thus not be contraries, for contraries mutually destroy each other. On the other hand, one may be true and the other false, as in "Man is an animal" and "Man is not an animal," and thus by reason of what is signified seem to have a certain kind of contrariety.

But this does not seem to be related to what Aristotle has said: first, because the Philosopher has not yet taken up the point of truth and falsity of enunciations; secondly, because this very thing can also be said of particular enunciations.

21.   Others, following Porphyry, relate this to the contrariety of the predicate. For sometimes the predicate may be denied of the subject because of the presence of the contrary in it, as when we say, "Man is not white" because he is black; thus it could be the contrary that is signified by "is not white."

This is not always the case, however, for we remove something from a subject even when it is not a contrary that is present in it but some mean between contraries, as in saying, "So-and-so is not white" because he is pale; or when there is a privation of act or habit or potency, as in saying, "So-and-so is nonseeing" because he lacks the power of sight or has an impediment so that he cannot see, or even because something is not of such a nature as to see, as in saying, "A stone does not see." It is therefore possible for the things signified to be contraries, but the enunciations themselves not to be; for as is said near the end of this book, opinions that are about contraries are not contrary,[127] for example, an opinion that something is good and an opinion that something is evil.

22.   This does not seem to relate to what Aristotle has proposed either, for he is not treating here of contrariety of things or opinions, but of contrariety of enunciations. For this reason it seems better here to follow the exposition of Alexander.

According to his exposition, in indefinite enunciations it is not determined whether the predicate is attributed to the subject universally (which would constitute contrariety of enunciations), or particularly (which would not constitute contrariety of enunciations). Accordingly, enunciations of this kind are not contrary in mode of expression. However, sometimes they have contrariety by reason of what is signified, i.e., when something is attributed to a universal in virtue of the universal nature although the universal sign is not added, as in "Man is an animal" and "Man is not an animal," for in virtue of what is signified these enunciations have the same force as "Every man is an animal" and "No man is an animal."

23.   When he says, *But as regards the predicate the universal universally predicated is not true*, etc., he precludes a certain difficulty. He has already stated that there is a diversity in the opposition of enunciations because of the universal being taken either universally or not universally on the part of the subject. Someone might think, as a consequence, that a similar diversity would arise on the part of the predicate, i.e., that the universal could be predicated both universally and not universally. To exclude this he says that in the case in which a universal is predicated it is not true that the universal is predicated universally.

There are two reasons for this. The first is that such a mode of predicating seems to be repugnant to the predicate in relation to its status in the enunciation; for, as has been said, the predicate is a quasi-formal part of the enunciation, while the subject is a material part of it.[128] Now when a universal is asserted universally the universal itself is taken according to the relationship it has to the singulars contained under it, and when it is asserted particularly the universal is taken according to the relationship it has to some one of what is contained under it. Thus both pertain to the material determination of the universal. This is why it is not appropriate to add either the universal or particular sign to the predicate, but rather to the subject; for it is more appropriate to say, "No man is an ass" than "Every man is no ass"; and likewise, to say, "Some man is white" than, "Man is some white."

[127] Cf. 23b 7.   [128] Cf. n. 10 of this lesson.

[86]

However, sometimes philosophers put the particular sign next to the predicate to indicate that the predicate is in more[129] than the subject, and this especially when they have a genus in mind and are investigating the differences which complete the species. There is an instance of this in II *De anima* where Aristotle says that the soul is a certain act.[130]

The other reason is related to the truth of enunciations. This has a special place in affirmations, which would be false if the predicate were predicated universally.[131] Hence to manifest what he has stated, he adds, *for there is no affirmation in which*, i.e., truly, *a universal predicate will be predicated universally*,[132] i.e., in which a universal predicate is used to predicate universally, for example, "Every man is every animal." If this could be done, the predicate "animal" according to the singulars contained under it would have to be predicated of the singulars contained under "man"; but such predication could not be true, whether the predicate is in more than the subject or is convertible with the subject; for then any one man would have to be all animals or all risible beings, which is repugnant to the notion of the singular, which is taken under the universal.[133]

The truth of the enunciation "Every man is susceptible of every discipline" is not an instance that can be used as an objection to this position, for it is not "discipline" that is predicated of man but "susceptible of discipline." It would be repugnant to truth if it were said that "Every man is everything susceptible of discipline."

24.   On the other hand, although the negative universal sign or the particular affirmative sign are more appropriately posited on the part of the subject, it is not repugnant to truth if they are posited on the part of the predicate, for such enunciations may be true in some matter. The enunciation "Every man is no stone," for example, is true, and so is "Every man is some animal." But the enunciation "Every man

---

[129] That is, is more universal.

[130] *De Anima* II, 1, 412a 22; St. Thomas, Lesson I.

[131] The editors of the Leonine have substituted here the reading in all the texts except the Piana. The Piana reads: ". . . et ista specialiter habet locum in affirmationibus quae falsae sunt significatum universaliter praedicaretur."

[132] The translation of the Greek text here is: ". . . for no affirmation *will be true* in which a universal predicate is predicated universally." (Ital-

ics added.)

[133] In the two reasons given for not predicating the predicate universally, the universal is taken as it is real, i.e., in personal (or absolute) supposition, not in simple supposition. Consequently, if the predicate were predicated universally it would mean that the singulars under the universal subject would be all of the singulars under the universal predicate; i.e., man would be every animal, and hence, so would Peter, who is a man, be every animal.

[87]

is every animal," in whatever matter it occurs, is false. There are other enunciations of this kind that are always false, such as, "Some man is every animal" (which is false for the same reason as "Every man is every animal" is false). And if there are any others like these, they are always false; and the reason is the same in every case. And, therefore, in rejecting the enunciation "Every man is every animal," the Philosopher meant it to be understood that all similar enunciations are to be rejected.

The Opposition of Universal and Particular Enunciations and the Relation of an Opposed Affirmation and Negation to Truth and Falsity

17b 16   Affirmation is opposed to negation in the way I call contradictory when the one signifying universally is opposed to the same one not signifying universally, as in "Every man is white" and "Not every man is white"; "No man is white" and "Some man is white."[134]

17b 20   They are opposed contrarily when the universal affirmation is opposed to the universal negation; as in "Every man is just" and "No man is just."

17b 22   Hence in the case of the latter it is impossible that both be at once true, but it is possible for the contradictories of these contraries to be at once true with respect to the same subject, as in "Not every man is white" and "Some man is white."

17b 26   Whenever there are contradictions with respect to universals signifying universally, one must be true, the other false; this is also the case when there are contradictions with respect to singulars, as in "Socrates is white" and "Socrates is not white."

17b 29   But when the contradictions are of universals not signifying universally, one is not always true and the other false; for it is at once true to say that man is white and man is not white, and man is beautiful and man is not beautiful.

17b 33   For if he is ugly, he is not beautiful; and if he is becoming something, he is not yet it.

17b 34   At first sight this might seem paradoxical, because "Man is not white" seems to signify the same thing as "No man is white"; but it neither signifies this, nor are they at once true necessarily.

---

1.   Now that he has determined the opposition of enunciations by comparing universal enunciations with indefinite enunciations, Aris-

---

134 The Oxford and Loeb texts translate this sentence in such a way that there could only be one pair of contradictories, i.e., only the universal affirmative and the particular negative is a pair of contradictories. The Oxford translation is: "An affirmation is opposed to a denial in the sense which I denote by the term 'contradictory,' when, while the

totle determines the opposition of enunciations by comparing universals to particulars. It should be noted that there is a twofold opposition in these enunciations, one of universal to particular, and he touches upon this first; the other is the opposition of universal to universal, and this

17b20 he takes up next, where he says, *They are opposed contrarily when the universal affirmation is opposed to the universal negation,* etc.

2.   The particular affirmative and particular negative do not have opposition properly speaking, because opposition is concerned with the same subject. But the subject of a particular enunciation is the universal taken particularly, not for a determinate singular but indeterminately for any singular. For this reason, when something is affirmed or denied of the universal particularly taken, the mode of enunciating is not such that the affirmation and negation are of the same thing; hence what is required for the opposition of affirmation and negation is lacking.[135]

3.   First he says that the enunciation that signifies the universal, i.e., universally, is opposed contradictorily to the one that does not signify universally but particularly, if one of them is affirmative and the other negative (whether the universal is affirmative and the particular negative or conversely), as in "Every man is white," "Not every man is white." For, the "not every" is used in place of the particular negative sign; consequently, "Not every man is white" is equivalent to "Some man is not white." In a parallel way "no," which signifies the same thing as "not any" or "not some," is the universal negative sign; consequently, the two enunciations, "Some man is white," which is the particular affirmative, and "No man is white," which is the universal negative, are contradictories.

4.   The reason for this is that contradiction consists in the mere removal of the affirmation by a negation. Now the universal affirmative is removed by merely the negation of the particular and nothing else is required of necessity; but the particular affirmative can only be removed by the universal negative because, as has already been said, the particular negative is not properly opposed to the particular affirmative.[136] Consequently, the particular negative is opposed contradictorily to the universal affirmative and the universal negative to the particular affirmative.

17b20 5.   When he says, *They are opposed contrarily when the universal*

subject remains the same, *the affirmation is of universal character and the denial is not.*" (Italics added.) The Greek text reads: "Ἀντικεῖσθαι μὲν οὖν κατάφασιν ἀποφάσει λέγω

ἀντιφατικῶς τὴν τὸ καθόλου σημαίνουσαν τῷ αὐτῷ ὅτι οὐ καθόλου . . ."
[135] 17a 34; St. Thomas, Lesson IX, n. 8 *supra.*
[136] Cf. n. 2 of this lesson.

[90]

affirmation is opposed to the universal negation, etc., he touches on the opposition of universal enunciations. The universal affirmative and universal negative, he says, are contraries, as in "Every man is just," "No man is just"; for the universal negative not only removes the universal affirmative but also designates an extreme of distance between them inasmuch as it denies the whole that the affirmation posits; and this belongs to the notion of contrariety. The particular affirmative and particular negative, for this reason, are related as a mean between contraries.

6.   He shows how the opposed affirmation and negation are related   17b22
to truth and falsity when he says, *Hence in the case of the latter it is impossible that both be at once true,* etc. He shows this first in regard to contraries; secondly, in regard to contradictories, where he says, *Whenever there are contradictions with respect to universals signifying*   17b26
universally, etc.; thirdly, in regard to those that seem contradictory but are not, where he says, *But when the contradictions are of universals*   17b29
not signifying universally, etc.

First, he says that because the universal affirmative and universal negative are contraries, it is impossible for them to be simultaneously true, for contraries mutually remove each other. However, the particular enunciations that are contradictorily opposed to the universal contraries, can be verified at the same time in the same thing, for example, "Not every man is white" (which is opposed contradictorily to "Every man is white") and "Some man is white" (which is opposed contradictorily to "No man is white").

A parallel to this is found in the contrariety of things, for white and black can never be in the same thing at the same time; but the remotion of white and black can be in the same thing at the same time, for a thing may be neither white nor black, as is evident in something yellow. In a similar way, contrary enunciations cannot be at once true, but their contradictories, by which they are removed, can be true simultaneously.

7.   Then he says, *Whenever there are contradictions with respect*   17b26
to universals signifying universally, one must be true and the other false, etc. Here he shows how truth and falsity are related in contradictories. As was said above, in contradictories the negation does no more than remove the affirmation,[137] and this in two ways: in one way when one of them is universal, the other particular; in another way when each is singular. In the case of the singular, the negation is necessarily referred to the same thing—which is not the case in particulars and indefinites—

---

[137] Cf. n. 4 of this lesson.

and cannot extend to more than removing the affirmation. Accordingly, the singular affirmative is always contradictory to the singular negative, the identity of subject and predicate being supposed.

Aristotle says, therefore, that whether we take the contradiction of universals universally (i.e., one of the universals being taken universally) or the contradiction of singular enunciations, one of them must always be true and the other false. It is not possible for them to be at once true or at once false because to be true is nothing other than to say of what is, that it is, or of what is not that it is not; to be false, to say of what is not, that it is, or of what is, that it is not, as is evident in IV *Metaphysicorum*.[138]

17b29 8. When he says, *But when the contradictions are of universals not signifying universally*, etc., he shows how truth and falsity are related to enunciations that seem to be contradictory, but are not. First
17b33 he proposes how they are related; then he proves it where he says, *For if he is ugly, he is not beautiful*, etc.; finally, he excludes a possible dif-
17b34 ficulty where he says, *At first sight this might seem paradoxical*, etc.

With respect to the first point we should note that affirmation and negation in indefinite propositions seem to be opposed contradictorily because there is one subject in both of them and it is not determined by a particular sign. Hence, the affirmation and negation seem to be about the same thing. To exclude this, the Philosopher says that in the case of affirmative and negative enunciations of universals not taken universally, one need not always be true and the other false, but they can be at once true. For it is true to say both that "Man is white" and that "Man is not white," and that "Man is honorable" and "Man is not honorable."

9. On this point, as Ammonius reports,[139] some men, maintaining that the indefinite negative is always to be taken for the universal negative, have taken a position contradictory to Aristotle's. They argued their position in the following way. The indefinite, since it is indeterminate, partakes of the nature of matter; but matter considered in itself is regarded as what is less worthy. Now the universal affirmative is more worthy than the particular affirmative and therefore they said that the indefinite affirmative was to be taken for the particular affirmative. But, they said, the universal negative, which destroys the whole, is less worthy than the particular negative, which destroys the part (just as universal corruption is worse than particular corruption); therefore,

---

138 *Metaph.*, Γ, 7, 1011b 25 ff.; St. Thomas, Bk. V, Lesson IX.
139 Ammonius, *In Aristotelis De interpretatione Commentarius* fol. 16, verso, col. 2, Venetiis, 1546; Boethius, *Comment. in librum Aristotelis* Περὶ ἑρμηνείας, I, p. 352.

they said that the indefinite negative was to be taken for the universal negative.

They went on to say in support of their position that philosophers, and even Aristotle himself, used indefinite negatives as universals. Thus, in the book *Physicorum* Aristotle says that there is not movement apart from the thing;[140] and in the book *De anima,* that there are not more than five senses.[141]

However, these reasons are not cogent. What they say about matter—that considered in itself it is taken for what is less worthy—is true according to the opinion of Plato, who did not distinguish privation from matter; however, it is not true according to Aristotle, who says in I *Physicae,* that the evil and ugly and other things of this kind pertaining to defect, are said of matter only accidentally.[142] Therefore the indefinite need not stand always for the more ignoble.

Even supposing it is necessary that the indefinite be taken for the less worthy, it ought not to be taken for the universal negative; for just as the universal affirmative is more powerful than the particular in the genus of affirmation, as containing the particular affirmative, so also the universal negative is more powerful in the genus of negations. Now in each genus one must consider what is more powerful in that genus, not what is more powerful simply.

Further, if we took the position that the particular negative is more powerful than all other modes, the reasoning still would not follow, for the indefinite affirmative is not taken for the particular affirmative because it is less worthy, but because something can be affirmed of the universal by reason of itself, or by reason of the part contained under it;[143] whence it suffices for the truth of the particular affirmative that the predicate belongs to one part (which is designated by the particular sign); for this reason the truth of the particular affirmative suffices for the truth of the indefinite affirmative. For a similar reason the truth of the particular negative suffices for the truth of the indefinite negative, because in like manner, something can be denied of a universal either by reason of itself, or by reason of its part.

Apropos of the examples cited for their argument, it should be noted that philosophers sometimes use indefinite negatives for universals in the case of things that are per se removed from universals; and they use indefinite affirmatives for universals in the case of things that are per se predicated of universals.

[140] *Phys.* III, 1, 200b 32; St. Thomas, Lesson I.

[141] *De Anima* III, 1, 424b 20; St. Thomas, Lesson I.

[142] *Phys.* I, 9, 192a 3 and 192a 22; St. Thomas, Lesson XV.

[143] Cf. Lesson X, n. 13.

17b33 10.   When he says, *For if he is ugly, he is not beautiful*, etc., he proves what he has proposed by something conceded by everyone, namely, that the indefinite affirmative is verified if the particular affirmative is true. We may take two indefinite affirmatives, one of which includes the negation of the other, as for example when they have opposed predicates. Now this opposition can happen in two ways. It can be according to perfect contrariety, as shameful (i.e., dishonorable) is opposed to worthy (i.e., honorable) and ugly (i.e., deformed in body) is opposed to beautiful. But the reasoning by which the affirmative enunciation, "Man is worthy," is true, i.e., by some worthy man existing, is the same as the reasoning by which "Man is shameful" is true, i.e., by a shameful man existing. Therefore these two enunciations are at once true, "Man is worthy" and "Man is shameful." But the enunciation, "Man is not worthy," follows upon "Man is shameful." Therefore the two enunciations, "Man is worthy," and "Man is not worthy," are at once true; and by the same reasoning these two, "Man is beautiful" and "Man is not beautiful."

The other opposition is according to the complete and incomplete, as *to be in movement* is opposed to *to have been moved*, and *becoming* to *to have become*.[144] Whence the nonbeing of that which is coming to be in permanent things, whose being is complete, follows upon the becoming but this is not so in successive things, whose being is incomplete. Thus, "Man is white" is true by the fact that a white man exists; by the same reasoning, because a man is becoming white, the enunciation "Man is becoming white" is true, upon which follows, "Man is not white." Therefore, the two enunciations, "Man is white" and "Man is not white" are at once true.

17b34 11.   Then when he says, *At first sight this might seem paradoxical*, etc., he excludes what might present a difficulty in relation to what has been said. *At first sight*, he says, what has been stated seems to be inconsistent; for "Man is not white" seems to signify the same thing as "No man is white." But he rejects this when he says that they neither signify the same thing, nor are they at once true necessarily, as is evident from what has been said.

---

[144] Cf. St. Thomas, *Quaestiones Disputatae De Veritate* VIII, 14 and XXVIII, 9 ad 10; also, *In I Phys.* Lesson IV, n. 2.

LESSON XII

There Is Only One Negation Opposed to One Affirmation

17b 37   It is evident also that there is one negation of one affirmation;

17b 39   for the negation must deny the same thing that the affirmation affirms, and of the same subject, either something singular, or something universal, and either universally or not universally.

18a 2   For example, the negation of "Socrates is white" is "Socrates is not white." (If something else is said of the same subject or the same thing of a different subject, it will not be opposed to it but different from it.) The negation opposed to "Every man is white" is "Not every man is white"; to "Some man is white," "No man is white"; to "Man is white," "Man is not white."

18a 7   We have said that there is one negation opposed contradictorily to one affirmation, and what these are; and that the others are contraries, and what these are; and that in every contradiction one is not always true and the other false,[145] and what the reason is for this, and when it is the case that one is true and the other false.

18a 12   Affirmation or negation is one when one thing is signified of one thing, whether the subject is universal and is taken universally or not; as in "Every man is white" and "Not every man is white"; "Man is white" and "Man is not white"; "No man is white" and "Some man is white"; provided the "white" signifies one thing.

18a 18   But if one name is imposed for two things, from which there is not one thing, the affirmation is not one. For example, if someone were to impose the name "cloak" on horse and man, the enunciation "Cloak is white" would not be one affirmation, nor would "Cloak is not white" be one negation.

18a 21   For this is no different from saying "Horse and man is white," and this no different from saying, "Horse is white" and "Man is white." If, then, these signify many things and are many, it is evident that the first enunciation ["Cloak is white"] signifies many things—or nothing, for there is not such a thing as a horse-man.

18a 26   Consequently, in such enunciations it is not necessary that one contradictory be true and the other false.

---

[145] The contradictions of contraries may both be true (cf. 17b 23).

1.   Having distinguished the diverse modes of opposition in enunciations, the Philosopher now proposes to show that there is one negation opposed to one affirmation. First he shows that there is one negation opposed to one affirmation; then he manifests what one affirmation

18a12   and negation are, where he says, *Affirmation or negation is one when one thing is signified of one thing,* etc. With respect to what he intends to do he first proposes the point; then he manifests it where he says,

17b39   *for the negation must deny the same thing that the affirmation affirms,* etc. Finally, he gives a summary of what has been said, where he says,

18a7   *We have said that there is one negation opposed contradictorily to one affirmation,* etc.[146]

2.   He says, then, that it is evident that there is only one negation of one affirmation. It is necessary to make this point here because he has posited many kinds of opposition and it might appear that two negations are opposed to one affirmation. Thus it might seem that the negative enunciations, "No man is white" and "Some man is not white" are both opposed to the affirmative enunciation, "Every man is white." But if one carefully examines what has been said it will be evident that the only negative opposed to "Every man is white" is "Some man is not white," which merely removes it, as is clear from its equivalent, "Not every man is white." It is true that the negation of the universal affirmative is included in the understanding of the universal negative inasmuch as the universal negative includes the particular negative, but the universal negative adds something over and beyond this inasmuch as it not only brings about the removal of universality but removes every part of it. Thus it is evident that there is only one negation of a universal affirmation, and the same thing is evident in the others.

17b39   3.   When he says, *for the negation must deny the same thing that the affirmation affirms,* etc., he manifests what he has said: first, from reason; secondly, by example.

The reasoning is taken from what has already been said, namely, that negation is opposed to affirmation when the enunciations are of the same thing of the same subject.[147] Here he says that the negation must deny the same predicate the affirmation affirms, and of the same subject, whether that subject be something singular or something uni-

---

[146] This is the text as it is in Aristotle. St. Thomas quotes here: "Manifestum est ergo . . .," which is in neither the Greek nor the Latin version of Aristotle. When St. Thomas begins the actual commentary on this section in n. 6 he quotes the correct Latin version of Aristotle's text: "Quod igitur una affirmatio . . ." But Codices A, B, and C have the "Manifestum est ergo . . ." here. The latter seems to be from an ancient version of Aristotle which was probably available to St. Thomas (cf. p. 57 n. ε of the Leonine).

[147] 17a 34; St. Thomas, Lesson IX, n. 8.

[96]

versal, either taken universally or not taken universally. But this can only be done in one way, i.e., when the negation denies what the affirmation posits, and nothing else. Therefore there is only one negation opposed to one affirmation.

4.   In manifesting this by example, where he says, *For example,* 18a2 *the negation of "Socrates is white,"* etc., he first takes examples of singulars. Thus, "Socrates is not white" is the proper negation opposed to "Socrates is white." If there were another predicate or another subject, it would not be the opposed negation, but wholly different. For example, "Socrates is not musical" is not opposed to "Socrates is white," nor is "Plato is white" opposed to "Socrates is not white."

Then he manifests the same thing in an affirmation with a universal universally taken as the subject. Thus, "Not every man is white," which is equivalent to the particular negative, is the proper negation opposed to the affirmation, "Every man is white."

Thirdly, he gives an example in which the subject of the affirmation is a universal taken particularly. The proper negation opposed to the affirmation "Some man is white" is "No man is white," for to say "no" is to say "not any," i.e., "not some."

Finally, he gives as an example enunciations in which the subject of the affirmation is the universal taken indefinitely; "Man is not white" is the proper negation opposed to the affirmation "Man is white."

5.   The last example used to manifest his point seems to be contrary to what he has already said, namely, that the indefinite negative and the indefinite affirmative can be simultaneously verified;[148] but a negation and its opposite affirmation cannot be simultaneously verified, since it is not possible to affirm and deny of the same subject.

But what Aristotle is saying here must be understood of the negation when it is referred to the same thing the affirmation contained, and this is possible in two ways: in one way, when something is affirmed to belong to man by reason of what he is (which is per se to be predicated of the same thing), and this very thing the negation denies; secondly, when something is affirmed of the universal by reason of its singular, and the same thing is denied of it.

6.   He concludes by summarizing what has been said: *We have* 18a7 *said that there is one negation opposed contradictorily to one affirmation,* etc. He considers it evident from what has been said that one negation is opposed to one affirmation; and that of opposite affirmations and negations, one kind are contraries, the other contradictories; and that what

---

[148] 17b 29 ff.; St. Thomas, Lesson XI,
    n. 8 ff.

each kind is has been stated. He does not speak of subcontraries because it is not accurate to say that they are opposites, as was said above.[149] He also says here that it has been shown that not every contradiction is true or false,[150] "contradiction" being taken here broadly for any kind of opposition of affirmation and negation; for in enunciations that are truly contradictory one is always true and the other false. The reason why this may not be verified in some kinds of opposites has already been stated, namely, because some are not contradictories but contraries, and these can be false at the same time. It is also possible for affirmation and negation not to be properly opposed and consequently to be true at the same time.[151] It has been stated, however, when one is always true and the other false, namely, in those that are truly contradictories.[152]

7.   The Philosopher explains what one affirmation or negation is where he says, *Affirmation or negation is one when one thing is signified of one thing,* etc. He did in fact state this earlier when he said that an enunciation is one when it signifies one thing,[153] but because the enunciation in which something is predicated of a universal, either universally or not universally, contains under it many things, he is going to show here that unity of enunciation is not impeded by this.

18a12

First he shows that unity of enunciation is not impeded by the multitude contained under the universal, whose notion is one. Then he shows that unity of enunciation is impeded by the multitude contained under the unity of a name only, where he says, *But if one name is imposed for two things,* etc.

18a18

He says, then, that an affirmation or negation is one when one thing is signified of one thing, whether the one thing that is subjected be a universal taken universally, or not, i.e., it may be a universal taken particularly or indefinitely, or even a singular. He gives examples of the different kinds: such as, the universal affirmative "Every man is white" and the particular negative, which is its negation, "Not every man is white," each of which is one. There are other examples which are evident. At the end he states a condition that is required for any of them to be one, i.e., *provided the "white,"* which is the predicate, *signifies one thing;* for a multiple predicate with a subject signifying one thing would also impede the unity of an enunciation. The universal proposition is therefore one, even though it comprehends a multitude

18a17

---

149 St. Thomas, Lesson XI, n. 2.
150 17b 29; St. Thomas, Lesson XI, n. 8.
151 17b 22; St. Thomas, Lesson XI, n. 6.
152 17b 26; St. Thomas, Lesson XI, n. 7.
153 17a 15; St. Thomas, Lesson VIII, n. 13.

of singulars under it, for the predicate is not attributed to many singulars according as each is divided from the other, but according as they are united in one common thing.

8.   When he says, *But if one name is imposed for two things,* he shows that unity of name alone does not suffice for unity of an enunciation. He first makes the point; secondly, he gives an example, where he says, *if someone were to impose the name "cloak" on horse and man,* etc.; thirdly, he proves it where he says, *For this is no different from saying "Horse and man is white,"* etc.; finally, he infers a corollary from what has been said, where he says, *Consequently, in such enunciations, it is not necessary,* etc. 18a18 18a21 18a26

If one name is imposed for two things, he says, from which one thing is not formed, there is not one affirmation. The *from which one thing is not formed*[154] can be understood in two ways. It can be understood as excluding the many that are contained under one universal, as man and horse under animal, for the name "animal" signifies both, not as they are many and different from each other but as they are united in the nature of the genus. It can also be understood—and this would be more accurate—as excluding the many parts from which something one is formed, whether the parts of the notion as known, as the genus and the difference, which are parts of the definition, or the integral parts of some composite, as the stones and wood from which a house is made. If, then, there is such a predicate which is attributed to a thing, the many that are signified must concur in one thing according to some of the modes mentioned in order that there be one enunciation; unity of vocal sound alone would not suffice. However, if there is such a predicate which is referred to vocal sound, unity of vocal sound would suffice, as in " 'Dog' is a name."

9.   He gives an example of what he means where he says, *For example, if someone were to impose the name "cloak,"* etc. That is, if someone were to impose the name "cloak" to signify man and horse and then said, "Cloak is white," there would not be one affirmation, nor would there be one negation. 18a19

He proves this where he says, *For this is no different from saying,* etc. His argument is as follows. If "cloak" signifies man and horse there is no difference between saying "Cloak is white" and saying, "Man is white, and, Horse is white." But "Man is white, and, horse is white" signify many and are many enunciations. Therefore, the enunciation, "Cloak is white," signifies many things. This is the case if "cloak" signi- 18a21

---

[154] In the Greek text the verb used in this phrase is ἐστιν and in the Latin version of it *est* and not *fit;* hence it reads, ". . . from which there is not one thing."

[99]

fies man and horse as diverse things; but if it signifies man and horse as one thing, it signifies nothing, for there is not any thing composed of man and horse.

When Aristotle says that there is no difference between saying "Cloak is white" and, "Man is white, and, horse is white," it is not to be understood with respect to truth and falsity. For the copulative enunciation "Man is white and horse is white" cannot be true unless each part is true; but the enunciation "Cloak is white," under the condition given, can be true even when one is false; otherwise it would not be necessary to distinguish multiple propositions to solve sophistic arguments. Rather, it is to be understood with respect to unity and multiplicity, for just as in "Man is white and horse is white" there is not some one thing to which the predicate is attributed, so also in "Cloak is white."

18a26   10.   When he says, *Consequently, it is not necessary in such enunciations,* etc., he concludes from what has been said that in affirmations and negations that use an equivocal subject, one need not always be true and the other false since the negation may deny something other than the affirmation affirms.

LESSON XIII

Truth and Falsity in Opposed Singular Propositions About the Future in Contingent Matter

18a 28   In enunciations about that which is or has taken place, the affirmation or the negation must be true or false. And in enunciations of universals as universal, one is always true and the other false, and also in enunciations of singulars, as has been said; but in enunciations of universals not taken universally, it is not necessary that one be true and the other false. We have already spoken of these.

However, in enunciations about future singular things the case is not the same.

18a 34   For if every affirmation or negation is true or false, then everything belongs or does not belong to a thing necessarily;

18a 35   for if one person says a thing will be such, and another says it will not be this very thing, clearly one of them must be speaking the truth if every affirmation is true or false. For it will not both belong and not belong to the thing simultaneously in such cases.

18a 39   For if it is true to say that a thing is white or is not white, it must necessarily be white or not white. And if it is white or not white, it was true to affirm or deny it. And if it does not belong to it, it is false to say that it does, and if it is false to say that it does, then it does not belong to it. Consequently, it is necessary that either the affirmation or negation be true. If this is so, then nothing either is, or takes place fortuitously or indeterminately in relation to two alternatives, or will be or will not be; but everything takes place of necessity and is not indeterminate to either of two alternatives (for the supposition is that either the one who affirms it or the one who denies it is speaking the truth). Whereas if everything does not take place of necessity, it could take place or not take place as well, for what is indeterminate to either of two alternatives happens or will happen no more in this way than not.

18b 9   Furthermore, on such a supposition, if something is now white, it was true to say formerly that it will be white; therefore it was always true to say of anything that has taken place that it will be. But if it was always true to say that it is or will be, it is not possible for this not to be, nor that it will not be; and when a thing cannot not take place, it is impossible that it not take place, and when it is impossible that it not take place, it is necessary that it take place; all things that will be, then, must necessarily take place. Therefore, nothing will be indeterminate to either of two alternatives, nor fortuitous; for if it were fortuitous it would not take place of necessity.

[101]

18b 17   But still it is not possible to say that neither is true; that is, to say that a thing neither will take place nor will not take place.

18b 18   In the first place, though the affirmation be false, the negation will not be true, and though the negation be false, the affirmation will not be true.

18b 20   Secondly, if it is true to say that a thing is white and large, both necessarily belong to it; and if they will belong to it the next day, they will necessarily belong to it the next day. But if a thing neither will be nor will not be tomorrow, it would not be indeterminate to either of two alternatives. For example, in the case of a naval battle, it would be necessary that the naval battle neither take place nor not take place tomorrow.

---

1.   Now that he has treated opposition of enunciations and has shown the way in which opposed enunciations divide truth and falsity, the Philosopher inquires about a question that might arise, namely, whether what has been said is found to be so in all enunciations or not. And first he proposes a dissimilarity in enunciations with regard to 18a34   dividing truth and falsity, then proves it where he says, *For if every affirmation or negation is true or false,* etc.

2.   In relation to the dissimilarity which he intends to prove we should recall that the Philosopher has given three divisions of the enunciation. The first was in relation to the unity of enunciation, and according to this it is divided into one simply and one by conjunction; the second was in relation to quality, and according to this it is divided into affirmative and negative; the third was in relation to quantity, and according to this it is either universal, particular, indefinite, or singular.

3.   Here he treats of a fourth division of enunciation, a division according to time. Some enunciations are about the present, some about the past, some about the future. This division could be seen in what Aristotle has already said, namely, that every enunciation must have a verb or a mode of a verb,[155] the verb being that which signifies the present time, the modes with past or future time.

In addition, a fifth division of the enunciation can be made, a division in regard to matter. It is taken from the relationship of the predicate to the subject. If the predicate is per se in the subject, it will be said to be an enunciation in necessary or natural matter. Examples of this are "Man is an animal" and "Man is risible." If the predicate is per se repugnant to the subject, as excluding the notion of it, it is said

[155] 17a 9; St. Thomas, Lesson VIII, n. 8.

[102]

to be an enunciation in impossible or remote matter; for example, the enunciation "Man is an ass." If the predicate is related to the subject in a way midway between these two, being neither per se repugnant to the subject nor per se in it, the enunciation is said to be in possible or contingent matter.

4.   Given these differences of enunciations, the judgment of truth and falsity is not alike in all. Accordingly, the Philosopher says, as a conclusion from what has been established:: *In enunciations about that*   18a28 *which is,* i.e., in propositions about the present, *or has taken place,* i.e., in enunciations about the past, the affirmation or the negation must be determinately true or false. However, this differs according to the different quantity of the enunciations. In enunciations in which something is universally predicated of universal subjects, one must always be true, either the affirmative or negative, and the other false, i.e., the one opposed to it. For as was said above,[156] the negation of a universal enunciation in which something is predicated universally, is not the universal negative, but the particular negative, and conversely, the universal negative is not directly the negation of the universal affirmative, but the particular negative. According to the foregoing, then, one of these must always be true and the other false in any matter whatever. And the same is the case in singular enunciations, which are also opposed contradictorily.[157] However, in enunciations in which something is predicated of a universal but not universally, it is not necessary that one always be true and the other false, for both could be at once true.[158]

5.   The case as it was just stated has to do with propositions about the past or the present. Enunciations about the future that are of universals taken either universally or not universally are also related in the same way in regard to oppositions. In necessary matter all affirmative enunciations are determinately true; this holds for enunciations in future time as well as in past and present time; and negative enunciations are determinately false. In impossible matter the contrary is the case. In contingent matter, however, universal enunciations are false and particular enunciations true. This is the case in enunciations about the future as well as those of the past and present. In indefinite enunciations, both are at once true in future enunciations as well as in those of the present or the past.

6.   In singular future enunciations, however, there is a difference. In past and present singular enunciations, one of the opposites must

[156] 17b 16 and 17b 26; St. Thomas, Lesson XI, n. 3 ff.
[157] 17b 28; St. Thomas, Lesson XI,
[158] 17b 29; St. Thomas, Lesson XI, n. 8.
n. 7.

be determinately true and the other false in any matter whatsoever, but in singulars that are about the future, it is not necessary that one be determinately true and the other false. This holds with respect to contingent matter; with respect to necessary and impossible matter the rule is the same as in enunciations about the present and the past.

Aristotle has not mentioned contingent matter until now because those things that take place contingently pertain exclusively to singulars, whereas those that per se belong or are repugnant are attributed to singulars according to the notions of their universals.

Aristotle is therefore wholly concerned here with this question: whether in singular enunciations about the future in contingent matter it is necessary that one of the opposites be determinately true and the other determinately false.

7.   He proves that there is a difference between these opposites
18a34   and the others where he says, *For if every affirmation or negation is true or false,* etc. First he proves it by showing that the opposite position leads to what is unlikely; secondly, he shows that what follows from
18b26   this position is impossible, where he says, *These absurd consequences and others like them,* etc.[159] In his proof he first shows that in enunciations about future singulars, truth cannot always be determinately attributed to one of the opposites, and then he shows that both cannot lack
18b17   truth, where he says, *But still it is not possible to say that neither is true,* etc. He gives two arguments with respect to the first point. In the first of these he states a certain consequence, namely, that if every affirmation or negation is determinately true or false, in future singulars as in the others, it follows that all things must determinately *be* or *not be.*
18a35   He proves this consequence where he says, *wherefore, if one person says,* etc., or as it is in the Greek, *for if one person says something will be,* etc.[160] Let us suppose, he argues, that there are two men, one of whom says something will take place in the future, for instance, that Socrates will run, and the other says this same thing will not take place. If the foregoing position is supposed—that in singular future enunciations one of them will be true, either the affirmative or the negative— it would follow that only one of them is saying what is true, because in singular future propositions both cannot be at once true, that is, both the affirmative and the negative. This occurs only in indefinite propositions. Moreover, from the fact that one of them must be speaking the

<hr />

[159] Lesson XIV.

[160] There are some slight variations in the text here. The Oxford Greek text has: ". . . εἰ γὰρ ὅ μὲν . . ." etc. In the Leonine Greek version it is, ". . . ὥστε εἰ ὁ μὲν . . ." etc; and in the Latin version ". . . quare si hic quidem . . ." etc. Here in the commentary St. Thomas gives still another version of it: ". . . si itaque hic quidem . . ." etc.

truth, it follows that it must determinately be or not be. Then he proves this from the fact that these two follow upon each other convertibly, namely, truth is that which is said and which is so in reality. And this is what he manifests when he says that, *if it is true to say that a thing is white*, it necessarily follows that it is so in reality; and if it is true to deny it, it necessarily follows that it is not so. And conversely, for if it is so in reality, or is not, it necessarily follows that it is true to affirm or deny it. The same convertibility is also evident in what is false, for if someone lies, saying what is false, it necessarily follows that in reality it is not as he affirms or denies it to be; and conversely, if it is not in reality as he affirms or denies it to be, it follows that in affirming or denying it he lies. 18a39

8.   The process of Aristotle's reasoning is as follows. If it is necessary that every affirmation or negation about future singulars is true or false, it is necessary that everyone who affirms or denies, determinately says what is true or false. From this it follows that it is necessary that everything be or not be. Therefore, if every affirmation or negation is determinately true, it is necessary that everything determinately be or not be. From this he concludes further that all things are of necessity. This would exclude the three kinds of contingent things.

9.   The three kinds of contingent things are these: some, the ones that happen by chance or fortune, happen infrequently; others are indeterminate to either of two alternatives because they are not inclined more to one part than to another, and these proceed from choice; still others occur for the most part, for example, men becoming gray in old age, which is caused by nature. If, however, everything took place of necessity, there would be none of these kinds of contingent things. Therefore, Aristotle says, *nothing is* with respect to the very permanence 18b5 of those things that are contingently permanent; *or takes place* with respect to those that are caused contingently; *by chance*[161] with respect to those that take place for the least part, or infrequently; *or is indeterminate to either of two alternatives* with respect to those that are related equally to either of two, i.e., to being or to nonbeing, and are determined to neither of these, which he signifies when he adds, *or will be, or will not be.*

    For of that which is more determined to one part we can truly and determinately say that it will be or will not be, as for example, the physician truly says of the convalescent, "He will be restored to health," although perchance by some accident his cure may be impeded. The

[161] St. Thomas uses "by chance" here in place of the "fortuitously" in the Greek text; perhaps it is because "chance" is the more common and is therefore used to cover both chance and fortune.

[105]

Philosopher makes this same point when he says in II *De generatione,* "A man about to walk might not walk."[162] For it can be truly said of someone who has the determined intention to walk that he will walk, although by some accident his walking might be impeded. But in the case of that which is indeterminate to either of two, it cannot determinately be said of it either that it will be or that it will not be, for it is proper to it not to be determined more to one than to another.

Then he manifests how it follows from the foregoing hypothesis that nothing is indeterminate to either of two when he adds that if every affirmation or negation is determinately true, then either the one who affirms or the one who denies must be speaking the truth. That which is indeterminate to either of two is therefore destroyed, for if there is something indeterminate to either of two, it would be related alike to taking place or not taking place, and no more to one than to the other.

It should be noted that the Philosopher is not expressly excluding the contingent that is for the most part. There are two reasons for this. In the first place, this kind of contingency still excludes the determinate truth of one of the opposite enunciations and the falsity of the other, as has been said.[163] Secondly, when the contingent that is infrequent, i.e., that which takes place by chance, is removed, the contingent that is for the most part is removed as a consequence, for there is no difference between that which is for the most part and that which is infrequent except that the former fails for the least part.

18b9 10.   When he says, *Furthermore, on such a supposition, if something is now white, it was true to say formerly that it will be white,* etc., he gives a second argument to show the dissimilarity of enunciations about future singulars. This argument is by reduction to the impossible. If truth and falsity are related in like manner in present and in future enunciations, it follows that whatever is true of the present was also true of the future, in the way in which it is true of the present. But it is now determinately true to say of some singular that it is white; therefore formerly, i.e., before it became white, it was true to say that this will be white. Now the same reasoning seems to hold for the proximate and the remote. Therefore, if yesterday it was true to say that this will be white, it follows that it was always true to say of anything that has taken place that it will be. And if it is always true to say of the present that *it is,* or of the future that *it will be,* it is not possible that this not be, or, that it will not be. The reason for this consequence is evident, for these two cannot stand together, that something truly be said to be, and that it not be; for this is included in the signification of the true, that

162 *De Generatione et Corruptione,* II,   163 *Supra* in this number, i.e., n. 9.
    11, 337b 7.

that which is said, is. If therefore that which is said concerning the present or the future is posited to be true, it is not possible that this not be in the present or future. But that which cannot not take place signifies the same thing as that which is impossible not to take place. And that which is impossible not to take place signifies the same thing as that which necessarily takes place, as will be explained more fully in the second book. It follows, therefore, that all things that are future must necessarily take place. From this it follows further, that there is nothing that is indeterminate to either of two or that takes place by chance, for what happens by chance does not take place of necessity but happens infrequently. But this is unlikely. Therefore the first proposition is false, i.e., that of everything of which it is true that it is, it was determinately true to say that it would be.

11.   For clarification of this point, we must consider the following. Since "true" signifies that something is said to be what it is, something is true in the manner in which it has being. Now, when something is in the present it exists in itself, and hence it can be truly said of it that it is. But as long as something is future, it does not yet exist in itself, but it is in a certain way in its cause, and this in a threefold way. It may be in its cause in such a way that it comes from it necessarily. In this case it has being determinately in its cause, and therefore it can be determinately said of it that it will be. In another way, something is in its cause as it has an inclination to its effect but can be impeded. This, then, is determined in its cause, but changeably, and hence it can be truly said of it that it will be but not with complete certainty. Thirdly, something is in its cause purely in potency. This is the case in which the cause is as yet not determined more to one thing than to another, and consequently it cannot in any way be said determinately of these that it is going to be, but that it is or is not going to be.[164]

---

[164] "But that it is or is not": The editors of the Leonine edition have substituted here the reading of all other codices and the Veneta edition of 1447 for the Piana edition. This substituted reading is "but that it is or is not [going to be]." In the note of explanation (p. 62, n. ν) they point out that the sense of the Piana text ("nor that it is or is not going to be") is that a future event is neither determinately going to be, nor determinately not going to be; and of the codices that it is *either* going to be *or* not going to be. In an indeterminate, o r disjunctive sense, the editors say, the latter is true, since there is no medium between "is going to be" and "is not going to be." However, if the members of the disjunction are taken absolutely, it is not possible that one or the other is determinately going to be, or that it is determinately not going to be, which is what the Piana reading signifies (cf. Lesson XV, n. 4). The editors think the reading of the codices is better in the context, since, having just said "of none of these can it be determinately said

18b17 12.   Then Aristotle says, *But still it is not possible to say that neither is true*, etc. Here he shows that truth is not altogether lacking to both of the opposites in singular future enunciations. First he says that just as it is not true to say that in such enunciations one of the opposites is determinately true, so it is not true to say that neither is true; as if we could say *that a thing neither will take place nor will not take place.*

18b18   Then when he says, *In the first place, though the affirmation be false*, etc., he gives two arguments to prove his point. The first is as follows. Affirmation and negation divide the true and the false. This is evident from the definition of true and false, for to be true is to be what in fact is, or not to be what in fact is not; and to be false is to be what in fact is not, or not to be what in fact is. Consequently, if the affirmation is false, the negation must be true, and conversely. But if the position is taken that neither is true, the affirmation, "This will be" is false, yet the negation is not true; likewise the negation will be false and the affirmation not be true. Therefore, the aforesaid position is impossible, i.e., that truth is lacking to both of the opposites.

18b20   The second argument begins where he says, *Secondly, if it is true to say that a thing is white and large,* etc. The argument is as follows. If it is true to say something, it follows that it is. For example, if it is true to say that something is large and white, it follows that it is both. And this is so of the future as of the present, for if it is true to say that it will be tomorrow, it follows that it will be tomorrow. Therefore, if the position that it neither will be or not be tomorrow is true, it will be necessary that it neither happen nor not happen, which is contrary to the nature of that which is indeterminate to either of two, for that which is indeterminate to either of two is related to either; for example, a naval battle will take place tomorrow, or will not. The same unlikely things follow, then, from this as from the first argument.

that it is going to be," it is useless to repeat, "nor that it is . . ." etc., i.e., the truth of the hypothetical disjunctive, that it is or is not going to be, which is going to be proved next, is the meaning to be taken here.

Contingency in Things and the Roots of Contingency
in Relation to Singular Propositions About
the Future in Contingent Matter

18b 26   These absurd consequences and others like them result if of every affirmation and negation, whether in regard to universals taken universally or in regard to singulars, one of the opposites must be true and the other false: that nothing is indeterminate to either of two in things that come about but all are and take place of necessity; consequently, there will be no need to deliberate nor to take pains about something, as though if we were to do this, such a thing would follow and if we were not to do this, it would not follow.

18b 33   For nothing prevents one person from saying that this will be so in ten thousand years and another person saying it will not; and on the aforesaid supposition, whichever of these was truly said at that time will take place of necessity.

18b 36   Moreover, it makes no difference whether people have actually made the contradictory statements or not; for it is evident that things either will take place or will not even if one person has not affirmed and the other denied it. For it is not because of the affirming or denying that it will be or will not be, whether in ten thousand years or any other space of time.

Therefore, if throughout all time it was the case that one thing or the other was truly said, it would be necessary that this take place; and of every one of the things that takes place it was always the case that it would necessarily take place. For what anyone truly says will be, cannot not take place; and of that which takes place, it was always true to say that it would be.

19a 6   But these things appear to be impossible; for we see that both our deliberation about doing something and our action are principles of future events;

19a 9 and that universally in the things not always in act there is a potentiality to be and not to be. In these there is the possibility either of being or not being, and so they may either take place or not take place.

19a 12   We can point to many clear instances of this. For example, this cloak could be cut in half, and yet might not be but wear out first; likewise it is possible that it not be cut in half, for it could not wear out first if it were not possible that it not be cut.

19a 16 So it is, too, in other things that are said to take place according to this kind of potentiality.

19a 18 It is evident, then, that not all things are or take place of necessity, but some are indeterminate to either of two, in which case the affirmation is no more true than the negation; others take place more in one way than another, as in that which takes place for the most part, and yet it is possible for the other one to take place and the more frequent one not.

----

1. The Philosopher has shown—by leading the opposite position to what is unlikely—that in singular future enunciations truth or falsity is not determinately in one of the opposites, as it is in other enunciations. Now he is going to show that the unlikely things to which it has led are impossibilities. First he shows that the things that followed are impossibilities; then he concludes what the truth is, where he says, 19a23 *Now that which is, when it is, necessarily is,* etc.[165]

2. With respect to the impossibilities that follow he first states the unlikely things that follow from the opposite position, then shows that 18b33 these follow from the aforesaid position, where he says, *For nothing prevents one person from saying that this will be so in ten thousand years,* etc. Finally he shows that these are impossibilities where he says, 19a6 *But these things appear to be impossible,* etc.

He says, then, concluding from the preceding reasoning, that these unlikely things follow—if the position is taken that of opposed enunciations one of the two must be determinately true and the other false in the same way in singular as in universal enunciations—namely, that in things that come about nothing is indeterminate to either of two, but all things are and take place of necessity. From this he infers two other unlikely things that follow. First, it will not be necessary to deliberate about anything; whereas he proved in III *Ethicorum* that counsel is not concerned with things that take place necessarily but only with contingent things, i.e., things which can be or not be.[166]

Secondly, all human actions that are for the sake of some end (for example, a business transaction to acquire riches) will be superfluous, because what we intend will take place whether we take pains to bring it about or not—if all things come about of necessity. This, however, is in opposition to the intention of men, for they seem to deliberate and to transact business with the intention that if they do this there will be such a result, but if they do something else, there will be another result.

[165] Cf. Lesson XV.   [166] *Nic. Eth.* III, 3, 1112a 19 ff.

3.   Where he says, *For nothing prevents one person from saying that*   18b33
this will be so in ten thousand years, etc., he proves that the said unlikely
things follow from the said position. First he shows that the unlikely
things follow from the positing of a certain possibility; then he shows
that the same unlikely things follow even if that possibility is not posited,
where he says, *Moreover, it makes no difference whether people have*   18b36
actually made the contradictory statements or not, etc.

He says, then, that it is not impossible that a thousand years
before, when men neither knew nor ordained any of the things that are
taking place now, a man said, "This will be," for example, that such a
state would be overthrown, and another man said, "This will not be."
But if every affirmation or negation is determinately true, one of them
must have spoken the truth. Therefore one of them had to take place of
necessity; and this same reasoning holds for all other things. Therefore
everything takes place of necessity.

4.   Then he shows that the same thing follows if this possibility is
not posited where he says, *Moreover, it makes no difference whether peo-*   18b36
ple have actually made the contradictory statements or not, etc. It makes
no difference in relation to the existence or outcome of things whether
a person denies that this is going to take place when it is affirmed, or
not; for as was previously said, the event will either take place or not
whether the affirmation and denial have been made or not. That something is or is not does not result from a change in the course of things
to correspond to our affirmation or denial, for the truth of our enunciation is not the cause of the existence of things, but rather the converse.
Nor does it make any difference to the outcome of what is now being
done whether it was affirmed or denied a thousand years before, or at
any other time before. Therefore, if in all past time, the truth of enunciations was such that one of the opposites had to have been truly said
and if upon the necessity of something being truly said it follows that
this must be or take place, it will follow that everything that takes place
is such that it takes place of necessity. The reason he assigns for this
consequence is the following. If it is posited that someone truly says
this will be, it is not possible that it will not be, just as having supposed
that man is, he cannot not be a rational mortal animal. For to be truly
said means that it is such as is said. Moreover, the relationship of what
is said now to what will be is the same as the relationship of what was
said previously to what is in the present or the past. Therefore, all things
have necessarily happened, and they are necessarily happening, and
they will necessarily happen, for of what is accomplished now, as existing in the present or in the past, it was always true to say that it would
be.

[111]

19a6 5.   When he says, *But these things appear to be impossible,* etc.,
he shows that what has been said is impossible. He shows this first by
19a12 reason, secondly by sensible examples, where he says, *We can point to
many clear instances of this,* etc.

First he argues that the position taken is impossible in relation
to human affairs, for clearly man seems to be the principle of the future
things that he does insofar as he is the master of his own actions and
has the power to act or not to act. Indeed, to reject this principle would
be to do away with the whole order of human association and all the
principles of moral philosophy. For men are attracted to good and
withdrawn from evil by persuasion and threat, and by punishment and
reward; but rejection of this principle would make these useless and
thus nullify the whole of civil science.

Here the Philosopher accepts it as an evident principle that
man is the principle of future things. However, he is not the principle
of future things unless he deliberates about a thing and then does it.
In those things that men do without deliberation they do not have
dominion over their acts, i.e., they do not judge freely about things to
be done, but are moved to act by a kind of natural instinct such as is
evident in the case of brute animals. Hence, the conclusion that it is
not necessary for us to take pains about something or to deliberate is
impossible; likewise what it followed from is impossible, i.e., that all
things take place of necessity.

6.   Then he shows that this is also the case in other things where
19a9 he says, *and that universally in the things not always in act, there is a
potentiality to be and not to be,* etc. In natural things, too, it is evident
that there are some things not always in act; it is therefore possible for
them to be or not be, otherwise they would either always be or always
not be. Now that which is not begins to be something by becoming it;
as for example, that which is not white begins to be white by becoming
white. But if it does not become white it continues not to be white.
Therefore, in things that have the possibility of being and not being,
there is also the possibility of becoming and not becoming. Such things
neither are nor come to be of necessity but there is in them the kind
of possibility which disposes them to becoming and not becoming, to
being and not being.

7.   Next he shows the impossibility of what was said by examples
19a12 perceptible to the senses, where he says, *We can point to many clear
instances of this,* etc. Take a new garment for example. It is evident
that it is possible to cut it, for nothing stands in the way of cutting it
either on the part of the agent or the patient. He proves it is at once
possible that it be cut and that it not be cut in the same way he has

[112]

already proved that two opposed indefinite enunciations are at once true, i.e., by the assumption of contraries. Just as it is possible that the garment be cut, so it is possible that it wear out, i.e., be corrupted in the course of time. But if it wears out it is not cut. Therefore both are possible, i.e., that it be cut and that it not be cut. From this he concludes universally in regard to other future things which are not always in act, but are in potency, that not all are or take place of necessity; some are indeterminate to either of two, and therefore are not related any more to affirmation than to negation; there are others in which one possibility happens for the most part, although it is possible, but for the least part, that the other part be true, and not the part which happens for the most part.

8.   With regard to this question about the possible and the necessary, there have been different opinions, as Boethius says in his *Commentary*, and these will have to be considered.[167] Some who distinguished them according to result—for example, Diodorus—said that the impossible is that which never will be, the necessary, that which always will be, and the possible, that which sometimes will be, sometimes not.

The Stoics distinguished them according to exterior restraints. They said the necessary was that which could not be prevented from being true, the impossible, that which is always prevented from being true, and the possible, that which can be prevented or not be prevented.

However, the distinctions in both of those cases seem to be inadequate. The first distinctions are a posteriori, for something is not necessary because it always will be, but rather, it always will be because it is necessary; this holds for the possible as well as the impossible. The second designation is taken from what is external and accidental, for something is not necessary because it does not have an impediment, but it does not have an impediment because it is necessary.

Others distinguished these better by basing their distinction on the nature of things. They said that the necessary is that which in its nature is determined only to being, the impossible, that which is determined only to nonbeing, and the possible, that which is not altogether determined to either, whether related more to one than to another or related equally to both. The latter is known as that which is indeterminate to either of two.

Boethius attributes these distinctions to Philo. However, this is clearly the opinion of Aristotle here, for he gives as the reason for the possibility and contingency in the things we do the fact that we de-

---

[167] Boethius, *Comment. in librum Aristotelis* Περὶ ἑρμηνείας, III, pp. 373 ff.

liberate, and in other things the fact that matter is in potency to either of two opposites.

9. But this reasoning does not seem to be adequate either. While it is true that in corruptible bodies matter is in potency to being and nonbeing, and in celestial bodies there is potency to diverse location; nevertheless nothing happens contingently in celestial bodies, but only of necessity. Consequently, we have to say that the potentiality of matter to either of two, if we are speaking generally, does not suffice as a reason for contingency unless we add on the part of the active potency that it is not wholly determined to one; for if it is so determined to one that it cannot be impeded, it follows that it necessarily reduces into act the passive potency in the same mode.

10. Considering this, some maintained that the very potency which is in natural things receives necessity from some cause determined to one. This cause they called fate. The Stoics, for example, held that fate was to be found in a series or interconnection of causes on the assumption that everything that happens has a cause; but when a cause has been posited the effect is posited of necessity, and if one per se cause does not suffice, many causes concurring for this take on the nature of one sufficient cause; so, they concluded, everything happens of necessity.

11. Aristotle refutes this reasoning in VI *Metaphysicae* by destroying each of the assumed propositions.[168] He says there that not everything that takes place has a cause, but only what is per se has a cause. What is accidental does not have a cause, for it is not properly being but is more like nonbeing, as Plato also held. Whence, *to be musical* has a cause and likewise *to be white*, but to be *musical white* does not have a cause; and the same is the case with all others of this kind.

It is also false that when a cause has been posited—even a sufficient one—the effect must be posited, for not every cause (even if it is sufficient) is such that its effect cannot be impeded. For example, fire is a sufficient cause of the combustion of wood, but if water is poured on it the combustion is impeded.

12. However, if both of the aforesaid propositions were true, it would follow infallibly that everything happens necessarily. For if every effect has a cause, then it would be possible to reduce an effect (which is going to take place in five days or whatever time) to some prior cause, and so on until it reaches a cause which is now in the present or already has been in the past. Moreover, if when the cause is posited it is neces-

168 *Metaph.* E, 2, 1026a 33 ff; St. Thomas, Lesson III.

sary that the effect be posited, the necessity would reach through an order of causes all the way to the ultimate effect. For instance, if someone eats salty food, he will be thirsty; if he is thirsty, he will go outside to drink; if he goes outside to drink, he will be killed by robbers. Therefore, once he has eaten salty food, it is necessary that he be killed. To exclude this position, Aristotle shows that both of these propositions are false.

13.   However, some persons object to this on the grounds that everything accidental is reduced to something per se and therefore an effect that is accidental must be reduced to a per se cause.

Those who argue in this way fail to take into account that the accidental is reduced to the per se inasmuch as it is accidental to that which is per se; for example, musical is accidental to Socrates, and every accident to some subject existing per se. Similarly, everything accidental in some effect is considered in relation to some per se effect, which effect, in relation to that which is per se, has a per se cause, but in relation to what is in it accidentally does not have a per se cause but an accidental one. The reason for this is that the effect must be proportionately referred to its cause, as is said in II *Physicorum* and in V *Metaphysicae*.[169]

14.   Some, however, not considering the difference between accidental and per se effects, tried to reduce all the effects that come about in this world to some per se cause. They posited as this cause the power of the heavenly bodies and assumed fate to be dependent on this power —fate being, according to them, nothing else but the power of the position of the constellations.

But such a cause cannot bring about necessity in all the things accomplished in this world, since many things come about from intellect and will, which are not subject per se and directly to the power of the heavenly bodies. For the intellect, or reason, and the will which is in reason, are not acts of a corporeal organ (as is proved in the treatise *De anima*[170]) and consequently cannot be directly subject to the power of the heavenly bodies, since a corporeal force, of itself, can only act on a corporeal thing. The sensitive powers, on the other hand, inasmuch as they are acts of corporeal organs, are accidentally subject to the action of the heavenly bodies. Hence, the Philosopher in his book *De anima* ascribes the opinion that the will of man is subject to the movement of the heavens to those who hold the position that the intellect does not differ from sense.[171] The power of the heavenly bodies, how-

[169] *Phys.* II, 3, 195b 25-28; St. Thomas, Lesson VI; and *Metaph.* Δ, 2, 1013b 28 ff.; St. Thomas, Lesson III.

[170] *De Anima* III, 4, 429a 18; St. Thomas, Lesson VII.

ever, does indirectly redound to the intellect and will inasmuch as the intellect and will use the sensitive powers. But clearly the passions of the sensitive powers do not induce necessity of reason and will, for the continent man has wrong desires but is not seduced by them, as is shown in VII *Ethicorum*.[172] Therefore, we may conclude that the power of the heavenly bodies does not bring about necessity in the things done through reason and will.

This is also the case in other corporeal effects of corruptible things, in which many things happen accidentally. What is accidental cannot be reduced to a per se cause in a natural power because the power of nature is directed to some one thing; but what is accidental is not one; whence it was said above that the enunciation "Socrates is a white musical being" is not one because it does not signify one thing.[173] This is the reason the Philosopher says in the book *De somno et vigilia* that many things of which the signs pre-exist in the heavenly bodies—for example in storm clouds and tempests—do not take place because they are accidentally impeded.[174] And although this impediment considered as such is reduced to some celestial cause, the concurrence of these, since it is accidental, cannot be reduced to a cause acting naturally.

15.   However, what is accidental can be taken as one by the intellect. For example, "the white is musical," which as such is not one, the intellect takes as one, i.e., insofar as it forms one enunciation by composing. And in accordance with this it is possible to reduce what in itself happens accidentally and fortuitously to a preordaining intellect. For example, the meeting of two servants at a certain place may be accidental and fortuitous with respect to them, since neither knew the other would be there, but be per se intended by their master who sent each of them to encounter the other in a certain place.

16.   Accordingly, some have maintained that everything whatever that is effected in this world—even the things that seem fortuitous and casual—is reduced to the order of divine providence on which they said fate depends. Other foolish men have denied this, judging of the Divine Intellect in the mode of our intellect which does not know singulars. But the position of the latter is false, for His divine thinking and willing is His very being. Hence, just as His being by its power comprehends all that is in any way (i.e., inasmuch as it *is* through participation of

---

[171] *De Anima* III, 3, 427a 21; St. Thomas, Lesson IV.

[172] *Nic. Eth.* VII, 3, 1146a 5 ff.; St. Thomas, Lesson I.

[173] Cf. Lesson V, n. 11 *supra*.

[174] *On Prophesying by Dreams*, 2, 463b 23. (St. Thomas' reference appears to be wrong.)

Him) so also His thinking and what He thinks comprehend all knowing and everything knowable, and His willing and what He wills comprehend all desiring and every desirable good; in other words, whatever is knowable falls under His knowledge and whatever is good falls under His will, just as whatever is falls under His active power, which He comprehends perfectly, since He acts by His intellect.

17.   It may be objected, however, that if Divine Providence is the per se cause of everything that happens in this world, at least of good things, it would look as though everything takes place of necessity: first on the part of His knowledge, for His knowledge cannot be fallible, and so it would seem that what He knows happens necessarily; secondly, on the part of the will, for the will of God cannot be inefficacious; it would seem, therefore, that everything He wills happens of necessity.

18.   These objections arise from judging of the cognition of the divine intellect and the operation of the divine will in the way in which these are in us, when in fact they are very dissimilar.

19.   On the part of cognition or knowledge it should be noted that in knowing things that take place according to the order of time, the cognitive power that is contained in any way under the order of time is related to them in another way than the cognitive power that is totally outside of the order of time. The order of place provides a suitable example of this. According to the Philosopher in IV *Physicorum,* before and after in movement, and consequently in time, corresponds to before and after in magnitude.[175] Therefore, if there are many men passing along some road, any one of those in the ranks has knowledge of those preceding and following as preceding and following, which pertains to the order of place. Hence any one of them sees those who are next to him and some of those who precede him; but he cannot see those who follow behind him. If, however, there were someone outside of the whole order of those passing along the road, for instance, stationed in some high tower where he could see the whole road, he would at once see all those who were on the road—not under the formality of preceding and subsequent (i.e., in relation to his view) but all at the same time and how one precedes another.

Now, our cognition falls under the order of time, either per se or accidentally; whence the soul in composing and dividing necessarily includes time, as is said in III *De anima.*[176] Consequently, things are subject to our cognition under the aspect of present, past, and future. Hence the soul knows present things as existing in act and perceptible

---

[175] *Phys.* IV, 11, 219a 14; St. Thomas,   [176] *De Anima* III, 6, 430a 32 ff.; St.
Lesson XVII.   Thomas, Lesson XI.

by sense in some way; past things it knows as remembered; future things are not known in themselves because they do not yet exist, but can be known in their causes—with certitude if they are totally determined in their causes so that they will take place of necessity; by conjecture if they are not so determined that they cannot be impeded, as in the case of those things that are for the most part; in no way if in their causes they are wholly in potency, i.e., not more determined to one than to another, as in the case of those that are indeterminate to either of two. The reason for this is that a thing is not knowable according as it is in potency, but only according as it is in act, as the Philosopher shows in IX *Metaphysicae*.[177]

20.   God, however, is wholly outside the order of time, stationed as it were at the summit of eternity, which is wholly simultaneous, and to Him the whole course of time is subjected in one simple intuition. For this reason, He sees in one glance everything that is effected in the evolution of time, and each thing as it is in itself, and it is not future to Him in relation to His view as it is in the order of its causes alone (although He also sees the very order of the causes), but each of the things that are in whatever time is seen wholly eternally as the human eye sees Socrates sitting, not in its causes but in itself.

21.   Now from the fact that man sees Socrates sitting, the contingency of his sitting which concerns the order of cause to effect, is not destroyed; yet the eye of man most certainly and infallibly sees Socrates sitting while he is sitting, since each thing as it is in itself is already determined. Hence it follows that God knows all things that take place in time most certainly and infallibly, and yet the things that happen in time neither are nor take place of necessity, but contingently.

22.   There is likewise a difference to be noted on the part of the divine will, for the divine will must be understood as existing outside of the order of beings, as a cause producing the whole of being and all its differences. Now the possible and the necessary are differences of being, and therefore necessity and contingency in things and the distinction of each according to the nature of their proximate causes originate from the divine will itself, for He disposes necessary causes for the effects that He wills to be necessary, and He ordains causes acting contingently (i.e., able to fail) for the effects that He wills to be contingent. And according to the condition of these causes, effects are called either necessary or contingent, although all depend on the divine

---

[177] *Metaph.* Θ, 9, 1051a 22 ff.;   St. Thomas, Lesson X.

will as on a first cause, which transcends the order of necessity and contingency.

This, however, cannot be said of the human will, nor of any other cause, for every other cause already falls under the order of necessity or contingency; hence, either the cause itself must be able to fail or, if not, its effect is not contingent, but necessary. The divine will, on the other hand, is unfailing; yet not all its effects are necessary, but some are contingent.

23.   Some men, in their desire to show that the will in choosing is necessarily moved by the desirable, argued in such a way as to destroy the other root of contingency the Philosopher posits here, based on our deliberation. Since the good is the object of the will, they argue, it cannot (as is evident) be diverted so as not to seek that which seems good to it; as also it is not possible to divert reason so that it does not assent to that which seems true to it. So it seems that choice, which follows upon deliberation, always takes place of necessity; thus all things of which we are the principle through deliberation and choice, will take place of necessity.

24.   In regard to this point there is a similar diversity with respect to the good and with respect to the true that must be noted. There are some truths that are known per se, such as the first indemonstrable principles; these the intellect assents to of necessity. There are others, however, which are not known per se, but through other truths. The condition of these is twofold. Some follow necessarily from the principles, i.e., so that they cannot be false when the principles are true. This is the case with all the conclusions of demonstrations, and the intellect assents necessarily to truths of this kind after it has perceived their order to the principles, but not before. There are others that do not follow necessarily from the principles, and these can be false even though the principles be true. This is the case with things about which there can be opinion. To these the intellect does not assent necessarily, although it may be inclined by some motive more to one side than another.

Similarly, there is a good that is desirable for its own sake, such as happiness, which has the nature of an ultimate end. The will necessarily adheres to a good of this kind, for all men seek to be happy by a certain kind of natural necessity. There are other good things that are desirable for the sake of the end. These are related to the end as conclusions are to principles. The Philosopher makes this point clear in II *Physicorum*.[178] If, then, there were some good things without the

---

[178] *Phys.* II, 7, 198a 35 ff.; St. Thomas, Lesson XV.

existence of which one could not be happy, these would be desirable of necessity, and especially by the person who perceives such an order. Perhaps to be, to live, and to think, and other similar things, if there are any, are of this kind. However, particular good things with which human acts are concerned are not of this kind nor are they apprehended as being such that without them happiness is impossible, for instance, to eat this food or that, or abstain from it. Such things, nevertheless, do have in them that whereby they move the appetite according to some good considered in them. The will, therefore, is not induced to choose these of necessity. And on this account the Philosopher expressly designates the root of the contingency of things effected by us on the part of deliberation—which is concerned with those things that are for the end and yet are not determined. In those things in which the means are determined there is no need for deliberation, as is said in III *Ethicorum*.[179]

These things have been stated to save the roots of contingency that Aristotle posits here, although they may seem to exceed the mode of logical matter.

[179] *Nic. Eth.* III, 3, 1112a 30-1113a 14; St. Thomas, Lesson VII.

It Is Concluded that Propositions Are True as They Correspond to the Way in Which Things Are in Reality

19a 23   Now that which is, when it is, necessarily is, and that which is not, when it is not, necessarily is not. But it is not necessary for everything that is, to be, nor is it necessary for that which is not, not to be. For these are not the same: that everything be necessarily when it is and to be simply from necessity. And the case is similar with respect to that which is not.

19a 27   And this is also the case with respect to contradiction. It is necessary that everything be or not be; and that it will be or will not be; however, taking them separately, it is not possible to say one of the two is necessary. For example, it is necessary that there will or will not be a naval battle tomorrow; however, it is not necessary that a naval battle take place tomorrow, nor is it necessary that it not take place. Yet it is necessary that it either take place or not take place.

19a 32   And so, since speech is true as it corresponds to things, it is clear that when things are such that they are indeterminate to either of two, and opposites are possible, the corresponding contradiction must be similar. This is the case in those things that do not always exist or always not exist. Of these it is necessary that one part of the contradiction be true or false, not however this or that part, but either of the two indeterminately. One may be more likely to be true, but it is not yet actually true or false.

19a 39   Therefore it is clear that it is not necessary that of every affirmation and negation of opposites, one is true and one false. For the case is not the same in regard to those things that are and those that are not but could be or not be. It is as we have just stated.

---

1.   Now that the Philosopher has shown the impossibilities that follow from the foresaid arguments, he concludes what the truth is on this point. In arguing to the impossibility of the position, he proceeded from enunciations to things, and has already rejected the unlikely consequences in respect to things. Now, in the converse order, he first shows the way in which there is truth about things; secondly, the way in which there is truth in enunciations, where he says, *And so, since speech is true* 19a32 *as it corresponds to things,* etc. With respect to truth about things he first shows the way in which there is truth and necessity about things absolutely considered; secondly, the way in which there is truth and

necessity about things through a comparing of their opposites, where he

19a27 says, *And this is also the case with respect to contradiction,* etc.

2.　　　　He begins, then, as though concluding from premises: if the foresaid things are unlikely (namely, that all things take place of necessity), then the case with respect to things must be this: everything that is must be *when* it is, and everything that is not, necessarily not be *when* it is not. This necessity is founded on the principle that it is impossible at once to be and not be; for if something is, it is impossible that it at the same time not be; therefore it is necessary that it be at that time. For "impossible not to be" signifies the same thing as "necessary to be," as Aristotle says in the second book.[180]

Similarly, if something is not, it is impossible that it at the same time be. Therefore it is necessary that it not be, for they also signify the same thing. Clearly it is true, then, that everything that is must be when it is, and everything that is not must not be when it is not.

This is not absolute necessity, but necessity by supposition. Consequently, it cannot be said absolutely and simply that everything that is must be, and that everything that is not must not be. For "every being, when it is, necessarily is" does not signify the same thing as "every being necessarily is, *simply.*" The first signifies necessity by supposition, the second, absolute necessity.

What has been said about *to be* must be understood to apply also to *not to be,* for "necessarily not to be simply" and "necessarily not to be when it is not" are also different.

By this Aristotle seems to exclude what was said above, namely, that if in those things that are, one of the two is determinately true, then even before it takes place one of the two would determinately be going to be.[181]

3.　　　　He shows how truth and necessity is had about things through

19a27 the comparing of their opposites where he says, *This is also the case with respect to contradiction,* etc. The reasoning is the same, he says, in respect to contradiction and in respect to supposition. For just as that which is not absolutely necessary becomes necessary by supposition of the same (for it must be when it is), so also what in itself is not necessary absolutely, becomes necessary through the disjunction of the opposite, for of each thing it is necessary that it is or is not, and that it will or will not be in the future, and this under disjunction. This necessity is founded upon the principle that it is impossible for contradictories to be at once true and false. Accordingly, it is impossible that

---

Cf. 22a 20; Cajetan, Lesson X, *infra.*　　[181] Cf. 18b 9; St. Thomas, Lesson XIII, n. 10 *supra.*

[122]

a thing neither be nor not be; therefore it is necessary that it either be or not be. However if one of these is taken separately [i.e., divisively], it is not necessary that that one be absolutely. This he manifests by example: it is necessary that there will be or will not be a naval battle tomorrow; but it is not necessary that a naval battle will take place tomorrow, nor is it necessary that it will not take place, for this pertains to absolute necessity. It is necessary, however, that it will take place or will not take place tomorrow. This pertains to the necessity which is under disjunction.

4.   Then when he says, *And so, since speech is true as it corresponds*   19a32
to things, etc., he shows how truth in speech corresponds to the way things are. First he shows in what way truth of speech conforms to the being and nonbeing of things; secondly, and finally, he arrives at the truth of the whole question, where he says, *Therefore it is clear that it is*   19a39
not necessary that of every affirmation and negation of opposites, one is true and one false, etc.

He says, then, that enunciative speech is related to truth in the way the thing is to being or nonbeing (for from the fact that a thing is or is not, speech is true or false). It follows, therefore, that when things are such as to be indeterminate to either of two, and when they are such that their contradictories[182] could happen in whichever way, whether equally or one for the most part, the contradiction of enunciations must also be such.

He explains next what the things are in which contradictories can happen. They are those that neither always are (i.e., the necessary), nor always are not (i.e., the impossible), but sometimes are and sometimes are not. He shows further how this is maintained in contradictory enunciations. In those enunciations that are about contingent things, one part of the contradiction must be true or false under disjunction; but it is related to either, not to this or that determinately. If it should turn out that one part of the contradiction is more true, as happens in contingents that are for the most part, it is nevertheless not necessary on this account that one of them is determinately true or false.

5.   Then he says, *Therefore, it is clear that it is not necessary that*   19a39
of every affirmation and negation of opposites, one is true and one false,
etc. This is the conclusion he principally intended. It is evident from what has been said that it is not necessary in every genus of affirmation and negation of opposites that one is determinately true and the other false, for truth and falsity is not had in the same way in regard to things

---

[182] One manuscript (B) has "contraries" here.

that are already in the present and those that are not but which could be or not be. The position in regard to each has been explained. In those that are, it is necessary that one of them be determinately true and the other false; in things that are future, which could be or not be, the case is not the same. The first book ends with this.

The Distinction and Order of Simple Enunciations in Which the Finite or the Infinite Name Is Posited Only on the Part of the Subject

19b 5   Since an affirmation signifies something about something, and the subject is either the name or that which has no name, and one thing must be signified about one thing in an affirmation

19b 7   (we have already stated what a name is and that which has no name: I do not call "non-man" a name but an infinite name—for an infinite name also signifies one thing in a certain way—nor "non-matures" a verb, but an infinite verb),

19b 10   every affirmation will be made up of a name and a verb or an infinite name and a verb.

19b 12   There can be no affirmation or negation without a verb; for according to what has been established, "is," or "will be," or "was," or "becomes," or any others such as these are verbs since they signify with time.

19b 14   Therefore the primary affirmation and negation is "Man is," "Man is not"; then, "Non-man is," "Non-man is not"; and then "Every man is," "Not every man is"; "Every non-man is," "Not every non-man is"; and there are similar affirmations and negations with regard to times outside of the present.

––––––––––––––––

1.   In the first book, the Philosopher has dealt with the enunciation considered simply. Now he is going to treat of the enunciation as it is diversified by the addition of something to it.

There are three things that can be considered in the enunciation: first, the words that are predicated or subjected, which he has already distinguished into names and verbs; secondly, the composition, according to which there is truth or falsity in the affirmative or negative enunciation; finally, the opposition of one enunciation to another.

This book is divided into three parts which are related to these three things in the enunciation. In the first, he shows what happens to the enunciation when something is added to the words posited as the subject or predicate; in the second, what happens when something is added to determine the truth or falsity of the composition. He begins this where he says, *Having determined these things, we must consider* 21a34 *in what way negations and affirmations of the possible and not possible,*

etc.[1] In the third part he solves a question that arises about the oppositions of enunciations in which something is added to the simple enunci-

23a27 ation. This he takes up where he says, *There is a question as to whether
the contrary of an affirmation is a negation, or whether the contrary of
an affirmation is another affirmation,* etc.[2]

With respect to additions made to the words used in the enunciation, it should be noted that an addition made to the predicate or the
subject sometimes destroys the unity of the enunciation, and sometimes
not, the latter being the case in which the addition is a negative making
a word infinite. Consequently, he first shows what happens to the enunciation when the added negation makes a word infinite. Secondly, he
shows what happens when an addition destroys the unity of the enunci-

20b12 ation where he says, *Neither the affirmation nor the negation which affirms or denies one predicate of many subjects or many predicates of
one subject is one, unless something one is constituted from the many,*
etc.[3]

In relation to the first point he first investigates the simplest of
enunciations, in which a finite or infinite name is posited only on the
part of the subject. Then he considers the enunciation in which a finite
or infinite name is posited not only on the part of the subject, but also

19b19 on the part of the predicate, where he says, *But when "is" is predicated
as a third element in the enunciation,* etc.[4] Apropos of these simple enunciations, he proposes certain grounds for distinguishing such enuncia-

19b14 tions and then gives their distinction and order where he says, *Therefore
the primary affirmation and negation is "Man is," "Man is not,"* etc. And
first he gives the grounds for distinguishing enunciations on the part of
the name; secondly, he shows that there are not the same grounds for

19b12 a distinction on the part of the verb, where he says, *There can be no
affirmation or negation without a verb,* etc. First, then, he proposes the
grounds for distinguishing these enunciations; secondly, he explains this

19b7 where he says, *we have already stated what a name is,* etc.; finally, he
19b10 arrives at the conclusion he intended where he says, *every affirmation
will be made up of a name and a verb, or an infinite name and a verb.*

2. First of all, he goes back to what was said above in defining
17a25 affirmation, namely, that affirmation is *an enunciation signifying something about something;* and, since it is peculiar to the verb to be a sign
of what is predicated of another, it follows that that about which something is said pertains to the name; but the name is either finite or infinite; therefore, as if drawing a conclusion, he says that since affirma-

---

[1] 21a 34; Cajetan, Lesson VIII.   [4] 19b 19; St. Thomas, Book II, Lesson
[2] 23a 27; Cajetan, Lesson XIII.   II.
[3] 20b 12; Cajetan, Lesson V.

tion signifies something about something it follows that that about which something is signified, i.e., the subject of an affirmation, is either a finite name (which is properly called a name),[5] or unnamed, i.e., an infinite name. It is called "unnamed" because it does not name something with a determinate form but removes the determination of form. And lest anyone think that what is subjected in an affirmation is at once a name and unnamed, he adds, *and one thing must be signified about one thing in an affirmation*, i.e., in the enunciation of which we are speaking now; and hence the subject of such an affirmation must be either the name or the infinite name.

3.   When he says, *we have already stated what a name is*, etc., he 19b7 relates what he has previously said. We have already stated, he says, what a name is and what that which is unnamed is, i.e., the infinite name. "Non-man" is not a name but an infinite name, and "non-runs" is not a verb but an infinite verb. Then he interposes a point that is useful for the preclusion of a difficulty, i.e., that an infinite name in a certain way does signify one thing. It does not signify one thing simply as the finite name does, which signifies one form of a genus or species, or even of an individual; rather it signifies one thing insofar as it signifies the negation of a form, in which negation many things are united, as in something one according to reason. For something is said to be one in the same way it is said to be a being. Hence, just as nonbeing is said to be being, not simply, but according to something, i.e., according to reason, as is evident in IV *Metaphysicae*,[6] so also a negation is one according to something, i.e., according to reason. Aristotle introduces this point so that no one will say that an affirmation in which an infinite name is the subject does not signify one thing about one subject on the grounds that an infinite name does not signify something one.

4.   When he says, *every affirmation will be made up of a name and a 19b10 verb or an infinite name and a verb*, he concludes that the mode of affirmation is twofold. One consists of a name and a verb, the other of an infinite name and a verb. This follows from what has been said, namely, that that about which an affirmation signifies something is either a name or unnamed. The same difference can be taken on the part of negation, for of whatever something can be affirmed it can be denied, as was said in the first book.[7]

5.   When he says, *There can be no affirmation or negation without 19b12 a verb*, etc., he intends to show that enunciations cannot be differenti-

[5] Cf. 16a 29; St. Thomas, Lesson IV, n. 13.

[6] Metaph. Γ, 21; 1003b 6 ff; St. Thomas, Book IV, Lessons I and II.

[7] 17a 26; St. Thomas, Lesson IX, n. 6.

ated on the part of the verb. He made the point earlier that there is no affirmation or negation without a verb. However there can be an affirmation or negation without a name, i.e., when an infinite name is posited in place of a name.[8] An infinite verb, on the other hand, cannot be posited in an enunciation in place of a verb, and this for two reasons. First of all, the infinite verb is constituted by the addition of an infinite particle which, when added to a verb said by itself (i.e., posited outside of the enunciation), removes it absolutely, just as it removes the form of the name absolutely when added to it. Therefore, outside of the enunciation, the infinite verb, as well as the infinite name, can be taken in the mode of one word.[9] But when a negation is added to the verb in an enunciation it removes the verb from something and thus makes the enunciation negative, which is not the case with respect to the name. For an enunciation is made negative by denying the composition which the verb introduces; hence, an infinite verb posited in the enunciation becomes a negative verb. Secondly, whichever way we use the negative particle, whether as making the verb infinite or as making a negative enunciation, the truth of the enunciation is not changed. The negative particle, therefore, is always taken in the more absolute sense, as being clearer. This, then, is why Aristotle does not diversify the affirmation as made up of a verb or infinite verb, but as made up of a name or an infinite name.

It should also be noted that besides the difference of finite and infinite there is the difference of nominative and oblique cases. The cases of names even with a verb added do not constitute an enunciation signifying truth or falsity, as was said in the first book,[10] for the nominative is not included in an oblique name. The verb of present time, however, is included in the cases of the verb, for the past and future, which the cases of the verb signify, are said with respect to the present. Whence, if we say, "This will be," it is the same as if we were to say, "This is future"; and "This has been" the same as "This is past." A name, then, and a case of the verb do constitute an enunciation. Therefore Aristotle adds that "is," or "will be," or "was," or any other verb of this kind that we use are of the number of the foresaid verbs without which an enunciation cannot be made, since they all signify with time and past and future time are said with respect to the present.

19b14   6.   When he says, *Therefore the primary affirmation and negation is,* etc., he infers from the premises the distinction of enunciations in which the finite and infinite name is posited only on the part of the subject. Among these there is a threefold difference to be noted: the first,

---

[8] 17a 9; St. Thomas, Lesson VIII, n. 8.   [10] Cf. St. Thomas, Lesson IV n. 15.
[9] Cf. St. Thomas, Lesson V, n. 11.

according to affirmation and negation; the second, according to finite and infinite subject; the third, according as the subject is posited universally or not universally. Now the finite name is prior in notion to the infinite name just as affirmation is prior to negation. Accordingly, he posits "Man is" as the first affirmation and "Man is not" as the first negation. Then he posits the second affirmation, "Non-man is," and the second negation, "Non-man is not." Finally he posits the enunciations in which the subject is universally posited. These are four, as are those in which the subject is not universally posited.

The reason he does not give examples of the enunciation with a singular subject, such as "Socrates is" and "Socrates is not," is that no sign is added to singular names, and hence not every difference can be found in them. Nor does he give examples of the enunciation in which the subject is taken particularly, for such a subject in a certain way has the same force as a universal subject not universally taken.

He does not posit any difference on the part of the verb according to its cases because, as he himself says, affirmations and negations in regard to extrinsic times, i.e., past and future time which surround the present, are similar to these, as has already been said.

[129]

LESSON II

The Number and Relationship of Simple Enunciations in Which the Verb "Is" Is Predicated As a Third Element and the Subject Is the Finite Name Not Universally Taken

19b 19 But when "is" is predicated as a third element in the enunciation, there are two oppositions.

19b 20 I mean by this that in an enunciation such as "Man is just," the "is" is a third name or verb contained in the affirmation.

19b 22 In this case, therefore, there will be four enunciations, two of which will correspond in their sequence, in respect of affirmation and negation, with the privations but two will not.[11]

19b 24 I mean that the "is" will be added either to "just" or to "nonjust"; and so also in the case of the negative. Thus there will be four.

19b 27 The following diagram will make this clear.

Man is just
(Affirmation)
↓

Man is not just
(Negation)

Man is not nonjust
(Negation)

Man is nonjust
(Affirmation)
↑

Here the "is" and the "is not" are added to "just" and "nonjust." This, then, is the way these are arranged, as we have said in the *Analytics*.[12]

---

1. After distinguishing enunciations in which either a finite or an infinite name is posited only on the part of the subject, the Philosopher begins here to distinguish enunciations in which either a finite or an infinite name is posited as the subject and as the predicate. First he distinguishes these enunciations, and then he manifests certain things that might be doubtful in relation to them where he says, *Since the* 20a16 *negation contrary to "Every animal is just," is the one signifying "No animal is just,"* etc.[13] With respect to their distinction he first deals with enunciations in which the name is predicated with the verb "is"; 20a3 secondly, with those in which other verbs are used, where he says, *In enunciations in which "is" does not join the predicate to the subject, for example, when the verb "matures" or "walks" is used,* etc.[14]

[11] Cf. *Prior Analytics*, I, 46, 51b 5 ff.
[12] *Prior Anal.* I, 46, 51b 5 ff.
[13] 20a 16; Cajetan, Lesson IV.
[14] 20a 3; Cajetan, Lesson III.

[130]

He distinguishes these enunciations as he did the primary enunciations, according to a threefold difference on the part of the subject, first treating those in which the subject is a finite name not taken universally, secondly, those in which the subject is a finite name taken universally where he says, *The same is the case when the affirmation is of* 19b32 *a name taken universally,* etc.[15] Thirdly, he treats those in which an infinite name is the subject, where he says, *and there are two other pairs,* 19b37 *if something is added to "non-man" as a subject,* etc.[16] With respect to the first enunciations [in which the subject is a finite name not taken universally] he proposes a diversity of oppositions and then concludes as to their number and states their relationship, where he says, *In this case,* 19b22 *therefore, there will be four enunciations,* etc. Finally, he exemplifies this with a table.

2.   In relation to the first point two things have to be understood. First, what is meant by *"is" is predicated as a third element in the enunci-* 19b19 *ation.* To clarify this we must note that the verb "is" itself is sometimes predicated in an enunciation, as in "Socrates is." By this we intend to signify that Socrates really is. Sometimes, however, "is" is not predicated as the principal predicate, but is joined to the principal predicate to connect it to the subject, as in "Socrates is white." Here the intention is not to assert that Socrates really is, but to attribute whiteness to him by means of the verb "is." Hence, in such enunciations "is" is predicated as added to the principal predicate. It is said to be third, not because it is a third predicate, but because it is a third word posited in the enunciation, which together with the name predicated makes one predicate. The enunciation is thus divided into two parts and not three.

3.   Secondly, we must consider what he means by *when "is" is predicated as a third element in the enunciation,* in the mode in which we have explained, *there are two oppositions.* In the enunciations already treated, in which the name is posited only on the part of the subject, there was one opposition in relation to any subject. For example, if the subject was a finite name not taken universally there was only one opposition, "Man is," "Man is not." But when "is" is predicated in addition there are two oppositions with regard to the same subject corresponding to the difference of the predicate name, which can be finite or infinite. There is the opposition of "Man is just," "Man is not just," and the opposition, "Man is nonjust," "Man is not nonjust." For the negation is effected by applying the negative particle to the verb "is," which is a sign of a predication.

4.   When he says, *I mean by this that in an enunciation such as* 19b20

---

[15] 19b 32; Cajetan, Lesson III.   [16] 19b 37; Cajetan, Lesson III.

"*Man is just*," etc., he explains what he means by *when "is" is predicated as a third element in the enunciation*. When we say "Man is just," the verb "is" is added to the predicate as a third name or verb in the affirmation. Now "is," like any other word, may be called a name, and thus it is a third name, i.e., word. But because, according to common usage, a word signifying time is called a verb rather than a name Aristotle adds here, *or verb*, as if to say that with respect to the fact that it is a third thing, it does not matter whether it is called a name or a verb.

19b22   5.   He goes on to say, *In this case, therefore, there will be four enunciations, etc.* Here he concludes to the number of the enunciations, first giving the number, and then their relationship where he says, *two of which will correspond in their sequence, in respect of affirmation and negation, with the privations but two will not*. Finally, he explains the
19b24   reason for the number where he says, *I mean that the "is" will be added either to "just" or to "nonjust,"* etc.

He says first, then, that since there are two oppositions *when "is" is predicated as a third element in the enunciation*, and since every opposition is between two enunciations, it follows that there are four enunciations in which "is" is predicated as a third element when the subject is finite and is not taken universally. When he says, *two of which will correspond in their sequence*, etc., he shows their relationship. Two of these enunciations are related to affirmation and negation according to consequence (or according to correlation or proportion, as it is in the Greek[17]) like privations; the other two are not. Because this is said so briefly and obscurely, it has been explained in diverse ways.[18]

6.   Before we take up the various explanations of this passage there is a general point in relation to it that needs to be clarified. In this kind of enunciation a name can be predicated in three ways. We can predicate a finite name and by this we obtain two enunciations, one affirmative and one negative, "Man is just" and "Man is not just." These are called simple enunciations. Or, we can predicate an infinite name and by this we obtain two other enunciations, "Man is nonjust" and "Man is not nonjust." These are called infinite enunciations. Finally, we can predicate a privative name and again we will have two, "Man is unjust" and "Man is not unjust." These are called privative.

7.   Now the passage in question has been explained by some in the following way. Two of the enunciations he has given, those with an

---

[17] The Greek word used here is a form of στοιχέω, which means "to be drawn up in a line" or" to be in rows," in its first imposition.

[18] Boethius, *Commentarii in librum Aristotelis περὶ ἑρμηνείας*, IV, p. 388; Ammonius, *In Aristotelis De interpretione Commentarius* III, fol. 24, col. 2; fol. 25, col. 1.

infinite predicate, are related to the affirmation and negation of the finite predicate according to consequence or analogy, as are privations, i.e., as those with a privative predicate. For the two with an infinite predicate are related according to consequence to those with a finite predicate but in a transposed way, namely, affirmation to negation and negation to affirmation. That is, "Man is nonjust," the affirmation of the infinite predicate, corresponds according to consequence to the negative of the finite predicate, i.e., to "Man is not just"; the negative of the infinite predicate, "Man is not nonjust," corresponds to the affirmative of the finite predicate, i.e., to "Man is just." Theophrastus for this reason called those with the infinite predicate, "transposed."

The affirmative with a privative predicate also corresponds according to consequence to the negative with a finite predicate, i.e., "Man is unjust" to "Man is not just"; and the negative of the privative predicate to the affirmative of the finite predicate, "Man is not unjust" to "Man is just." These enunciations can therefore be placed in a table in the following way:

Man is just	Man is not just
Man is not nonjust	Man is nonjust
Man is not unjust	Man is unjust

This makes it clear that two, those with the infinite predicate, are related to the affirmation and negation of the finite predicate in the way privations are, i.e., as those that have a privative predicate.

It is also evident that there are two others that do not have a similar consequence, i.e., those with an infinite subject, "Non-man is just" and "Non-man is not just." This is the way Herminus explained the words *but two will not,* i.e., by referring it to enunciations with an infinite subject. This, however, is clearly contrary to the words of Aristotle, for after giving the four enunciations, two with a finite predicate and two with an infinite predicate, he adds *two of which . . . but two will not,* as though he were subdividing them, which can only mean that both pairs are comprised in what he is saying. He does not include among these the ones with an infinite subject but will mention them later. It is clear, then, that he is not speaking of these here.

8.   Since this exposition is not consonant with Aristotle's words, others, Ammonius says, have explained this in another way. According to them, two of the four propositions, those of the infinite predicate, are related to affirmation and negation, i.e., to the species itself of affirmation and negation, as privations, that is, as privative affirmations and negations. For the affirmation, "Man is nonjust," is not an affirmation simply, but relatively, as though according to privation; as a dead man is not a man simply, but according to privation. The same thing applies

[133]

to the negative enunciation with an infinite predicate. However, the two enunciations having finite predicates are not related to the species of affirmation and negation according to privation, but simply, for the enunciation "Man is just" is simply affirmative and "Man is not just" is simply negative.

But this meaning does not correspond to the words of Aristotle either, for he says further on: *This, then, is the way these are arranged, as we have said in the Analytics,* but there is nothing in that text pertaining to this meaning. Ammonius, therefore, interprets this differently and in accordance with what is said at the end of *I Priorum* about propositions having a finite or infinite or privative predicate.[19]

19b30

9.   To make Ammonius' explanation clear, it must be noted that, as Aristotle himself says, the enunciation, by some power, is related to that of which the whole of what is signified in the enunciation can be truly predicated. The enunciation, "Man is just," for example, is related to all those of which in any way "is a just man" can be truly said. So, too, the enunciation "Man is not just" is related to all those of which in any way "is not a just man" can be truly said.

According to this mode of speaking it is evident, then, that the simple negative is wider than the infinite affirmative which corresponds to it. Thus, "is a nonjust man" can truly be said of any man who does not have the habit of justice; but "is not a just man" can be said not only of a man not having the habit of justice, but also of what is not a man at all. For example, it is true to say "Wood is not a just man," but false to say, "Wood is a nonjust man." The simple negative, then, is wider than the infinite affirmative—just as animal is wider than man, since it is verified of more.

For a similar reason the simple negative is wider than the privative affirmative, for "is an unjust man" cannot be said of what is not man. But the infinite affirmative is wider than the private affirmative, for "is a nonjust man" can be truly said of a boy or of any man not yet having a habit of virtue or vice, but "is an unjust man" cannot. And the simple affirmative is narrower than the infinite negative, for "is not a nonjust man" can be said not only of a just man, but also of what is not man at all. Similarly, the privative negative is wider than the infinite negative. For "is not an unjust man" can be said not only of a man having the habit of justice and of what is not man at all—of which "is not a nonjust man" can be said—but over and beyond this can be said about all men who neither have the habit of justice nor the habit of injustice.

10.   With these points in mind it is easy to explain the present sentence in Aristotle. *Two of which,* i.e., *the infinites, will be related to*

[19] *Prior Anal.* I, 46, 51b 5ff.

[134]

the simple *affirmation and negation according to consequence*, i.e., in their mode of following upon the two simple enunciations, the infinitives will be related *as are privations*,[20] i.e., as the two privative enunciations. For just as the infinite negative follows upon the simple affirmative, and is not convertible with it (because the infinite negative is wider), so also the privative negative which is wider follows upon the simple affirmative and is not convertible. But just as the simple negative follows upon the infinite affirmative, which is narrower and is not convertible with it, so also the simple negative follows upon the privative affirmative, which is narrower and is not convertible. From this it is clear that there is the same relationship, with respect to consequence, of infinites to simple enunciations as there is of privatives.

11.   He goes on to say, *but two*, i.e., the simple enunciations that are left after the two infinite enunciations have been taken care of, *will not*, i.e., are not related to infinites according to consequence as privatives are related to them, because, on the one hand, the simple affirmative is narrower than the infinite negative, and the privative negative wider than the infinite negative; and on the other hand, the simple negative is wider than the infinite affirmative, and the privative affirmative narrower than the infinite affirmative. Thus it is clear that simple enunciations are not related to infinites in respect to consequence as privatives are related to infinites.

12.   But although this explains the words of the Philosopher in a subtle manner the explanation appears a bit forced. For the words of the Philosopher seem to say that diverse relationships will not apply in respect to diverse things; however, in the exposition we have just seen, first there is an explanation of a similitude of relationship to simple enunciations and then an explanation of a dissimilitude[21] of relationship in respect to infinites. The simpler exposition of this passage of Aristotle by Porphyry, which Boethius gives, is therefore more apposite.

According to Porphyry's explanation there is similitude and dissimilitude according to consequence of affirmatives and negatives. Thus Aristotle is saying: *Of which*, i.e., the four enunciations we are discussing, *two*, i.e., affirmatives, one simple and the other infinite, will be related according to consequence in regard to affirmation and negation, i.e., so that upon one affirmative follows the other negative, for the infinite negative follows upon the simple affirmative and the simple

[20] The text of Aristotle (19b 22) reads: ". . . two of which will correspond in their sequence, in respect of affirmation and negation, with the privations, but two will not."

[21] Codd, ABCE have "dissimilitude" here; P and D have "similitude."

negative upon the infinite affirmative.[22] *But two, i.e., the negatives, will not,* i.e., are not so related to affirmatives, i.e., so that affirmatives follow from negatives. And with respect to both, privatives are related in the same way as the infinites.

19b24   13.   Then Aristotle says, *I mean that the "is" will be added either to "just" or to "nonjust,"* etc. Here he shows how, under these circumstances, we get four enunciations. We are speaking now of enunciations in which the verb "is" is predicated as added to some finite or infinite name, for instance as it adjoins "just" in "Man is just," or "nonjust" in "Man is nonjust." Now since the negation is not applied to the verb in either of these, each is affirmative. However, there is a negation opposed to every affirmation as was shown in the first book.[23] Therefore, two negatives correspond to the two foresaid affirmative enunciations, making four simple enunciations.

19b27   14.   Then he says, *The following diagram will make this clear.* Here he manifests what he has said by a diagrammatic description; for, as he says, what has been stated can be understood from the following diagram. Take a four-sided figure and in one corner write the enunciation "Man is just." Opposite it write its negation "Man is not just," and under these the two infinite enunciations, "Man is nonjust," "Man is not nonjust."

Man is just   Man is not just

Man is not nonjust   Man is nonjust

It is evident from this table that the verb "is" whether affirmative or negative is adjoined to "just" and "nonjust." It is according to this that the four enunciations are diversified.

15.   Finally, he concludes that these enunciations are disposed according to an order of consequence that he has stated in the *Analytics,* i.e., in *I Priorum.*[24]

There is a variant reading of a previous portion of this text, namely, *I mean that "is" will be added either to "man" or to non-man,"*

---

[22] This is the relationship according to Porphyry's explanation of this passage:

[23] Lesson IX, n. 6.

[24] *Prior Anal.* I, 46, 51b 5 ff.

Simple affirmative   Infinite affirmative

Infinite negative   Simple negative

and in the diagram "is" is added to "man" and "non-man."[25] This cannot be understood to mean that "man" and "non-man" are taken on the part of the subject; for Aristotle is not treating here of enunciations with an infinite subject and hence "man" and "non-man" must be taken on the part of the predicate. This variant text seemed to Alexander to be corrupt, for the Philosopher has been explicating enunciations in which "just" and "nonjust" are posited on the part of the predicate. Others think it can be sustained and that Aristotle has intentionally varied the names to show that it makes no difference what names are used in the examples.

[25] Cf. Ammonius, *De interpret.* III, 1
fol. 25, col. 4; also, note π in the
Leonine edition, p. 85.

The Number and Relationship of Enunciations in Which the Verb "Is" Is Predicated and the Subject Is the Finite Name Taken Universally, or the Infinite Name, and of Those in Which the Adjective Verb is Predicated

19b 32 The same is the case when the affirmation is of a name taken universally, as in the following:

Every man is just (Affirmation)		Not every man is just (Negation)
Not every man is nonjust (Negation)		Every man is nonjust (Affirmation)

19b 35 But it is not possible, in the same way as in the former case, that those on the diagonal both be true; it is sometimes possible, however.

19b 36 These two pairs, then, are opposed; and there are two other pairs if something is added to "non-man" as a subject. Thus:

Non-man is just (Affirmation)	Non-man is not just (Negation)
Non-man is not nonjust (Negation)	Non-man is nonjust (Affirmation)

20a 1 There will be no more opposites than these.

20a 1 The latter, however, are separate from the former and distinct from them because of the use of "non-man" as a name.

20a 3 In enunciations in which "is" does not join the predicate to the subject, for example when the verb "matures" or "walks" is used, the same scheme applies, and they are arranged in the same way as when "is" was added. For example:

Every man matures (Affirmation)	Not every man matures (Negation)
Not every non-man matures (Negation)	Every non-man matures (Affirmation)

20a 7 We must not say "non-every man" but must add the negation to "man"; for the "every" does not signify a universal but that a universal is taken universally.

20a 10 This is evident from the following: "Man matures," "Man does not mature"; "Non-man matures," "Non-man does not mature." For these differ

[138]

from the former in that they are not taken universally; the "every" and the "no," then, only signify that the affirmation or negation is of a name universally.

20a 14 All else in enunciations in which "is" does not join the predicate to the subject will be the same as in the case in which "is" is the second element.

COMMENTARY BY CARDINAL CAJETAN

1.   Having distinguished enunciations in which the subject is an infinite name not taken universally,[26] Aristotle now distinguishes enunciations in which the subject is a finite name taken universally. He first proposes a similarity between these enunciations and the infinite enunciations already discussed, and then shows their difference where he says, *But it is not possible, in the same way as in the former case, that* 19b35 *those on the diagonal both be true,* etc. Finally, he concludes with the number of oppositions there are between these enunciations where he says, *These two pairs, then, are opposed,* etc.   19b36

He says first, then, that enunciations in which the affirmation is of a name taken universally are similar to those already discussed.

2.   It is to be noted in relation to Aristotle's first point that in indefinite enunciations there were two oppositions and four enunciations, the affirmatives inferring the negatives and not being inferred by them, as is clear in the exposition of Ammonius as well as of Porphyry. In enunciations in which the finite name universally taken is the subject there are also two oppositions and four enunciations, the affirmatives inferring the negatives and not the contrary. Hence, enunciations are related in a similar way if the affirmation is made universally of the name taken as the subject. For again, four enunciations will be made, two with a finite predicate—"Every man is just," and its negation, "Not every man is just"—and two with an infinite predicate—"Every man is nonjust" and its negation, "Not every man is nonjust." And since any affirmation together with its negation makes one whole opposition, two oppositions are made, as was also said of indefinite enunciations. There might seem to be an objection to his use of particulars when speaking of universal enunciations, but this cannot be objected to, for just as in dealing with indefinite enunciations he spoke of their negations, so now in dealing with universal affirmatives he is forced to speak of their ne-

[26] Actually the enunciation with an infinite name not taken universally is dealt with in this lesson. Aristotle has just finished treating the enunciation with the *finite* name not taken universally, i.e., the indefinite.

gations. The negation of the universal affirmative, however, is not the universal but the particular negative as was stated in the first book.[27]

3.   A table will make it evident that the consequence is similar in these and in indefinite enunciations. And lest what is clear be made obscure by prolixity let us first make a diagram of the indefinites posited in the last lesson, based upon the exposition of Porphyry.

Place the finite affirmative on one side and under it the infinite negative, and under this the privative negative. On the other side put the finite negative first, under it the infinite affirmative, and under this the privative affirmative. Then under this diagram make another similar to it but of universals. On one side put the universal affirmative of the finite predicate, under it the particular negative of the infinite predicate, and to complete the parallel put the particular negative of the privative predicate under this. On the other side, first put the particular negative of the infinite predicate,[28] under it the universal affirmative of the finite predicate,[29] and under this the universal affirmative of the privative predicate. Thus:

DIAGRAM OF THE INDEFINITES

Man is just	Man is not just
Man is not nonjust	Man is nonjust
Man is not unjust	Man is unjust

DIAGRAM OF THE UNIVERSALS

Every man is just	Not every man is just[30]
Not every man is nonjust	Every man is nonjust[31]
Not every man is unjust	Every man is unjust

In this disposition of enunciations, the consequence always follows in the second diagram just as it followed in regard to indefinites

[27] 17b 16; St. Thomas, Lesson XI, n. 3.

[28] In Cajetan this is "Not every man is nonjust," which is the same enunciation as the diagonal to it and hence cannot be correct, for in n. 4 when he explains what Aristotle means by diagonal enunciations, and again in n. 5 when he explains that the diagonals of indefinites are both true whereas this is only sometimes true of universals, it is evident that the diagonals cannot be the identical enunciation.

[29] The universal affirmative of the finite predicate would be "Every man is just," which is the same enunciation as the one placed first in this dia-gram. This enunciation, therefore, and the one placed just above it (cf. note 28) are not correctly given in the text. It is evident from Aristotle's text (19b 32) that the "non" attached to "nonjust" has been misplaced in these two enunciations: the first one on the side of the diagram we are now setting up should be "Not every man is just" instead of "Not every man is nonjust," and the second should be "Every man is nonjust" instead of "Every man is just." This correction has been made in Cajetan's table.

[30] Cf., notes 28 and 29.

[31] Cf., note 29.

in the first diagram. This is true if we follow the exposition of Ammonius in which infinites are related to finites as privatives are related to the same finites, and the finites not related to the infinite middle enunciations as privatives are related to those infinites. It is equally true if we follow the exposition of Porphyry, in which affirmatives infer negatives and not vice versa. That the tables serve both expositions will be clear to one studying them. These universal enunciations, therefore, are related in like manner to indefinite enunciations in three things: the number of propositions, the number of oppositions, and the mode of consequence.

4.   When he says, *But it is not possible, in the same way as in the* 19b35 *former case, that those on the diagonal both be true,* etc., he proposes a difference between the universals and the indefinites, i.e., that it is not possible for the diagonals to be true in the case of universals. First we will explain these words according to the exposition we believe Aristotle had in mind, then according to the opinion of others.

     Aristotle means by diagonal enunciations those that are diametrically opposed in the diagram above, i.e., the finite affirmative in one corner and the infinite affirmative or the privative in the other; and the finite negative in one corner and the infinite negative or privative in the other.

5.   Enunciations that are similar in quality, and called diagonal because diametrically distant, are dissimilar in truth, then, in the case of indefinites and universals. The indefinites on the corners, both on the diagonal of affirmations and the diagonal of negations can be simultaneously true, as is evident in the table of the indefinite enunciations. This is to be understood in regard to contingent matter. But diagonals of universals are not so related, for angulars on the diagonal of affirmations cannot be simultaneously true in any matter. Those on the diagonal of negations, however, can sometimes be true simultaneously, i.e., when they are in contingent matter. In necessary and remote matter it is impossible for both of these to be true. This is the exposition of Boethius, which we believe to be the true one.

6.   Herminus, however, according to Boethius,[32] explains this in another way. He takes the oppositions in one way in universals and in another in indefinites, although he holds that there is a likeness between universals and indefinites with respect to the number of enunciations and of oppositions. He arrives at the oppositions of indefinites we have, i.e., one between the affirmative and negative finites, and the other between the affirmative and negative infinites. But he disposes the

---

[32] Boethius, *De Interpret.* IV, p. 388.

oppositions of universals in another way, taking one between the finite universal affirmative and finite particular negative, "Every man is just" and "Not every man is just," and the other between the same finite universal affirmative and the infinite universal affirmative, "Every man is just" and "Every man is nonjust." Between the latter there is contrariety, between the former contradiction.

He also proposes the dissimilarity between universals and indefinites in another way. He does not base the dissimilarity between diagonals of universals and indefinites on the difference between affirmative and negative diagonals of universals, as we do, but on the difference between the diagonals of universals on both sides among themselves. Hence he forms his diagram in this way: under the finite universal affirmative he places the infinite universal affirmative, and on the other side, under the finite particular negative the infinite particular negative. Thus the diagonals are of different quality. He also diagrams the indefinites in this way.

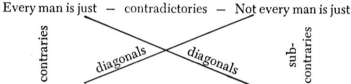

With enunciations disposed in this way he says their difference is this: that in indefinite enunciations, one on the diagonal is true as a necessary consequence of the truth of the other, so that the truth of one enunciation infers the truth of its diagonal from wherever you begin. But there is no such mutual necessary consequence in universals—from the truth of one on a diagonal to the other—since the necessity of inference fails in part. If you begin from any of the universals and proceed to its diagonal, the truth of the universal cannot be simultaneous with the truth of its diagonal so as to compel it to truth. For if the universal is true its universal contrary will be false, since they cannot be at once true; and if this universal contrary is false, its particular contradictory, which is the diagonal of the first universal assumed, will necessarily be true, since it is impossible for contradictories to be at once false; but if, conversely, you begin with a particular enunciation and proceed to its diagonal, the truth of the particular can so stand with the truth of its diagonal that it does not infer its truth necessarily. For this follows: the

[142]

particular is true, therefore its universal contradictory is false. But this does not follow: this universal contradictory is false, therefore its universal contrary, which is the diagonal of the particular assumed, is true. For contraries can be at once false.

7.   But the way in which oppositions are taken in this exposition does not seem to be what Aristotle had in mind. He did not intend to speak here of the opposition between finites and infinites, but of the opposition between finites themselves and infinites themselves. For if we meant to explain each mode of opposition, there would not be two but three oppositions: first, between finites; second, between infinites; and third, the one Herminus states between finite and infinite. Even the diagram Herminus makes is not like the one Aristotle makes at the end of *I Priorum,* to which Aristotle himself referred us in the last lesson when he said, *This, then, is the way these are arranged, as we have said in the Analytics;* for in Aristotle's diagram affirmatives are diagonal to affirmatives and negatives to negatives.

8.   Then Aristotle says, *These two pairs, then, are opposed,* etc.   19b36
Here he concludes to the number of propositions. What he says here can be interpreted in two ways. In the first way, "these" designates universals, and thus the meaning is that the finite and infinite universals have two oppositions, which we have explained above. In the second, "these" designates enunciations which are finite and infinite with respect to the predicate, whether universal or indefinite, and then the meaning is that these enunciations have two oppositions, one between the finite affirmation and its negation and the other between the infinite affirmation and its negation. The second exposition seems more satisfactory to me, for the brevity for which Aristotle strove allows for no repetition; hence, in terminating his treatment of the enunciations he had enumerated—those with a finite and infinite predicate according to diverse quantities—he meant to reduce all the oppositions to two.

9.   When he says, *and there are two other pairs if something is*   19b37
added to "non-man" as a subject, etc., he shows the diversity of enunciations when "is" is added as a third element and the subject is an infinite name. First, he proposes and distinguishes them; secondly, he shows that there are no more opposites than these where he says, *There*   20a1
will be no more opposites than these; thirdly, he shows the relationship of these to the others where he says, *The latter, however, are separate*   20a1
from the former and distinct from them, etc.
        With respect to the first point, it should be noted that there are three species of absolute [de inesse] enunciations in which the verb "is" is posited explicitly. Some have nothing added to the subject—which can

[143]

be either finite or infinite—beyond the verb, as in "Man is," "Non-man is." Some have, besides the verb, something either finite or infinite added to a finite subject, as in "Man is just," "Man is nonjust." Finally, some have, besides the verb, something either finite or infinite added to an infinite subject, as in "Non-man is just," "Non-man is nonjust." He has already treated the first two and now intends to take up the last ones. *And there are two other pairs,* he says, that have something, namely a predicate, added beside the verb "is" to "non-man" as if[33] to a subject, i.e., to an infinite subject. He says "as if" because the infinite name falls short of the notion of a subject insofar as it falls short of the notion of a name. Indeed, the signification of an infinite name is not properly submitted to composition with the predicate, which "is," the third element added, introduces.

Aristotle enumerates four enunciations and two oppositions in this order as he did in the former. In addition he distinguishes these from the former finiteness and infinity. First, he posits the opposition between affirmative and negative enunciations with an infinite subject and a finite predicate, "Non-man is just," "Non-man is not just." Then he posits another opposition between those with an infinite subject and an infinite predicate, "Non-man is nonjust," "Non-man is not nonjust."

20a1   10.   Then he says, *There will be no more opposites than these.* Here he points out that there are no more oppositions of enunciations than the ones he has already given. We should note, then, that simple [or absolute] enunciations—of which we have been speaking—in which the verb "is" is explicitly posited whether it is the second or third element added, cannot be more than the twelve posited. Consequently, their oppositions according to affirmation and negation are only six. For enunciations are divided into three orders: those with the second element added, those with the third element added to a finite subject, and those with the third element added to an infinite subject; and in any order there are four enunciations. And since their subject in any order can be quantified in four ways, i.e., by universality, particularity, singularity, and indefiniteness, these twelve will be increased to forty-eight (four twelves being forty-eight). Nor is it possible to imagine more than these.

Aristotle has only expressed twenty of these, eight in the first order, eight in the second, and four in the third, but through them he intended the rest to be understood. They are to be enumerated and disposed according to each order so that the primary negation is placed

---

[33] The Latin text of Aristotle, which Cajetan quotes here has "quasi ad subjectum." The Greek ὡς ὑποκειμενόν"; both the *quasi* and the ὡς can of course be translated as "as" or "as if." Cajetan takes it in this latter meaning.

The following diagram will make this clear.

FIRST ORDER

Socrates is
Some man is
Man is
Every man is

Non-Socrates is
Some non-man is
Non-man is
Every non-man is

Socrates is not
Some man is not
Man is not
No man is

Non-Socrates is not
Some non-man is not
Non-man is not
No non-man is

SECOND ORDER

Socrates is just
Some man is just
Man is just
Every man is just

Socrates is nonjust
Some man is nonjust
Man is nonjust
Every man is nonjust

Socrates is not just
Some man is not just
Man is not just
No man is just

Socrates is not nonjust
Some man is not nonjust
Man is not nonjust
No man is nonjust

THIRD ORDER

Non-Socrates is just
Some non-man is just
Non-man is just
Every non-man is just

Non-Socrates is nonjust
Some non-man is nonjust
Non-man is nonjust
Every non-man is nonjust

Non-Socrates is not just
Some non-man is not just
Non-man is not just
No non-man is just

Non-Socrates is not nonjust
Some non-man is not nonjust
Non-man is not nonjust
No non-man is nonjust

opposite an affirmation in order to make the relation of opposition more evident. Thus, the universal negative should not be ordered as opposite to the universal affirmative, but the particular negative, which is its negation. Conversely, the particular negative should not be ordered as opposite to the particular affirmative, but the universal negative, which is its negation. For a clearer look at their number all those of similar quantity should be co-ordered in a straight line and in the three distinct orders given above.

It is evident that there are no more than these, for the subject and the predicate cannot be varied in any other way with respect to finite and infinite. Nor can the finite and infinite subject be varied in any other way, for the enunciation with a second adjoining element cannot be varied with a finite and infinite predicate but only in respect to the subject. This is clear enough. But enunciations with a third adjoining element can be varied in four ways: they may have either a finite subject and predicate, or an infinite subject and predicate, or a finite subject and infinite predicate, or an infinite subject and finite predicate. These variations are all evident in the above table.

20a1   11.   Then when he says, *The latter, however, are separate from the former and distinct from them,* etc., he shows the relationship of those we have put in the third order to those in the second order. The former, he says, are distinct from the latter because they do not follow upon the latter, nor conversely. He assigns the reason when he adds: *because of the use of "non-man" as a name,* i.e., the former are separate from the latter because the former use an infinite name in place of a name, since they all have an infinite subject. It should be noted that he says enunciations of an infinite subject use an infinite name as a name; for to be subjected in an enunciation is proper to a name, to be predicated common to a name and a verb, and therefore every subject of an enunciation is subjected as a name.

12.   Next he takes up enunciations in which adjective verbs are
20a3   posited, when he says, *In enunciations in which "is" does not join the predicate to the subject,* etc. First, he distinguishes these adjective verbs;
20a7   secondly, he answers an implied question where he says, *We must not say "non-every man,"* etc.; thirdly, he concludes with their conditions
20a14   where he says, *All else in the enunciations in which "is" does not join the predicate to the subject will be the same,* etc.

It is necessary to note here that there is a difference between enunciations in which "is" is posited as a second adjoining element and those in which it is posited as a third element. In those with "is" as a second element oppositions are simple, i.e., varied only on the part of the subject by finite and infinite. In those having "is" as a third element

[146]

oppositions are made in two ways—on the part of the predicate and on the part of the subject—for both can be varied by finite and infinite. Hence we made only one order of enunciations with "is" as the second element. It had four enunciations quantified in diverse ways, and two oppositions. But enunciations with "is" as a third element must be divided into two orders, because in them there are four oppositions and eight enunciations, as we said above. Enunciations with adjective verbs are made equivalent in signification to enunciations with "is" as the third element by resolving the adjective verb into its proper participle and "is," which may always be done because a substantive verb is contained in every adjective verb. For example, "Every man runs" signifies the same thing as "Every man is running." Because of this Boethius calls enunciations having an adjective verb "enunciations of the second adjoining element according to vocal sound, but of the third adjoining element according to power." He designates them in this manner because they can be resolved into enunciations with a third adjoining element to which they are equivalent.

With respect to the number and oppositions of enunciations, those with an adjective verb, formally taken, are not equivalent to those with a third adjoining element but to those in which "is" is posited as the second element. For oppositions cannot be made in two ways in adjectival enunciations as they are in the case of substantival enunciations with a third adjoining element, namely, on the part of the subject and predicate, because the verb which is predicated in adjectival enunciations cannot be made infinite. Hence oppositions of adjectival enunciations are made simply, i.e., only by the subject quantified in diverse ways being varied by finite and infinite, as was done above in substantival enunciations with a second adjoining element, and for the same reason, i.e., there can be no affirmation or negation without a verb but there can be without a name.

Since the present treatment is not of *significations* but of the *number* of enunciations and oppositions, Aristotle determines that adjectival enunciations are to be diversified according to the mode in which enunciations with "is" as the second adjoining element are distinguished. And he says that in enunciations in which the verb "is" is not posited formally, but some other verb, such as "matures" or "walks," i.e., in adjectival enunciations, the name and verb form the same scheme with respect to the number of oppositions and enunciations as when "is" as a second adjoining element is added to the name as a subject. For these adjectival enunciations, like the ones in which "is" is posited, have only two oppositions, one between the finites, as in "Every man runs," "Not every man runs," the other between the infinites with respect to subject, as in "Every non-man runs," "Not every non-man runs."

[147]

20a7   13.   Then he answers an implied question when he says, *We must not say "non-every man" but must add the negation to man,* etc. First he states the solution of the question, then he proves it where he says,

20a10   *This is evident from the following,* etc.

     The question is this: Why is the negation that makes a word infinite never added to the universal or particular sign? For example, when we wish to make "Every man runs" infinite, why do we do it in this way ,"Every non-man runs," and not in this, "Non-every man runs."

     He answers the question by saying that to be capable of being made infinite a name has to signify something universal or singular. "Every" and similar signs, however, do not signify something universal or singular, but that something is taken universally or particularly. Therefore, we should not say "non-every man" if we wish to infinitize (although it may be used if we wish to deny the quantity of an enunciation), but must add the infinitizing negation to "man," which signifies something universal, and say "every non-man."

20a10   14.   Where he says, *This is evident from the following,* etc., he proves that "every" and similar words do not signify a universal but *that a universal is taken universally.* His argument is the following: That by which enunciations having or not having the "every" differ is not the universal; rather, they differ in that the universal is taken universally. But that by which enunciations having and not having the "every" differ is signified by the "every." Therefore, that which is signified by the "every" is not a universal but *that the universal is taken universally.* The minor of the argument is evident, though not explicitly given in the text: that in which the having of some term differs from the not having of it, other things being equal, is the signification of that term. The major is made evident by examples. The enunciations "Man matures" and "Every man matures" differ precisely by the fact that in one there is an "every," in the other not. However, they do not differ in such a way by this that one is universal, the other not universal, for both have the universal subject, "man"; they differ because in the one in which "every" is posited, the enunciation is of the subject universally, but in the other not universally. For when I say, "Man matures," I attribute maturing to "man" as universal or common but not to man as to the whole human race; when I say, "Every man matures," however, I signify maturing to be present to man according to all the inferiors. This is evident, too, in the three other examples of enunciations in Aristotle's text. For example, "Non-man matures" when its universal is taken universally becomes "Every non-man matures," and so of the others.[34] It follows,

[34] Cajetan actually has here "Homo non currit" and "Omnis homo non   currit" as examples. But if these are translated as "Man is not running"

therefore, that "every" and "no" and similar signs do not signify a universal but only signify that they affirm or deny of man universally.

15.   Two things should be noted here: first, that Aristotle does not say "every" and "no" signify universally, but that the universal is taken universally; secondly, that he adds, *they affirm or deny of man.*[35] The 20a13 reason for the first is that the distributive sign does not signify the mode of universality or of particularity absolutely, but the mode applied to a distributed term. When I say, "every man" the "every" denotes that universality is applied to the term "man." Hence, when Aristotle says "every" signifies that a universal is taken universally, by the "that" he conveys the application in actual exercise of the universality denoted by the "every," just as in I *Posteriorum* in the definition of "to know," namely, *To know scientifically is to know a thing through its cause and that this is its cause,* he signifies by the word "that" the application of the cause.[36]

The reason for the second is to imply the difference between categorematic and syncategorematic terms. The former apply what is signified to the terms absolutely; the latter apply what they signify to the terms in relation to the predicates. For example, in "white man" the "white" denominates man in himself apart from any regard to something to be added; but in "every man," although the "every" distributes "man," the distribution does not confirm the intellect unless it is understood in relation to some predicate. A sign of this is that when we say "Every man runs" we do not intend to distribute "man" in its whole universality absolutely, but only in relation to "running." When we say "White man runs," on the other hand, we designate man in himself as "white" and not in relation to "running."

and "Every man is not running" they will not correspond to what Cajetan is saying, since the latter is not the universal universally taken. Nor can they be, "Man nonruns" and "Every man nonruns," because Cajetan has ruled out the infinite adjective verb in n. 12 of this lesson. They could, of course, be translated as "Man is nonrunning" and "Every man is nonrunning," but this would not be a very exact duplication of Aristotle's examples which have an infinite name with an adjective verb. Hence, Aristotle's examples have been substituted here for Cajetan's. It is not clear either why Cajetan

mentions *three* other examples—only two more are given here by Aristotle—unless he is thinking of all of the examples used in this lesson.
[35] The Greek reads: ". . . ὥστε τὸ πᾶς ἢ μηδείς οὐδὲν ἄλλο προσσημαίνει ἢ ὅτι καθόλου τοῦ ὀνόματος κατάφησιν ἢ ἀπόφησιν"; ("the 'every' and the 'no,' then, signify nothing other than that they affirm or deny universally of a name"). In the present translation this is rendered as, "The 'every' and the 'no,' then, only signify that the affirmation or negation is of a name universally."
[36] *Post. Anal.* I, 2, 71b 10.

Therefore, since "every" and "no" and the other syncategorematic terms do nothing except determine the subject in relation to the predicate in the enunciation, and this cannot be done without affirmation and negation, Aristotle says that they only signify that the affirmation or negation is of a name, i.e., of a subject, universally, i.e., they prescribe the affirmation or negation that is being formed, and by this he separates them from categorematic terms. *They affirm or deny* can also be referred to the signs themselves, i.e., "every" and "no," one of which distributes positively, the other distributes by removing.

20a14   16.   When he says *All else in enunciations in which "is" does not join the predicate to the subject,* etc., he concludes the treatment of the conditions of adjectival enunciations. He has already stated that adjectival enunciations are the same with respect to the number of oppositions as substantival enunciations with "is" as the second element, and has clarified this by a table showing the number of oppositions. Now, since upon this conformity follows conformity both with respect to finiteness of predicates and with respect to the diverse quantity of subjects, and also—if any enunciations of this kind are enumerated—their multiplication in sets of four, he concludes, *Therefore also the other things,*[37] which are to be observed in them, *are to be considered the same,* i.e., similar to these.

[37] In the Greek this part of the sentence reads: ". . . τὰ οὖν ἄλλα τὰ αὐτὰ δεῖ προστιθέναι." The Latin translation of it: "Ergo et cetera eadem oportet apponi."

Some Doubts About What Has Been Said
Are Presented and Solved

20a 16   Since the negation contrary to "Every animal is just," is the one signifying "No animal is just," it is evident that these will never be at once true, or in reference to the same thing, but the opposites of these will sometimes be true, i.e., "Not every animal is just" and "Some animal is just."

20a 20   Now the enunciation "No man is just" follows upon the enunciation "Every man is nonjust"; and "Not every man is nonjust," which is its opposite, follows upon "Some man is just," for its opposite [i.e. the opposite of "every man"] must be "some man."

20a 23   And it is also clear with respect to the singular that if a question is asked and a negative answer is the true one, there is also a true affirmation. Take the example, "Is Socrates wise?" and the answer, "No"; then, "Socrates is nonwise." But in the case of universals, the affirmative inference is not true, but the negation is true. For example, in the question, "Is every man wise?" and the true answer, "No," the inference "Then every man is nonwise" is clearly false, but "Not every man is wise" is true. The latter is the opposite, the former the contrary.

20a 31   The antitheses in infinite names and verbs, as in "non-man" and "nonjust," might seem to be negations without a name or a verb; they are not, however. For the negation must always be either true or false; but the person who says "non-man" says nothing more than one who says "man," and he is even further from saying something true or false if something is not added.

20a 37   Moreover, "Every non-man is just" does not signify the same thing as any of the other enunciations, nor does the opposite of this, "Not every non-man is just."

20a 39   But "Every non-man is nonjust" signifies the same thing as "No non-man is just."

20b 1   When the names and verbs are transposed, the enunciations signify the same thing; for example, "Man is white" and "White is man."

20b 3 For if this is not the case there will be more than one negation of the same enunciation; but it has been shown that there is only one negation of one affirmation,[38] for the negation of "Man is white" is "Man is not white," and if "White is man" is not the same as "Man is white," the negation of it

[38] Cf. 17b 38.

["White is man"] will be "White is not non-man" and "White is not man." The former, however, is the negation of "White is non-man"; the latter of "Man is white." Therefore, there will be two [negations] of one [affirmation]. It is clear, therefore, that when the name and the verb are transposed the signification of the affirmation and negation is the same.

---

1.   Having treated the diversity of enunciations Aristotle now answers certain questions about them. He takes up six points related to the number of difficulties. These will become evident as we come to them.

Since he has said that in universal enunciations the diagonals in one case cannot be at once true but can be in another, for the diagonal affirmatives cannot be at once true but the negatives can,[39] someone might raise a question as to the cause of this diversity. Therefore, it is his intention now to assign the cause of this: namely, that the diagonal affirmatives are contrary to each other, and contraries cannot be at once true in any matter; but the diagonal negatives are subcontraries opposed to these and can be at once true.

In relation to this he first states the conditions for contraries and subcontraries. Then he shows that diagonal affirmatives are contraries
20a20   and that diagonal negatives are subcontraries where he says, *Now the enunciation "No man is just" follows upon the enunciation "Every man is nonjust,"* etc.

By way of resumé, therefore, he says that in the first book it was said that the negative enunciation contrary to the universal affirmative "Every animal is just" is "No animal is just." It is evident that these cannot be at once true, i.e., at the same time, nor *of the same thing*, i.e., of the same subject. But the opposites of these, i.e., the subcontraries, can sometimes be at once true, i.e., in contingent matter, as in "Some animal is just" and "Not every animal is just."

20a20   2.   When he says, *Now the enunciation, "No man is just" follows upon the enunciation "Every man is nonjust,"* etc., he shows that the diagonal affirmatives previously posited are contraries, the negatives subcontraries. First he manifests this from the fact that the infinite universal affirmative and the simple universal negative are equal in meaning, and consequently each of them is contrary to the simple universal

[39] See Aristotle, 19b 35, Book II, Lesson III. Aristotle's diagram makes this point clear.

The diagonal affirmatives cannot be at once true but the diagonal negatives can be.

Every man is just ⟍ ⟋ Not every man is just

Not every man is nonjust ⟋ ⟍ Every man is nonjust

[152]

affirmative, which is the other diagonal. Hence, he says that the infinite universal affirmative "Every man is nonjust" follows upon the finite universal negative "No man is just," equivalently.[40]

Secondly he shows this from the fact that the finite particular affirmative and the infinite particular negative are equal in meaning, and consequently each of these is subcontrary to the simple particular negative, which is the other diagonal. This you can see in the previous diagram. He says, then, that the opposite "Not every man is nonjust" follows upon the finite particular "Some man is just" equivalently (understand "the opposite" not of this particular but of the infinite universal affirmative, for this is its contradictory).

In order to see clearly how these enunciations are equivalent, make a four-sided figure, putting the finite universal negative in one corner and under it the contradictory, the finite particular affirmative. On the other side, put the infinite universal affirmative and under it the contradictory, the infinite particular negative. Now indicate the contradiction between diagonals and the contradiction between collaterals.

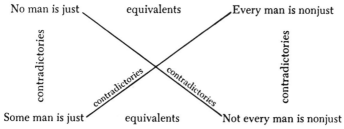

This arrangement makes the mutual consequence of the universals in truth and falsity evident, for if one of them is true, its diagonal contradictory is false; and if this is false, its collateral contradictory, which is the other universal, will be true. With respect to the falsity of the particulars the procedure is the same. Their mutual consequence is made evident in the same way, for if one of them is true, its diagonal contradictory is false, and if this is false, its contradictory collateral, which is the other particular, will be true; the procedure is the same with respect to falsity.

3.   However, a question arises with respect to this. At the end of I *Priorum*, Aristotle determines from what he has proposed that the judgment of the universal negative and the infinite universal affirmative is not the same.[41] Furthermore, in the second book of the present work, in relation to the phrase *Of which two are related according to*

[40] In the Greek text the universal negative follows upon the infinite universal affirmative.

[41] Cf. *Prior Anal.* I, 46, 51b 5 ff.

consequence, two are not. Ammonius, Porphyry, Boethius, and St. Thomas say that the simple negative follows upon the infinite affirmative and not conversely.[42]

Albert answers this latter difficulty by pointing out that the infinite affirmative follows upon the finite negative when the subject is constant, but the simple negative follows upon the affirmative absolutely. Hence both positions are verified, for with a constant subject there is a mutual consequence between them, but there is not a mutual consequence between them absolutely.

We could also answer this difficulty in this way. In Book II, Lesson II we were speaking of the infinite enunciation with the whole of what it signified reduced to the form of the predicate, and according to this there was not a mutual consequence, since the finite negative is superior to the infinite affirmative. But here we are speaking of the infinite itself formally taken. Hence St. Thomas, when he introduced the exposition of Ammonius in his commentary on the above passage, said that according to this mode of speaking the simple negative is wider than the infinite affirmative.

In the above mentioned text in I *Priorum*, Aristotle is speaking of finite and infinite enunciations in relation to the syllogism.[43] It is evident, however, that the universal affirmative, whether finite or infinite is only inferred in the first mode of the first figure, while any universal negative whatever is inferred in the second mode of the first figure and in the first and second modes of the second figure.

20a23   4.   When he says, *And it is also clear with respect to the singular that if a question is asked and a negative answer is the true one, there is also a true affirmation,* etc., he presents a difficulty relating to the varying position of the negation, i.e., whether there is a difference as to truth and falsity when the negation is a part of the predicate or a part of the verb. This difficulty arises from what he has just said, namely, that it is of no consequence as to truth or falsity whether you say, "Every man is nonjust" or "Every man is not just";[44] yet in one case the negation is a part of the predicate, in the other part of the copula, and this makes a great deal of difference with respect to affirmation and negation.

---

[42] The phrase of Aristotle referred to here reads: ". . . two of which will correspond in their sequence, in respect of affirmation and negation . . . but two will not" (19b 22). See Book II, Lesson II, n. 5 ff., for the commentary on this passage.

[43] Cf. *Prior Anal.* I, 46, 52a 36 ff.

[44] Cf. 19b32. In Latin the two enunciations are "Omnis homo est non justus" and "Omnis homo non est justus"; that is, the negation is placed after the copula or before it.

[154]

To solve this problem Aristotle makes a distinction: in singular enunciations, the singular negation and infinite affirmation of the same subject are of the same truth, but in universals this is not so. For if the negation of the universal is true it is not necessary that the infinite affirmation of the universal is true. The negation of the universal is the contradictory particular, but if it is true [i.e., the contradictory particular] it is not necessary that the subaltern, which is the contrary of the contradictory, be true, for two contraries can be at once false. Hence he says that in singular enunciations it is evident that if it is true to deny the thing asked, i.e., if the negation of a singular enunciation, which has been made into an interrogation, is true, there will also be a true affirmation, i.e., the infinite affirmation of the same singular will be true. For example, if the question "Do you think Socrates is wise?" has "No" as a true response, then "Socrates is nonwise," i.e., the infinite affirmation "Socrates is nonwise" will be true.

But in the case of universals the affirmative inference is not true, 20a26 i.e., from the truth of a negation to a universal affirmative question, the truth of the infinite universal affirmative (which is similar in quantity and quality to the enunciation asked) does not follow. *But the negation is true,* i.e., from the truth of the negative response it follows that its negation is true, i.e., the negation of the universal asked, which is the particular negative. Consider, for example, the question "Do you think every man is wise?" If the response "No" is true, one would be tempted to infer the affirmative similar to the question asked, i.e., then "Every man is nonwise." This, however, does not follow from the negation, for this is false as it follows from that response. Rather, what must be inferred is "Then not every man is wise." And the reason for both is that the particular enunciation inferred last is the opposite, i.e., the contradictory of the universal question, which, being falsified by the negative response, makes the contradictory of the universal affirmative true, for of contradictories, if one is false the other is true.

The infinite universal affirmative first inferred, however, is contrary to the same universal question. Should it not also be true? No, because it is not necessary in the case of universals that if one is false the other is true.

The cause of the diversity between singulars and universals is now clear. In singulars the varying position of the negation does not vary the quantity of the enunciation, but in universals it does. Therefore there is not the same truth in enunciations denying a universal when in one the negation is a part of the predicate and in the other a part of the verb.

[155]

20a31 5.   Then he says, *The antitheses in infinite names and verbs, as in "non-man" and "nonjust," might seem to be negations without a name or a verb*, etc. Here he raises the third difficulty, i.e., whether infinite names or verbs are negations. This question arises from his having said that the negative and infinite are equivalent and from having just said that in singular enunciations it makes no difference whether the negative is a part of the predicate or a part of the verb. For if the infinite name is a negation, then the enunciation having an infinite subject or predicate will be negative and not affirmative.

He resolves this question by an interpretation which proves that neither infinite names nor verbs are negations although they seem to be. First he proposes the solution saying, *The antitheses in infinite names and verbs*, i.e., words contraposed, e.g., "non-man," and "nonjust man" and "just man"; or this may be read as, *Those* (namely, words) *corresponding to infinites*, i.e., corresponding to the nature of infinites, *placed in opposition to names or verbs* (namely, removing what the names and verbs signify, as in "non-man," "nonjust," and "nonruns," which are opposed to "man," "just" and "runs"), would seem at first sight to be quasi-negations without name and verb, because, as related to the names and verbs before which they are placed, they remove them; they are not truly negations however. He says *without a name or a verb* because the infinite name lacks the nature of a name and the infinite verb does not have the nature of a verb. He says *quasi* because the infinite name does not fall short of the notion of the name in every way, nor the infinite verb of the nature of the verb.[45] Hence, if it is thought that they are negations, they will be regarded as without a name or a verb, not in every way but *as though* they were without a name or a verb.

He proves that infinitizing signs of separation are not negations by pointing out that it is always necessary for the negation to be true or false since a negation is an enunciation of something separated from something. The infinite name, however, does not assert what is true or false. Therefore the infinite word is not a negation. He manifests the minor when he says that the one who says "non-man" says nothing more of man than the one who says "man." Clearly this is so with respect to what is signified, for "non-man" adds nothing beyond "man"; rather, it removes "man." Moreover, with respect to a conception of truth or

---

[45] The ὥσπερ in the Greek text (*quasi* in the Latin) to which Cajetan refers here appeared to be sufficiently understood in "seems to be," and hence has been omitted from the translation of Aristotle's text. In this passage Aristotle could also mean that an infinite name alone is not a negation, nor is an infinite verb alone, i.e., there must be both a name and verb for a negative enunciation.

[156]

falsity, it is of no more use to say "non-man" than to say "man" if something else is not added; rather, it is less true or false, i.e., one who says "non-man" is more removed from truth and falsity than one who says "man," for both truth and falsity depend on composition, and the finite word which posits something is closer to composition than the infinite word, which neither posits nor composes, i.e., it implies neither positing nor composition.

6.   When he says, Moreover, "Every non-man is just" does not sig-   20a37
nify the same thing as any of the other enunciations, etc., he answers a fourth difficulty, i.e., how the earlier statement concerning enunciations having an infinite subject is to be understood. The statement was that   20a1 these stand by themselves and are distinct from the former [in consequence of using the name "non-man"]. This is to be understood not just with respect to the enunciations themselves formally, but with respect to the consequence of what is signified. Hence, giving two examples of enunciations with an infinite subject, the universal affirmative and universal negative,[46] he says that neither of these signifies the same thing as any of those, namely of those having a finite subject. The universal affirmative "Every non-man is just" does not signify the same thing as any of the enunciations with a finite subject; for it does not signify "Every man is just" nor "Every man is nonjust." Nor do the opposite negation, or the universal negative having an infinite subject which is contrarily opposed to the universal affirmative, signify the same thing as enunciations with a finite subject; i.e., "Not every non-man is just" and "No non-man is just," do not signify the same thing as any of those with a finite subject. This is evident from the diversity of subject in the latter and the former.

7.   When he says, But "Every non-man is nonjust" signifies the same   20a39
thing as "No non-man is just," he answers a fifth difficulty, i.e., is there a consequence among enunciations with an infinite subject? This question arises from the fact that consequences were assigned among them earlier.[47] He says, therefore, that there is a consequence even among these, for the universal affirmative with an infinite subject and predicate and the universal negative with an infinite subject but a finite predicate are equivalent, i.e., "Every non-man is nonjust" signifies the same thing as "No non-man is just." This is also the case in particular infinites and singulars which are similar to the foresaid, for no matter what their quantity, the affirmative with both extremes infinite and the negative with an infinite subject and a finite predicate are always equivalent, as

[46] Aristotle's examples are the universal   every non-man is just."
affirmative and the particular enun-   [47] Cf. 20a 20.
ciation opposed to this, i.e., "Not

may be easily seen by examples. Hence, Aristotle in giving the universals intends the others to be understood from these.

20b1   8.   When he says, *When the names and verbs are transposed, the enunciations signify the same thing,* etc., he resolves a sixth difficulty: whether the signification of the enunciation is varied because of the transposition of names or verbs. This question arises from his having shown that the transposition of the negation varies the signification of the enunciation.[48] "Every man is nonjust,"[49] he said, does not signify the same thing as "Not every man is just." This raises the question as to whether a similar thing happens when we transpose names. Would this vary the enunciation as the transposed negation does?

First he states the solution, saying that transposed names and verbs signify the same thing, e.g., "Man is white" signifies the same thing as "White is man." Transposed verbs also signify the same thing, as in "Man is white" and "Man white is."

20b3   9.   Then he proves the solution from the number of contradictory negations when he says, *For if this is not the case there will be more than one negation of the same enunciation,* etc. He does this by a reduction to the impossible and his reasoning is as follows. If this is not so, i.e., if transposed names diversify enunciations, there will be two negations of the same affirmation. But in the first book it was shown that there is only one negation of one affirmation.[50] Going, then, from the destruction of the consequent to the destruction of the antecedent, transposed names do not vary the enunciation.

To clarify the proof of the consequent, make a figure in which both of the affirmations posited above, with the names transposed are located on one side. Put the two negatives similar to them in respect to terms and position on the opposite side. Then leaving a little space, under the affirmatives put the affirmation with an infinite subject and under the negatives the negation of it. Mark the contradiction between the first affirmation and the first two negations and between the second affirmation and all three negations, but in the latter case mark the contradiction between it and the lowest negation as not true but imaginary. Mark, also, the contradiction between the third affirmation and negation.

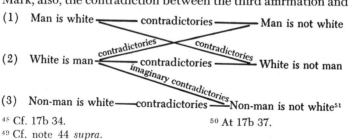

(1)   Man is white ———— contradictories ———— Man is not white

(2)   White is man ⟨contradictories / contradictories⟩ contradictories ———— White is not man

(3)   Non-man is white ——— imaginary contradictories ——— contradictories ⟶ Non-man is not white[51]

[48] Cf. 17b 34.   [50] At 17b 37.
[49] Cf. note 44 *supra*.

Now we can see how Aristotle proves the consequent. The negation of the affirmation "Man is white" is "Man is not white." But if the second affirmation, "White is man," is not the same as "Man is white," because of the transposition of the names, its negation, [i.e., of "White is man"] will be either of these two: "Non-man is not white," or "White is not man." But each of these has another opposed affirmation than that assigned, namely, than "White is man." For one of the negations, namely, "Non-man is not white," is the negation of "Non-man is white"; the other, "White is not man" is the negation of the affirmation "Man is white," which was the first affirmation. Therefore whatever negation is given as contradictory to the middle enunciation, it follows that there are two of one, i.e., two affirmations of one negation, and two negations of one affirmation, which is impossible. And this, as has been said, follows upon an erroneously set up hypothesis, i.e., that these affirmations are diverse because of the transposition of names.

51 There are differences between the enunciations Aristotle gives as examples and those of Cajetan. If we were to make a diagram of Aristotle's enunciations, modelling it upon Cajetan's it would appear thus: proved, whereas the original text seems to beg the question as the translator of the Ross edition points out in a footnote, Cf. "De interpretatione," 20b 1, n. 3 *The Works of Aristotle,* ed. W. D. Ross (London:

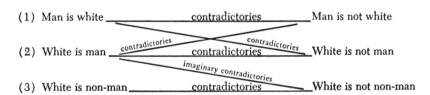

(1) Man is white _____ contradictories _____ Man is not white

(2) White is man ___contradictories___ contradictories ___contradictories___ White is not man

imaginary contradictories

(3) White is non-man _____ contradictories _____ White is not non-man

Cajetan has used for the last two enunciations "Non-man is white" and "Non-man is not white," i.e., an infinite name on the part of the subject rather than the predicate. Perhaps Cajetan wanted to emphasize the "imaginary" quality of the last contradictory, and obviate the difficulty caused by Aristotle's "White is not non-man" (the last enunciation in the diagram above but given in the text as the first contradictory of "White is man," which is the obversion of "White is man" and therefore equivalent to it. For with Cajetan's changes Aristotle's point seems to be more cogently Oxford University Press, 1937). It should also be noted that when Aristotle speaks of enunciations signifying the same thing with names and verbs transposed, he means with names transposed they signify the same thing, and when the verb is transposed they signify the same thing. Actually he only shows this about names because it is the more difficult and is almost impossible to see in English because of our rigid word order. His examples make this clear, the first of which, literally translated, are, "is man white" and "is white man," i.e., the words are only positionally changed.

10.   Notice first that Aristotle through these two negations, "Non-man is not white" and "White is not man," taken under disjunction to find the negation of the affirmation "Man is white," has comprehended other things. It is as though he said: The negation which will be taken will either be the true negation of such an affirmation or some extraneous negation; and whichever is taken, it always follows, given the hypothesis, that there are many negations of one affirmation—one which is the contradictory of it, having equal truth with the one having its name transposed, and the other which you accept as distinct, or you imagine falsely. And conversely, there is a single negation of many affirmations, as is clear in the diagram. Hence, from whichever of these four you begin, you see two opposed to it. It is significant, therefore, that Aristotle concludes indeterminately: *Therefore, there will be two* [negations] *of one* [affirmation].

11.   Note secondly that Aristotle does not consider it important to prove that the contradictory of the first affirmation is the contradictory of the second, and similarly that the contradictory of the second affirmation is the contradictory of the first. This he accepts as self-evident since they can neither be true at the same time nor false at the same time. This is manifestly clear when a singular term is placed first, for "Socrates is a white man" and "Socrates is not a white man" cannot be maintained at the same time in any mode. You should not be disturbed by the fact that he does not propose these singulars here, for he was undoubtedly aware that he had already stated in the first book which affirmation and negation are contradictories and which not[52] and for this reason felt that a careful elaboration of the examples was not necessary here.

        It is therefore evident that since negations of affirmations with transposed names are not diverse the affirmations themselves are not diverse, and hence transposed names and verbs signify the same thing.

12.   A doubt does arise, however, about the point Aristotle is making here, for it does not seem true that with transposed names the affirmation is the same. This, for example, is not valid: "Every man is an animal"; therefore, "Every animal is a man." Nor is the following example with a transposed verb valid: "Man is a rational animal and (taking "is" as the second element), therefore "Man animal rational is"; for although it is nugatory as a whole combination, nevertheless it does not follow upon the first.

        The answer to this is as follows. Just as there is a twofold transmutation in natural things, i.e., local, from place to place, and formal, from form to form, so in enunciations there is a twofold transmutation:

[52] At 17b 16ff.

a positional transmutation when a term placed before is placed after, and conversely, and a formal transmutation when a term that was a predicate is made a subject, and conversely, or in whatever mode, simply, etc. And just as in natural things sometimes a purely local transmutation is made (for instance, when a thing is transferred from place to place, with no other variation made) and sometimes a transmutation is made according to place—not simply but with a formal variation—(as when a thing passes from a cold place to a hot place), so in enunciations a transmutation is sometimes made which is purely positional, i.e., when the name and verb are varied only in vocal position, and sometimes a transmutation is made which is at once formal and positional, as when the predicate becomes the subject, or the verb which is the third element added becomes the second.

Aristotle's purpose here was to treat of the purely positional transmutation of names and verbs, as the vocabulary of the transposition indicates; when he says, then, that transposed names and verbs signify the same thing, he intends to imply that if nothing other than the transposition of name and verb takes place in the enunciation, what is said remains the same. Hence, the response to the present objection is clear, for in both examples there is not only a transposition but a transmutation—of subject to predicate in one case, and from an enunciation with a third element to one with a second element in the other. The response to similar questions is evident from this.

Ways in Which An Enunciation May
Be Many Rather than One

20b 12   Neither the affirmation nor the negation which affirms or denies one predicate of many subjects or many predicates of one subject is one, unless something one is constituted from the many. I do not use "one" of those things which, although one name may be imposed, do not constitute something one. For example, man probably is animal and biped and civilized,[53] but there is also something one formed from these; whereas from "white" and "man" and "walking" there is not. Consequently, if someone affirms something one of these latter there will not be one affirmation, except in vocal sound; on the contrary, there will be many affirmations. Nor will there be one affirmation if someone affirms these of one subject; in this case too there will be many.

20b 22   In fact, if dialectical interrogation is a request for an answer, i.e., either for the admission of a premise or one part of a contradiction—and a premise is a part of one contradiction—there would not be one answer in reference to the above predicates. There would not be one answer even if there is a true answer, for there would not be a single question.

20b 26 But we have spoken about these things in the *Topics*.[54]

At the same time it is clear that the question "What is it?" is not a dialectical one. For the dialectical interrogation must provide for choosing whichever part of a contradiction one wishes to enunciate. For this the interrogator must specifically word the question so that the parts of the contradiction are clear; for example, by asking whether man is this or not.

———————

1.   After the Philosopher has treated the diversity in an enunciation arising from the addition of the infinite negation, he explains what hap-

---

[53] In this sentence Aristotle uses "and" (καὶ) as a conjunction between the predicates and "probably" (ἴσως) to qualify them in relation to the subject. The sentence could be interpreted to mean that these are many that are one. In this case, the conjunctions are used to emphasize the many, for biped civilized animal is a natural definition of man, the

"biped" and "civilized" being universals *ut nunc*, used as a difference until a better, i.e., essential difference, is found. Hence, taken with "animal" this constitutes a dialectical definition of man and for this reason Aristotle qualifies the predicates with "probably."

[54] *Topics* VIII, 7.

pens to an enunciation when something is added to the subject or predicate which takes away its unity. He first determines their diversity, and then proves that all the enunciations are many[55] where he says, *In fact, if dialectical interrogation is a request for an answer*, etc. Secondly, he determines their consequences, where he says, *Some things predicated separately are such that they unite to form one predicate*, etc.[56]   20b22

20b31

He begins by taking up something he said in the first book: there is not one affirmative enunciation nor one negative enunciation when one thing is affirmed or denied of many or many of one, if one thing is not constituted from the many.[57] Then he explains what he means by the subject or predicate having to be one where he says, *I do not use "one" of those things which, although one name may be imposed, do not constitute something one*, i.e., a subject or predicate is one, not from the unity of the name, but from the unity of what is signified. For when many things are brought together under one name in such a way that what is signified by that name is not one, then the unity is only one of vocal sound. But when one name has been imposed for many, whether for subjective or for integral parts, so that it encloses them in the same signification, then there is unity both of vocal sound and what is signified. In the latter case, unity of the enunciation is not impeded.   20b15

2.   Then he adds, *For example, man probably is an animal and biped and civilized*.[58] This, however, is obscure, for it can be understood as an example of the opposite, as if he were saying, "I do not mean by 'one' such a 'one' as the unity of the name imposed upon many from which one thing is not constituted, for instance, 'man' as 'one' from the parts of the definition, animal and civilized and biped.'" And to prevent anyone from thinking these are true parts of the definition of the name he interposes *perhaps*.   20b16

Porphyry, however, referred to with approval by Boethius, separates these parts of the text. He says Aristotle first states that that enunciation is many in which many are subjected to one, or many are predicated of one, when one thing is not constituted from these. And when he says, *For example, man perhaps is*, etc., he intends to show that an enunciation is *many* when many from which one thing is constituted are subjected or predicated, as in the example "Man is an animal and civilized and biped," with copulas interjected or a pause such as orators

[55] What Cajetan must mean here is "all such enunciations" or "all of these" are many.
[56] At the beginning of the following Lesson.
[57] Cf. 17a 15; St. Thomas, Lesson VIII, nn. 12 ff., especially beginning

with n. 15.
[58] *Supra*, n. 53. "Probably" has been used in the present translation of the Greek rather than "perhaps" to indicate more formally the dialectical character of the definition.

make. He added *perhaps,* they say, to imply that this could happen, but it need not.

3.   While agreeing with the opinion of Porphyry, Boethius, and Albert, we think a more subtle construction can be made of the text. According to it Aristotle makes four points here. First, he reviews what an enunciation is in general when he says, *The enunciation is many in which one is enunciated of many or many of one, unless from the many something one is constituted . . .* as he stated and explained in the first book.⁵⁹

20b15   Secondly, he clarifies the term "one," when he says, *I do not use "one" of those things,* etc., i.e., I call a name one, not by reason of the unity of vocal sound, but of signification, as was said above.⁶⁰

Thirdly, he manifests (by dividing) and divides (by manifesting) the number of ways in which one name may be imposed on many things from which one thing is not constituted. From this he implies the diversity of the multiple enunciation. And he posits two ways in which one name may be imposed on many things from which one thing is not constituted: first, when one name is imposed upon many things from which one thing is constituted but not as one thing is constituted from them. In this case, materially and accidentally speaking, the name is imposed on many from which one thing is constituted, but it is formally and per se imposed on many from which one thing is not constituted; for it is not imposed upon them in the respect in which they constitute one thing; as perhaps the name "man" is imposed to signify animal and civilized and biped (i.e., parts of its definition) not as they are united in the one nature of man in the mode of act and potency, but as they are themselves distinct actualities. Aristotle implies that he is taking these parts of the definition as distinct by the conjunctions and by also adding
20b17   adversatively, *but if there is something one formed from these,*⁶¹ as if to say, "when however it holds that one thing is constituted from these."

He adds *perhaps* because the name "man" is not imposed to signify its definitive parts as they are distinct. But if it had been so imposed

---

⁵⁹ This quotation is not Aristotle's directly. It states positively what Aristotle states negatively in 20b 12. For the reference to Book I see note 57 *supra.*

⁶⁰ Aristotle treats the unity of the *name* beginning with 16a 22 (St. Thomas, Lesson IV, nn. 9 ff.) and beginning with 16b 30 (St. Thomas, Lesson VI, n. 6). However, Aristotle seems to be treating the unity of signification of *many names* here. In rela-

tion to this see 17a 13 (St. Thomas, Lesson VIII, n. 10); 17a 15 (St. Thomas, Lesson VIII, nn. 12 ff., especially n. 15); 17a 34 (St. Thomas, Lesson IX, nn. 8 ff.)

⁶¹ Neither the Greek nor the Latin text of Aristotle has the "if" that Cajetan puts into this phrase. The correct reading is: ". . . but there is something one formed from these."

[164]

or were imposed, it would be one name imposed on many things from which no one thing is constituted. And since the judgment with respect to such a name and those many things is the same, the many definitive parts can also be taken in two ways: first, in the mode of the actual and possible, and thus they constitute one thing, and formally speaking are called many from which one thing is constituted, and they are to be pronounced in continuous speech and they make one enunciation, for example, "A mortal rational animal is running." For this is one enunciation, just as is "Man is running." In the second way, the foresaid parts of the definition are taken as they are distinct actualities, and thus they do not constitute one thing, for one thing is not constituted from two acts as such, as Aristotle says in VII *Metaphysicae*.[62] In this case they constitute many enunciations and are pronounced either with conjunctions interposed or with a pause in the rhetorical manner, for example, "Man is an animal and civilized and biped" or "Man is an animal—civilized—biped." Each of these is a multiple enunciation. And so is the enunciation, "Socrates is a man" if "man" is imposed to signify animal, civilized, and biped as they are distinct actualities.

Aristotle takes up the second way in which one name is imposed on many from which one thing is not constituted where he says, *whereas*   20b18
from "white" and "man" and "walking" there is not [something one formed]. Since in no way can any one nature be constituted from "man," "white," and "walking" (as there can be from the definitive parts), it is evident that if a name were imposed on these it would be a name that does not signify one thing, as was said in the first book of the name "cloak" imposed for man and horse.

4.   We have, therefore, two modes of the many (i.e., the multiple enunciation) and since both are constituted in two ways, there will be four modes: first, when one name imposed on many from which one thing is constituted is subjected or predicated as though the name stands for many; the second, when the many from one which one thing is constituted are subjected or predicated as distinct actualities; the third, when one name is imposed for a many from which nothing one is constituted; the fourth, when many which do not constitute one thing are subjected or predicated. Note that the enunciation, according to the members of the division by which it has been divided into one and many, can be varied in four ways, i.e., one is predicated of one, one of many, many of one, and many of many. Aristotle has not spoken of the last one, either because its plurality is clear enough or because, as Albert says, he only intends to treat of the enunciation which is one in some way.

[62] *Metaph.* Z, 13, 1039a 5.

20b19 Finally [fourthly], he concludes with this summary: *Consequently, if someone affirms something one of these latter there will not be one affirmation* according to the thing: *vocally it will be one; significatively, it will not be one, but many.* And conversely, *if the many are affirmed of one subject, there will not be one affirmation.* For example, "Man is white, walking, and musical" implies three affirmations, i.e., "Man is white" and "is walking" and "is musical," as is clear from its contradiction, for a threefold negation is opposed to it, corresponding to the threefold affirmation.

20b22　5.　Then when he says, *In fact, if dialectical interrogation is a request for an answer,* etc., he proves a posteriori that the foresaid enunciations are many. First he states an argument to prove this by way of the consequent; then he proves the antecedent of the given consequent

20b26　where he says, *But we have spoken about these things in the Topics,* etc.

Now if dialectical questioning is a request for an answer, either a proposition or one part of a contradiction, none of the foresaid enunciations, put in the form of a question, will have one answer. Therefore, the question is not one, but many. Aristotle first states the antecedent of the argument, *if dialectical interrogation is a request for an answer,* etc. To understand this it should be noted that an enunciation, a question, and an answer sound the same. For when we say, "The region of heaven is animated," we call it an enunciation inasmuch as it enunciates a predicate of a subject, but when it is proposed to obtain an answer we call it an interrogation, and as applied to what was asked we call it a response. Therefore, to prove that there is not one response or one question or one enunciation will be the same thing.

It should also be noted that interrogation is twofold. One proposes either of the two parts of a contradiction to choose from. This is called dialectical interrogation because the dialectician knows the way to prove either part of a contradiction from probable positions. The other kind of interrogation seeks one determinate response. This is the demonstrative interrogation, for the demonstrator proceeds determinately toward a single alternative.

Note, finally, that it is possible to reply to a dialectical question in two ways. We may consent to the question, either affirmatively or negatively; for example, when someone asks, "Is the region of heaven animated," we may respond, "It is," or to the question "Is not God moved," we may say, "No." Such a response is called a proposition.

The second way of replying is by destroying; for example, when someone asks "Is the region of heaven animated?" and we respond, "No," or to the question, "Is not God moved?" we respond, "He is

[166]

moved." Such a response is called the other part of a contradiction, because a negation is given to an affirmation and an affirmation to a negation.

Dialectical interrogation, then, according to the exposition just given, which is that of Boethius, is a request for the admission of a response which is a proposition, or which is one part of a contradiction.

6.   He adds the proof of the consequent when he says, *and a*   20b23
proposition is a part of one contradiction.[63] In relation to this it should be noted that if a dialectical response could be many, it would not follow that a response to a multiple enunciation would not be dialectical. However, if the dialectical response can only be one enunciation then it follows that a response to a plural enunciation is not a dialectical response, for it is one [i.e., it inclines to one part of a contradiction at a time].

It should also be noted that if an enunciation is a part of many contradictions, it is thereby proven not to be one, for one contradicts only one. But if an enunciation is a part of only one contradiction, it is one by the same reasoning, i.e., because there is only one negation of one affirmation, and conversely.

Hence Aristotle proves the consequent from the fact that the proposition, i.e., the dialectical response, is a part of one contradiction, i.e., it is one affirmative or one negative enunciation. It follows from this, as has been said, that there is no dialectical response of a multiple enunciation, and consequently not one response.

It should not be overlooked that when he designates a proposition or one part of a contradiction as the response to a dialectical interrogation, it is only of the proposition that he adds that it is one, because the very wording shows the unity of the other. For when you hear one part of a contradiction, you immediately understand one affirmation or negation.

He puts the "therefore"[64] with the antecedent, either implying that this is taken from another place and he will explain in particular afterward, or having changed the structure, he places the sign of the consequent, which should be between the antecedent and consequent before the antecedent, as when one says, "Therefore if Socrates runs, he is moved," for "If Socrates runs, therefore he is moved."

---

[63] Aristotle uses "premise" rather than proposition." The latter in its first meaning is the conclusion of a syllogism.

[64] The οὖν used here by Aristotle is translated as "in fact" ("ergo" in the Latin text). Aristotle does not use οὖν to mean "therefore" except in a question (cf. Liddell and Scott, *Greek-English Lexicon*).

20b25   Then the consequent follows: *there will not be one answer to this*, etc.;[65] and the inference of the principal conclusion, *for there would not be a single question*. For if the response cannot be one, the question will not be one.

20b25   7.   He adds, *even if there is a true answer*, because someone might think that although one response cannot be given to a plural interrogation when the question concerns something that cannot be affirmed or denied of all of the many (for example, when someone asks, "Is a dog an animal?" no one response can be given, for we cannot truly say of every dog that it is an animal because of the star by that name; nor can we truly say of every dog that it is not an animal, because of the barking dog), nevertheless one response could be given when that which falls under the interrogation can be truly said of all. For example, when someone asks, "Is a dog a substance?" a single response can be given because it can truly be said of every dog that it is a substance, for to be a substance belongs to all dogs. Aristotle adds the phrase, *even if there is a true answer*, to remove such an erroneous judgment. For even if the response to the multiple enunciation is verified of all, it is nonetheless not one, since it does not signify one thing, nor is it a part of one contradiction. Rather, as is evident, this response has many contradictories.

20b26   8.   Where he says, *But we have spoken about these things in the Topics*, etc., he proves the antecedent in two ways. First, he proves it on the basis of what was said in the *Topics;* secondly, by a sign.

20b26   The sign is given first where he says, *Similarly*[66] *it is clear that the question "What is it?" is not a dialectical one*, etc. That is, given the doctrine in the *Topics*, it is clear (i.e., assuming the antecedent that the dialectical interrogation is a request for an affirmative or negative response) that the question "*What is it?*" is not a dialectical interrogation, e.g., when someone asks, "What is an animal?" he does not interrogate dialectically.

      Secondly, he gives the proof of what was assumed, namely, that the question "What is it?" is not a dialectical question. He states that a dialectical interrogation must offer to the one responding the option of whichever part of the contradiction he wishes. The question "What is it?" does not offer such liberty, for in saying "What is an animal?" the

---

65 The Greek for this and the phrase quoted in the following number is: ". . . οὐκ ἂν εἴη μία ἀπόκρισις πρὸς ταῦα· οὐδὲ γὰρ ἡ ἐρώτησις μία, οὐδ' ἂν ἦ ἀληθής." This has been translated as ". . . there would not be one answer in reference to the above predicates. There would not be one answer even if there is a true answer, for there would not be a single question."

66 The Greek text has ἅμα ("at the same time") for the "similarly" that Cajetan has here. The Latin text has *simul*.

one responding is forced to assign a definition, and a definition is not only determined to one but is also entirely devoid of contradiction, since it affirms neither being nor non-being. Therefore, the question "What is it?" is not a dialectical interrogation. Whence he says, *For the dialecti-* 20b27 *cal interrogation must provide,* i.e., from the proposed dialectical interrogation the one responding must be able to choose whichever part of the contradiction he wishes, which parts of the contradiction the *interrogator must specify,*[67] i.e., he must propose the question in this way: "Is this animal man or not?" wherein the wording of the question clearly offers an option to the one answering. Therefore, you have as a sign that a dialectical question is seeking a response of a proposition or of one part of a contradiction, the setting apart of the question "What is it?" from dialectical questions.

---

[67] The Greek for this phrase is "ἐρωτῶντα προσδιορίσαι," which in the present translation has been rendered freely as "For this the interrogator must specifically word the question so that the parts of the contradiction are clear," from the wording of this point as it is in the *Topics.*

Some Predicates Said Divisively of a Subject
Can Be Said Conjointly, Others Not

20b 31   Some things predicated separately are such that they unite to form one predicate; others, however, do not. What, then, is the difference? For it is true to say separately of man that he is an animal and that he is biped, and it is also true to say these as one. It is also true to say "man" and "white" separately of him and to say these as one. But if a man is a shoemaker and also good, it is not true to say that he is a good shoemaker.[68]

20b 36   For if we hold that whenever each is truly said of a subject, both together must also be true, many absurdities will follow. For example, it is true to say of man that he is man and that he is white; therefore these two taken together can also be truly said of him; again, if it is true to say that he is white and that he is also the two combined predicates above, he will be white white man; and so to infinity. Or, again, "musical," "white," and "walking" may be truly said of man; and these combined many times. Furthermore, if Socrates is Socrates and a man, Socrates is a Socrates man; and if he is man and biped, he is a biped man.

It is clear, therefore, that if anyone says these combinations can always be made simply, many absurd things follow. Now we will state how this must be resolved.

21a 7   Those things that are predicated—taken in relation to that to which they are joined in predication—[69] which are said accidentally, either of the same subject or one another, will not be one. For example, man is white and musical; but whiteness and being musical are not one, for both are accidental to the same thing. Even if it were true to say that whatever is white is musical, musical and white will not be one thing, for that which is musical is white accidentally; consequently, that which is white will not be musical.

21a 14   This is the reason "good" and "shoemaker" cannot be combined simply; but "biped" and "animal" can, for these are not accidental.

21a 16   Furthermore, predicates that are present in one another cannot be combined simply. This is the reason we cannot combine "white" many times, nor is "man" an "animal-man," or a "biped-man," for the notion *man* includes both biped and animal.

---

[68] In the Latin text "shoemaker" is changed to "lute player."
[69] The Greek here is: "τῶν δὴ κατηγορ-

ουμένων καὶ ἐφ' οἷς κατηγορεῖσθαι συμβαίνει. . . ." In order to show when predicates said of a subject

1.   Having explained the diversity of the multiple enunciation Aristotle now proposes to determine the consequences of this. He treats this in relation to two questions which he solves. The second begins where he says, *On the other hand, it is also true to say predicates of something singly,* etc.[70]   21a18

With respect to the other question, first he proposes it, then he shows that the question is a reasonable one where he says, *For if we hold that whenever each is truly said of a subject, both together must also be true, many absurdities will follow,* etc. Finally, he solves it where he says, *Those things that are predicated—taken in relation to that to which they are joined in predication,* etc.   20b36   21a7

The first question is this: Why is it that from some things predicated divisively of a subject an enunciation follows in which they are predicated of the same subject unitedly, and from others not? What is the reason for this diversity? For example, from "Socrates is an animal and he is biped" follows, "Therefore, Socrates is a biped animal"; and similarly, from "Socrates is a man and he is white" follows, "Therefore, Socrates is a white man." But from "Socrates is good and he is a lute player," the enunciation, "Therefore, he is a good lute player" does not follow. Hence in proposing the question Aristotle says, *Some things,* i.e., predicates, are so predicated when combined, that there is one predicate from what is predicated separately, i.e., from some things that are predicated separately, a united predication is made but from others this is not so. What is the difference between these; whence does such a diversity arise?

He adds the examples which we have already cited and applied to the question. Of these examples, the first contains predicates from which something one per se is formed, i.e., "animal" and "biped," a genus and difference; the second contains predicates from which something accidentally one is formed, namely, "white man"; the third con-

divisively can be said conjointly and when not, Aristotle makes the distinction here between per se and accidental predication, i.e., predicates in relation to that to which they are joined in predication are either per se or accidental. Some have taken this phrase to mean that both subjects and predicates are per se or accidental but there would not seem to be much point in saying that subjects are per se or accidental, for although the terms of a subject may be per se or accidentally united, the subject is always one;

if it does seem multiple, it is actually a multiplicity on the part of the predicate; e.g., "This distinguished man is a lawyer" is actually, "This man is a lawyer and distinguished." That Aristotle is speaking here of predicates in relation to subjects and not predicates *and* subjects is also born out by what he says in the next line, ". . . whichever are said accidentally of the same subject or of one another . . .," that is, in the latter case, one predicate of another predicate as in "white man."

[70] At the beginning of the next lesson.

tains predicates from which neither one per se nor one accidentally is formed, "lute player" and "good," as will be explained.

20b36   2.   When he says, *For if we hold that whenever each is truly said of a subject, both together must also be true,* etc., he shows that there truly is such a diversity among predicates and in so doing renders the question reasonable, for if there were not such a diversity among predicates the question would be pointless. He shows this by reasoning leading to an absurdity, i.e., to something nugatory.

Now, something nugatory is effected in two ways, explicitly and implicitly. Therefore, he first makes a deduction to the explicitly nugatory, secondly to the implicitly, where he says, *Furthermore, if Socrates is Socrates and a man, Socrates is a Socrates man,* etc.

21a2

If, he says, there is no difference between predicates, and it is supposed of any of them indifferently that because both are said separately both may be said conjointly, many absurdities will follow. For of some man, say Socrates, it is true to say separately that he is a man and he is white; therefore both together, i.e., we may also say conjointly, "Socrates is a white man." Again, of the same Socrates we can say separately that he is a white man and that he is white, and both together, i.e., therefore conjointly, "Socrates is a white white man." Here the nugatory expression is evident. Further, if of the same Socrates that you again say separately is a white white man it will be true and consistent to say that he is white, and according to this, if again repeating this separately, you will not deviate from a similar truth, and this will follow to infinity, then Socrates is a white white white man to infinity.

The same thing can be shown by another example. If someone says of Socrates that he is musical, white, and walking, since it is also possible to say separately that he is musical, and that he is white, and that he is walking, it will follow that Socrates is musical, white, walking, musical, white, walking. And since these can be enunciated many times separately, yet at the same time, the nugatory statement proceeds without end.

Then he makes a deduction to the implicitly nugatory. Since it can be truly said of Socrates separately that he is man and that he is biped, it will follow that Socrates is a biped man, if it is licit to infer conjointly. This is implicitly nugatory because the "biped," which indirectly expresses the difference of man in act and in understanding, is included in the notion of man. Hence, if we posit the definition of man in place of "man" (which it is licit to do, as Aristotle teaches in II *Topicorum*[71]) the nugatory character of the enunciation will be evident, for when we say "Socrates is a biped man," we are saying "Socrates is a

[71] *Topics* II, 2, 110a 5.

[172]

biped biped animal." From what has been said it is evident that many absurdities follow if anyone proposes that combinations, i.e., unions of predicates, be made simply, i.e., without any distinction.

Now, i.e., in what follows, we will state how this must be settled. 20a6 This particular text is not uniformly worded in the manuscripts, but since no discrepancy of thought is involved one may read it as he wishes.

3.   When he says, *Those things that are predicated—taken in rela-* 21a7 *tion to that to which they are joined in predication*, etc., he solves the proposed question. First he makes an answer with respect to the instances cited in proposing the question; secondly, he solves the problem as related to the instances posited in his proof where he says, *Further-* 21a16 *more, predicates that are present in one another cannot be combined simply*. In relation to the first answer, he states the true position first and then applies it to the instances where he says, *This is the reason* 21a14 *"good" and "shoemaker" cannot be combined simply*, etc.

He settles the question with this distinction: there are two kinds of multiple predicates and subjects.[72] Some are accidental, some per se. If they are accidental this occurs in two ways, either because both are said accidentally of a third thing or because they are predicated of each other accidentally. Now when the many predicated divisively are in any way accidental, a conjoined predicate does not follow from them; but when they are per se, a conjoined predicate does follow from them. In answering the question, therefore, Aristotle connects what he is saying with what has gone before: *Of those things that are predicated and* 21a7 *those of which they are predicated*, i.e., subjects,[73] *whichever are said accidentally* (by which he intimates the opposite member, i.e., per se), *either of the same subject*, i.e., they unite accidentally for the denomination of one third thing, *or of one another*, i.e., they denominate each other accidentally (and by this he posits the members of a two-fold division), *these*[74] (i.e., these many accidentally) *will not be one*, i.e., do not produce a conjoined predication.

4.   He explains both of these by examples. First, the many said accidentally of a third; for example, man is white and musical divisively. *But they are not the same*,[75] i.e., it does not follow unitedly that "Man is musical white" for both are accidental to the same third thing.

Then he explains the second member by an example. In it the many are predicated only of one another. *Even if it were true to say white is musical*,[76] i.e., even if these are predicated accidentally of each

---

[72] Aristotle is only speaking of predicates. Cf. *Supra*, note 69.

[73] *Supra*, note 69.

[74] "These" is not in the Greek text but is contained in "which."

[75] In the Greek text this is οὐχ ἕν, in the Latin *non est unum*, not *non est idem*, as Cajetan gives it here.

[76] In Aristotle this reads: "οὐδ' εἰ τὸ λευκόν μουσικὸν ἀληθὲς εἰπεῖν . . ."

[173]

other by reason of the subject in which they are united, so that we may say "Man is white and he is musical, and white is musical," it still does not follow that "musical white" is predicated as a unity when we say, "Therefore, man is musical white." He gives as the cause of this that "white" is said of "musical" accidentally and conversely.

5.   It must be noted here that although he has enumerated two accidental members, he explains both members by this single example so as to imply that the distinction is not one of different accidental predicates, but of the same predicates compared in different ways. "White" and "musical" compared to "man" fall under the first member, but compared with each other, under the second. Hence he has provided diversity of comparison by the plurality of the members, but identity of predicates by the unity of the example.

6.   To make this division evident it must also be noted that *accidentally* can be taken in two ways.

It may be taken as it is distinguished from "posterioristic perseity." This is not the way it is taken here, for "many predicates accidentally" would then mean that the "accidentally" determines a conjunction between predicates, and thus the rule would clearly be false,[77] for the first predicates he gave as examples are predicated accidentally in this way, namely, "biped animal," or "rational animal" (for a difference is not predicated of a genus in any mode of perseity, and yet Aristotle says in the text that these are not predicated accidentally, and has asserted that "He is an animal and biped, therefore he is a biped animal" is a good inference). Or it would mean that the "accidentally" determines a conjunction of the predicates with the subject, and thus also the rule would be false, for it is valid to say, "The wall is colored and it is visible," yet visible colored is not per se in the wall.

"Accidentally" taken in the second way is distinguished from what I call "on its own account," i.e., not because of something else; "accidentally" then means "through another." This is the way it is taken here, for whatever are of such a nature that they are joined because of something else, and not on their own account, do not admit of conjoined

which is translated as, "Even if it were true to say that whatever is white is musical . . . ." The Latin does not take account as accurately as does the Greek of the whiteness as a subject of musical here, at least in predication, for it reads: "Nec si album, musicus verum est dicere. . . ."

[77] The rule is: Those things that are predicated—taken in relation to that to which they are joined in predication—which are said accidentally, either of the same subject or of one another, will not be one." (Cf. 21a 7.)

inference, because a conjoined inference subjects one to the other, and denotes the things united on their own account as potency and act.

Therefore, the sense of the division is this: of many predicates, some are accidental, some per se, i.e., some are united among themselves on their own account, some on account of another. Those that are per se united infer conjointly; those that are united on account of another do not infer conjointly in any way.

7.   When he says, *This is the reason "good" and "shoemaker" cannot* $\quad$ 21a14
be combined simply, etc., he applies the truth he has stated to the parts of the question. He applies it first to the second part, i.e., why this does not follow: "He is good and he is a shoemaker, therefore he is a good shoemaker." Then he applies it to the other part of the question, i.e., why this follows: "He is an animal and he is biped, therefore he is a biped animal." He adds the reason in the case of the latter: "biped" and "animal" are not predicates accidentally conjoined among themselves, nor in a third thing, but per se. This also explains the other member of the first division which has not yet been explicitly posited.

Notice that he maintains the same judgment is to be made about lute player and good, and musical and white. He has concluded that "white" and "musical" do not infer a conjoined predicate; hence neither do "lute player" and "good" infer "good lute player" simply, i.e., conjointly. There is a reason for saying this. For although there is a difference between musical and white, and goodness and the art of lute-playing, they are also similar. Let us consider their difference first. Goodness is of such a nature that it denominates both a third subject, namely, man, and the art of lute-playing. This is the reason the falsity is clearly discernible when we say "He is good and a lute player, therefore he is a good lute player." Musical and whiteness, on the other hand, are of such a nature that they denominate only a third subject, and not each other, and hence, the error is less obvious in "He is white and he is musical, therefore he is musical white." Now it is this difference that makes Aristotle's process of reasoning appear somewhat inconclusive. However, they are similar. For if identity of predicates is kept in every way that is required for the same things divided to be inferred conjointly, then, just as "musical" does not denominate "whiteness," nor the contrary, so neither does "goodness," of which we are speaking when we say "Man is good," denominate the art of lute-playing, nor conversely. For "good" is equivocal—by choice though[78]—and therefore is said of the perfection of the lute player by means of one notion and of the per-

---

[78] That is, "good" is not sheerly equivocal, or equivocal by chance, but is systematically ambiguous, i.e., analogous. Cf. *Nic. Ethics* I, 6, 1096 b 27.

fection of man by means of another. For example, when we say, "Socrates is good" we understand moral goodness, which is the goodness of man absolutely (for the analogous term posited simply, stands for what is mainly so); but when good lute player is inferred, it is not the goodness of morality that is predicated but the goodness of art; whence identity of the terms is not saved. Therefore, Aristotle has adequately and subtly expressed the same judgment about both, i.e., "white" and "musical," and "good" and "lute player," for the reason here is the same as there.

8.　　　There is another point that must be mentioned. Aristotle in proposing the question draws three consequences: "He is an animal and biped, therefore he is a biped animal" and "He is a man and white, therefore he is a white man" and "He is a lute player and good, therefore he is a good lute player." Then he states that the first two consequences are good, the third not. His intention was to inquire into the cause of this diversity, but in solving the question he mentions only the first and third consequences, leaving the goodness or badness of the second consequence undiscussed. Why is this? I would say in answer to this that in these few words he has also implied the nature of the second consequence, for there is a more profound meaning to the statement in the text that *whiteness and being musical is not one*. It is a meaning that not only indicates what has already been explained but also its cause, and from this the nature of the second consequence is apparent. For the reason "white" and "musical" do not infer a conjoined predication is that in conjoined predication one part must be subjected to the other as potency to act such that in some way one thing is formed from them and one is denominated from the other (for the force of the conjoined predication requires this, as we have said above concerning the parts of the definition). "White" and "musical," however, do not in themselves form one thing per se, as is evident, nor do they form one thing accidentally. For while it is true that as united in a subject they are one in subject accidentally, nevertheless things that are united in one third subject do not form one thing accidentally among themselves: first, because neither informs the other (which is required for accidental unity of things among themselves, although not in a third thing); secondly, because, considered apart from the unity of a subject, which is outside of their notions, there is no cause of unity between them. Therefore, when Aristotle says that whiteness and being musical are not one, i.e., among themselves, in some measure he expresses the reason why a predicate is not conjointly inferred from them. And since the same discipline extends to opposites, the goodness of the second consequence is implied by these words. That is, man and white are related as potency

[176]

and act (and so, on its own account whiteness informs, denominates, and forms one thing with 'man'); therefore from these taken divisively a conjoined predication can be inferred, i.e., "He is man and white, therefore he is a white man"; just as, in the opposite case, it was said that "musical" and "white" do not infer a conjoined predicate because neither informs the other.

9.   There is no opposition between the position just stated and the fact that white forms an accidental unity with man. For we did not say that accidental unity of certain things impedes inferring a conjunction from divided things,[79] but that accidental unity of certain things *only* by reason of a third thing is the one that impedes. Things that are one accidentally only by reason of a third thing have no unity among themselves; and for this reason a conjunction, which implies unity, cannot be inferred, as we have said. But things that are one accidentally on their own account, i.e., among themselves, as for example, "white man," when taken conjointly, have the necessary unity because they have unity among themselves.

Notice that I have added "only." The reason is that if any two are one accidentally, namely, by reason of a third subject, and they not only have unity from this but also on their own account (because one informs the other), then from these taken divisively a conjoined inference can be made. For example, we can infer, "It is a quantity and it is colored, therefore it is a colored quantity," because color informs quantity.

10.   You can hold as true that this second consequence is good even though Aristotle has not explicitly confirmed it by returning to it, both from the fact that in proposing the question he has claimed it as good and also because there is no instance opposed to it. Moreover, Aristotle has implied that it is only such unity that impedes the conjoined inference where he says: *which are said accidentally, either of the same sub-*   21a9
ject or of one another. By *accidentally of the same subject,* he posits their unity to be only from union in a third thing (for only these are predicated accidentally of the same subject, as was said). When he adds, *or of one another*—positing mutual accidentality—no unity at all is left between them. Therefore, both kinds of accidental predicates, namely, in a third thing or in one another, that impede a conjoined inference have unity only in a third thing.

11.   Then when he says, *Furthermore, predicates that are present in*   21a16
one another cannot be combined simply, etc., he gives the solution for

---

[79] Cajetan's Latin here is "ex diversis" but what must be meant is "ex di-   visis," in view of the context.

the instances (both the explicitly nugatory and the implicitly nugatory) cited in the proof. It is not only not licit, he says, to infer a union from divided predicates when these are accidental, but it is not licit when the predicates *are present in one another.* That is, it is not licit to infer a conjoined predicate from divided predicates when the predicates include one another in such a way that one is included in the formal signification of another intrinsically, or explicitly, as "white" in "white," or implicitly, as "animal" and "biped" in "man." Therefore, "white" said repeatedly and divisively does not infer a conjoined predication, nor does "man" divisively enunciated from "animal" or "biped" infer "biped" or "animal" conjoined with man, such that we could say, "Therefore, Socrates is a biped-man" or "animal-man." For animal and biped are included in the notion of man in act and in understanding, although implicitly.

The solution of the question, then, is this: the inferring of a conjunction from divided predicates is impeded when there is unity of the many accidentally only in a third thing and when there is a nugatory result. Consequently, where neither of these is found it will be licit to infer a conjunction from divided predicates. It is to be understood that this applies when the divided predicates are at once true of the same subject.

Whether from an Enunciation Having Many Conjoined
Predicates It Is Licit to Infer an Enunciation
Which Contains the Same Predicates Divisively

21a 18   On the other hand, it is also true to say predicates of something
singly; for example, it is true to say that some man is a man, or that some
white man is white. However, this is not always the case.

21a 21   When something opposed is present in the adjunct, from which a
contradiction follows, it will not be true to predicate them singly, but false
e.g., to say that a dead man is a man. When something opposed is not
present in the adjunct, however, it is true to predicate them singly.

21a 24   Or, rather, when something opposed is present in it, it is never true;
but when something opposed is not present, it is not always true. For example,
Homer is something, say, a poet. Is it therefore true to say also that Homer *is*,
or not?

21a 26   The "is" here is predicated accidentally of Homer, for the "is" is
predicated of him with regard to the fact that he is a poet, not in itself.

21a 29   Therefore, in whatever predications no contrariety is present when
definitions are put in place of the names, and wherein predicates are predicated per se and not accidentally, it will also be true to predicate each one
singly.

21a 32   In the case of non-being, however, it is not true to say that because
it is a matter of opinion it *is* something; for the opinion of it is not that it is,
but that it is not.

---

1.   Aristotle now takes up the second question in relation to multiple enunciations. He first presents it, and then solves it where he says,
When something opposed is present in the adjunct, from which a con-   21a21
tradiction follows, it will not be true to predicate them singly, but false,
etc. Finally, he excludes an error where he says, *In the case of non-*   21a32
being, however, it is not true to say that because it is a matter of opinion,
it is something, etc.
        The second question is this: Is it licit to infer from an enunci-
ation having a conjoined predication, enunciations dividing that conjunction? This question is the contrary of the first question. The first
asked whether a conjoined predicate could be inferred from divided

predicates; the present one asks whether divided predicates follow from conjoined predicates.

21a18   When he presents the question he says, *On the other hand, it is also true to say predicates of something singly,* i.e., what was previously said conjointly may be said divisively; for example, that some white man is a man, or that some white man is white. That is, from "Socrates is a white man," follows divisively, "Therefore Socrates is a man," "Therefore Socrates is white." *However, this is not always the case,* i.e., sometimes it is not possible to infer divisively from conjoined predicates, for this does not follow: "Socrates is a good lute player, therefore he is good." Hence, sometimes it is licit, sometimes not.

     Note that in inferring each part divisively he takes as an example "white man." This is significant, for by it he means to imply that his intention is to investigate when each part can be inferred divisively from a conjoined predicate, and not when only one of the two can be inferred.

21a21 2.   When he says, *When something opposed is present in the adjunct,* etc., he solves the question, first by responding to the negative part of the question, i.e., when it is not licit; secondly, to the affirmative
21a29 part, i.e., when it is licit, where he says, *Therefore, in whatever predications no contrariety is present when definitions are put in place of the names, and wherein predicates are predicated per se and not accidentally,* etc.

     It should be noted, in relation to the negative part of the question, that a conjoined predicate may be formed in two ways: from opposites and from nonopposites. Therefore, he shows first that the parts in a conjoined predicate of opposites can never be inferred divisively. Secondly, he shows that this is not licit universally in a conjoined predi-
21a24 cate of nonopposites, where he says, *Or, rather, when*[80] *something opposed is present in it, it is never true; but when something opposed is not present, it is not always true.*

     Aristotle says, then, that when something that is an opposite is contained in the adjacent term, which results in a contradiction between the terms themselves, *it is not true,* namely, to infer divisively, *but false.* For example, when we say, "Caesar is a dead man," it does not follow, "Therefore he is a man," because the contradiction between "man" and "dead" which results from adding the "dead" to "man" is opposed to man, for if he is a man he is not dead, because he is not an

---

[80] Cajetan quotes only three words of this sentence, "Vel etiam quando. . . ." These words do not appear anywhere in Moerbeke's Latin text of Aristotle. Perhaps what is intended is "Aut quando insit quidem. . . .," the Latin equivalent of the Greek text at 21a 24.

[180]

inanimate body; and if he is dead he is not a man, because as dead he is an inanimate body.

When something opposed is not present, i.e., there is no such opposition, *it is true*, i.e., it is true to infer divisively. The reason a divided inference does not follow when there is opposition in the added term is that in a conjoined enunciation the other term is destroyed by the opposition of the added term. But that which has been destroyed is not inferred apart from the destruction, which is what the divided inference would signify.

3.   Two questions arise at this point. The first concerns something assumed here: how can it ever be true to make such a statement as "Caesar is a dead man," since an enunciation cannot be true in which two contradictories are predicated at the same time of something (for this is a first principle). But "man" and "dead," as is said in the text, include contradictory opposition, for in man is included life, and in dead, nonlife.

The second question concerns the consequent that Aristotle rejects, which appears to be good. The enunciation given as an example predicates terms that are opposed contradictorily. But from an enunciation predicating two contradictory terms, either both can be inferred (because it is equivalent to a copulative enunciation), or neither (because it destroys itself); therefore both parts seem to follow, since it is false that neither follows.

4.   These two questions can be answered simultaneously. It is one thing to speak of two terms in themselves, and another to speak of them as one stands under the determination of another. Taken in the first way, "man" and "dead" have a contradiction between them and it is impossible that they be found in the same thing at the same time. In the second way, however, "man" and "dead" are not opposed, since "man," changed by the destructive element introduced by "dead," no longer stands for what it signifies as such, but as determined by the term added, by which what is signified is removed. Aristotle, in order to imply both, says two things: that they have the opposition upon which contradiction follows if you regard what they signify in themselves; and, that one true enunciation is formed from them as in "Socrates is a dead man," if you regard their conjunction as destructive of one of them.

Accordingly, the answer to the two questions is evident. In a case such as this two contradictories are not enunciated of the same thing at the same time, but one term as it stands under dissolution or transmutation from the other, to which by itself it would be contradictory.

[181]

5.   There is also a question about something else that Aristotle says, namely, *something opposed is present . . . from which a contradiction follows*. The phrase *from which a contradiction follows* seems to be superfluous, for contradiction follows upon all opposites, as is evident in discoursing about singulars; for a father is not a son, and white is not black, and one seeing is not blind, etc.

Opposites, however, can be taken in two ways: formally, i.e., according to what they signify, and denominatively, or subjectively. For example, father and son can be taken for paternity and filiation, or they can be taken for the one who is denominated a father or a son. But, again, since every distinction is made by some opposition, as is said in X *Metaphysicae*,[81] it could be supposed that opposites are wholly distinct.

It must be pointed out, therefore, that although contradiction follows between all opposites or distinct things formally taken, nevertheless, contradiction does not follow upon all opposites denominatively taken. Father and son formally taken infer a mutual negation of one another, for paternity is not filiation and filiation is not paternity, but in respect to what is denominated they do not necessarily infer a contradiction. It does not follow, for example, that "Socrates is a father; therefore he is not a son," nor conversely. Aristotle, therefore, in order to establish that not all combined opposites prevent a divided inference (since those having a contradiction applying only formally do not prevent a divided inference, but those having a contradiction both formally and according to the thing denominated do prevent a divided inference) adds, *from which a contradiction follows*, namely, in the third thing denominated. And appropriately enough he uses the word *follows*, for the contradiction in the third thing denominated is in a certain way outside of the opposites themselves.

6.   When he says, *Or, rather, when something opposed is present in it, it is never true*, etc., he explains that the parts cannot universally be inferred divisively in the case of a conjoined predicate in which there is a nonopposite as the third thing denominated. He proposes this—*Or, rather, when something opposed is contained in it*, i.e., opposition between the terms conjoined—as if amending what he has just said, namely, *it is always false*, i.e., to infer divisively. What he is saying, then, is this: I have said that when there is inherent opposition it is not true but false to infer divisively; but when there is not such opposition it is true to infer divisively; or, even better, when there is opposition it is always false but when there is not such opposition it is not always true. That

---

81 *Metaph.* I, 3, 1054a 20 ff.

[182]

is, he modifies what he first said by the addition of "always" and "not always."

Then he adds an example to show that division does not always follow from nonopposites: *For example, Homer is something, say, a poet. Is it therefore true to say also that Homer "is," or not?* From the conjoined predicate, *is a poet,* enunciated of Homer, one part, *Therefore Homer is,* does not follow; yet it is evident that these two conjoined parts, "is" and "poet," do not have the opposition upon which contradiction follows. Therefore, in the case of conjoined nonopposites a divided inference does not always hold.

7.   When he says, *The "is" here is predicated accidentally of Homer,*   21a26
he proves what he has said. One part of this composite, namely, "is," is predicated of Homer in the antecedent conjunction *accidentally,* i.e., by reason of another, namely, with regard to the "poet" which is predicated of Homer; it is not predicated as such of Homer. Nevertheless, this is what is inferred when one concludes "Therefore Homer is."

To validate his negative conclusion, namely, that it is not always true to infer divisively from conjoined nonopposites, it was sufficient to give one instance of the opposite of the universal affirmative. To do this Aristotle introduces that genus of enunciation in which one part of the conjunction is something pertaining to an act of the mind (for we are speaking only of Homer living in his poems in the minds of men). In such enunciations the parts conjoined are not opposed in the third thing denominated; nevertheless it is not licit to infer each part divisively, for the fallacy of going from the relative to the absolute will be committed. For example, it is not valid to say, "Caesar is praiseworthy, therefore he is," which is a parallel case, i.e., of an effect whose existence requires maintenance.

Aristotle will explain in the following sections of the text how the reasoning in the above text is to be understood.

8.   When he says, *Therefore, in whatever predications no contrari-*   21a29
ety is present when definitions are put in place of the names, etc., he replies to the affirmative part of the question,[82] i.e., when it is licit to infer divisively from conjoined predicates. He maintains that two conditions—opposed to what has been said earlier in this portion of the text —must combine in one enunciation in order that such a consequence be effected: there must be no opposition between the parts conjoined, and they must be predicated per se.

He says, then, inferring from what has been said: *Therefore, in whatever predicaments,*[83] i.e., predicates joined in a certain order,

---

[82] See Cajetan, n. 2 of this lesson for this division of the question.

[83] In Greek this is "κατηγορίαις," which has been rendered as "predica-

no contrariety,[84] in virtue of which contradiction is posited in the third thing denominated (for contraries mutually remove each other from the same thing), *is present,* or universally, *no opposition is present,*[85] i.e., upon which a contradiction follows in the third thing denominated, *when definitions are taken*[86] *in place of the names.* . . . He says this because it may be the case that the opposition is not apparent from the names alone, as in "dead man," and again it may be, as in "living dead," but whether apparent or not it will be evident that we are putting together opposites if we posit the definitions of the names in place of the names. For example, in the case of "dead man," if we replace "man" and "dead," with their definitions, the contradiction will be evident, for what we are saying is "rational animate body, irrational inanimate body."

21a30   In whatever conjoined predicates, then, there is no opposition, and wherein predicates *are predicated per se and not accidentally, in these*[87] *it will also be true to predicate them singly,*[88] i.e., say divisively what had been enunciated conjointly.

9.   In order to make this second condition clear, it should be noted that "per se"[89] can be taken in two ways: positively, and thus it refers to "perseity" of the first, of the second, and of the fourth mode universally;[90] or negatively, and thus it means the same as not through something else.

It should also be noted that when Aristotle says of a conjoined predicate that it is predicated "per se," the "per se" can be referred to three things: to the parts of the conjunction among themselves, to the whole conjunction with respect to the subject, and to the parts of the conjoined predicate with respect to the subject. Now if "per se" is taken positively, although it will not be false, nevertheless in reference to any of these three the meaning will be found to be foreign to the mind of Aristotle. For, although these are valid: "He is a risible man, therefore he is man and he is risible" and "He is a rational animal, therefore he

tions"; "predicates" and predicaments" are also legitimate meanings of the word.

[84] The Greek is, ". . . μήτε ἐναντιότης ἔνεστιν . . ."; Moerbeke's Latin is, ". . . neque contrarietas, (aliqua aut nulla oppositis) inest. . . ."

[85] *Supra,* note 84.

[86] The Greek word used here is λέγωνται. This has been rendered as ". . . when definitions *are put* in place of names. . . ." The Latin of Moerbeke is *dicantur;* Cajetan uses *sumantur.*

[87] "In these" has been omitted from the translation of the Greek text because it is contained in ". . . in whatever predications. . . ."

[88] The Greek text reads: ". . . τὸ τὶ καὶ ἁπλῶς ἀληθὲς ἔσται εἰπεῖν" (". . . it will also be true to say [or predicate] each one simply").

[89] This is καθ' αὑτὰ in the Greek, i.e., *per se* as opposed to *per accidens;* in both Moerbeke's and Cajetan's Latin it is *secundum se,* which is a synonym for per se.

[90] Cf. *Post. Anal.* I, 4, 73a 35-74a 4.

is animal and he is rational," nevertheless the opposite kind of predication infers consequences in a similar way. For example, there is no "perseity" in "He is a white musician, therefore he is white and he is a musician"; rather, there is an accidental conjunction, not only between the parts among themselves and between the whole and the subject, but even between the parts and the subject. It is evident, therefore, that Aristotle is not taking "per se" positively, for an addition that does not differentiate this kind of predication from the opposed kind of predication would be useless. Why add "per se and not accidentally," if both those that are per se in the way explained and those that are conjoined accidentally infer divisively?

If "per se" is taken negatively, i.e., as not through another, and is referred to the parts of the conjoined predicate among themselves, the rule is found to be false. It is not licit, for example, to say, "He is a good lute player, therefore he is good and a lute player"; yet the art of lute-playing and its goodness are conjoined without anything as a medium. And the case is the same if it is referred to the whole conjoined predicate with respect to the subject, as is clear in the same example, for the whole, "good lute player," does not belong to man on account of another, and yet it does not infer the division, as has already been said. Therefore, "per se" is referred to the parts of the conjoined predicate with respect to the subject and the meaning is: when the predicates are conjointly predicated *per se,* i.e., *not through another,* i.e., each part is predicated of the subject, not on account of another but on account of itself and the subject, then a divided predication is inferred from the conjoined predication.

10.   This is the way in which Averroes and Boethius explain this and, explained in this way, a true rule is found, as can easily be manifested inductively; moreover, the reasoning is compelling. For, if the parts of some conjoined predicate so inhere in the subject that neither is in it on account of another, their separation produces nothing that could impede the truth of the divided predicates. And this meaning is consonant with the words of Aristotle, for by this he also distinguishes between enunciations in which the conjoined predicate infers a divided predicate, and those in which this consequence is not inherent. For besides the predicates having opposition in the additional determining element, there are those with a conjoined predicate wherein one part is a determination of the other in such a way that only through it does it regard the subject, as is evident in Aristotle's example, "Homer is a poet." The "is" does not regard Homer by reason of Homer himself, but precisely by reason of the poetry he left. Hence it is not licit to infer, "Therefore Homer is." The same is true with respect to negative enunci-

ations of this type, for it is not licit to infer from "Socrates is not a wall," "Therefore Socrates is not." And the reason is the same: "to be" is not denied of Socrates, but of "wallness" in Socrates.

11. Accordingly, it is evident how the reasoning in the text above is to be understood. "Per se" is taken negatively in the way explained here, and "accidentally" as "on account of another." The "accidentally" is used with the same signification in solving this and the preceding question. In both he understands "accidentally" to mean conjoined on account of another, but it is referred to diverse things. In the preceding question "accidentally" determines the way in which two predicates are conjoined among themselves; in the latter question it determines the way in which the part of the conjoined predicate is ordered to the subject. Hence, in the former, "white" and "musician" are numbered among the things that are accidental, but in the latter they are not.

12. This exposition seems a bit dubious, however. For if it is not licit to infer divisively from a conjoined predicate because one part of the conjoined predicate does not regard the subject on account of itself but on account of another part (as Aristotle says of the enunciation, "Homer is a poet"), it will follow that there will never be a good consequence from the third determinant to the second, since in every enunciation with a third determinant, "is" regards the subject on account of the predicate and not on account of itself.

13. To make this difficulty clear, we must first note a distinction. It is one thing to treat of the rule when inferring a second determinant from a third determinant, and when not; it is quite another thing when a divided inference is made from a conjoined predicate, and when not. The former is an additional point; the latter is the question we have been inquiring about. The former is compatible with variety of the terms, the latter not. For if one of the terms which is one part of a conjoined predicate will be varied according to signification, or supposition when taken separately, it is not inferred divisively from the conjoined predicate, but the other is.

Secondly, note this proposition: when a second determinant is inferred from a third, identity of the terms is not kept. This is evident with respect to the term "is." Indeed, St. Thomas said above that "is" as the second determinant implies one thing and "is" as the third determinant another. The former implies the act of being simply, the latter implies the relationship of inherence, or identity of the predicate with the subject. Therefore, when the second determinant is inferred from the third, one term is varied and consequently an inference is not made of the divided from the conjoined.

[186]

Accordingly, the response to the objection is clear, for although the second determinant can sometimes be inferred from the third, it is never licit for the second to be inferred from the third as divided from conjoined, because you cannot infer divisively when one part is destroyed by that very division. Therefore, let the consequence of the objection be denied and for proof let it be said that the conclusion—that such an inference is illicit under the limits of inferences which induce division from a conjoined predicate—is good, for this is what Aristotle is speaking of here.

14.   But the objection is raised against this that in the case of "Socrates is white, therefore he is," a divided inference can be made as from a conjoined predicate, in virtue of the argument that we can go from what is in the mode of part to its whole as long as the terms remain the same.[91]

The answer to this is as follows. It is true that white man is a part in the mode of man (because white diminishes nothing of the notion of man but posits man simply); is white, however, is not a part in the mode of is, because a part in the mode of its whole is a universal, the condition not diminishing the positing of it simply. But it is evident that white diminishes the notion of is, and does not posit it simply, for it contracts it to relative being. Whence when something becomes white, philosophers do not say that it is generated, but generated relatively.

15.   In accordance with this, the objection is raised that in saying "It is an animal, therefore it is," a divided inference is made in virtue of the same argument; for animal does not diminish the notion of is itself.

The answer to this is that if the is asserts the truth of a proposition, the fallacy is committed of going from the relative to the absolute; if the is asserts the act of being, the inference is good, but it is of the second determinant, not of the third.

16.   There is another doubt, this time about the principle in the exposition; for this follows, "It is a colored quantity, therefore it is a quantity and it is colored";[92] but "colored" regards the subject through the medium of quantity; therefore the exposition given above does not seem to be correct.

The answer to this and to similar objections is that "colored" is not so present in a subject by means of quantity that it is its determina-

[91] The implication is that if it is true to say "Socrates is white," it must also be true to say "Socrates exists"; for how could he be white if he did not exist, i.e., if white Socrates exists, then Socrates exists.

[92] Cf. Cajetan, Lesson VI, n. 9, (last paragraph).

tion, and by reason of such a determination denominates the subject; as "goodness," for instance, determines the art of lute-playing when we say "He is a good lute player." Rather, the subject itself is first denominated "colored" and quantity is called "colored" secondarily, although color is received through the medium of quantity. Hence, we made a point of saying earlier that one part of a conjoined predicate is predicated accidentally when it denominates the subject precisely because it denominates the other part.[93] This is not the case here nor in similar instances.

21a32 17.   When he says, *In the case of non-being, however, it is not true to say that it is something*, etc., he excludes the error of those who were satisfied to conclude that what is not, is.[94] This is the syllogism they use: "That which is, is 'opinionable'; that which is not, is 'opinionable'; therefore what is not, is." Aristotle destroys this process of reasoning by destroying the first proposition, which predicates divisively a part of what is conjoined in the subject, as if it said "It is 'opinionable,' therefore it is." Hence, assuming the subject of their conclusion, he says, *In the case of that which is not, however;* and he adds their middle term, *because it is a matter of opinion;* then he adds the major extreme, *it is not true to say that it is something.* He then assigns the cause: it is not because it is but rather because it is not, that there is such opinion.

---

93 Cf. Cajetan, Lesson VI, n. 10, (last paragraph).

94 Moerbeke's Latin is ". . . quod autem non est . . ."; the Greek, ". . . τὸ μὴ ὄν. . . ."

LESSON VIII
Modal Propositions and Their Opposition

21a 34   Having determined these things, we must consider in what way negations and affirmations of the possible and not possible, contingent and not contingent, and of the impossible and necessary are related to each other—a question of considerable difficulty.

21a 38   Let us grant that of mutually related enunciations,[95] contradictories are those opposed to each other by being related in a certain way according to "to be" and "not to be"; for example, the negation of "Man is" is "Man is not" and not, "Non-man is," and of "Man is white," "Man is not white," and not, "Man is nonwhite." For if this is not so, it will be true to say that "wood" is nonwhite man since of anything either the affirmation or the negation is true. Now in those in which "to be" is not the determining word added, that which is said in place of "to be" will effect the same thing; for example, the negation of "Man walks" will be "Man does not walk" and not, "Non-man walks." The reason, of course, is that there is no difference between "Man walks" and "Man is walking." And if this is always the case, then the negation of "possible to be" will be "possible not to be" and not, "not possible to be."

21b 12   However, it seems that the same thing is possible to be and possible not to be; for everything that has the possibility to be cut or to walk has the possibility not to be cut and not to walk; and the reason is that everything that is possible in this way is not always in act, and so the negation will also be inherent in it; for that which could walk could also not walk, and that which could be seen, not be seen. But it is impossible that opposed assertions in respect to the same thing be true. Therefore, the negation of "possible to be" is not, "possible not to be."

21b 19   For it follows from what we have said, either that the same thing is asserted and denied at once of the same subject or that assertions and denials of modals are not made by the addition of "to be" or "not to be" respectively. If the former alternative is impossible, the latter must obtain.

---

[95] The Greek for this phrase is, "εἰ γὰρ τῶν συμπλεκομένων. . . ." Aristotle means by this: Of mutually related enunciations [which embraces contradictories, contraries, and the contradictories of contraries, i.e., subcontraries], we are going to speak only of contradictories. However, this phrase could be translated as, "Of combined things . . .," which is the way Cajetan takes it, and in relation to it comments that by this Aristotle differentiates complex things, such an enunciations, from incomplex things, such as names or verbs. Cf. n. 12 of this lesson.

It should also be noted that the examples of the contradictories that

1.   Now that he has treated enunciations in which something added to the parts leaves the unity intact on the one hand, and varies it on the other, Aristotle begins to explain what happens to the enunciation when something is added, not to its parts, but to its composition. First, he explains their opposition; secondly, he treats of the consequences of their opposition where he says, *Logical sequences result from modals ordered thus*, etc.[96] With respect to the first point, he proposes the question he intends to consider and then begins his consideration where he says, *Let us grant that of mutually related enunciations, contradictories are those opposed to each other*, etc.

He proposes that we must now investigate the way in which affirmations and negations of the possible and not possible are related. He gives the reason when he adds, *for the question has many special difficulties.*[97]

However, before we proceed with the consideration of enunciations that are called modal, we must first see that there are such things as modal enunciations, and which and how many modes render propositions modal; we must also know what their subject is and their predicate, what the modal enunciation itself is, what the order is between modal enunciations and the enunciations already treated, and finally, why a special treatment of them is necessary.

2.   We can speak about things in two ways: in one, composing one thing with another; in the other, declaring the kind of composition that exists between the two things. To signify these two ways of speaking about things we form two kinds of enunciations. One kind enunciates that something belongs or does not belong to something. These are called absolute [de inesse] enunciations; these we have already discussed. The other enunciates the mode of composition of the predicate with the subject. These are called modal, from their principal part, the mode. For when we say, "That Socrates run is possible," it is not the running of Socrates that is enunciated but the kind of composition there is between running and Socrates—in this case, possible. I have said "mode of composition" expressly, for there are two kinds of mode posited in the enunciation. One modifies the verb, either with respect to what it signifies, as in "Socrates runs swiftly," or with respect to the time signified along

follow in the text, if literally translated from the Greek would actually be, "Man to be," "Man not to be" and "Non-man to be," etc., which correspond in mode of expression to the "possible to be," "possible not to be" and "not possible to be" spoken of later in this portion of the text.

96 22a 14; Lesson X, (at the beginning).

97 In the Greek this is, ". . . ἔχει γὰρ ἀπορίας τινάς." Moerbeke's Latin is exactly equivalent. Cajetan has, ". . . habent enim multas dubitationes speciales."

with the verb, as in "Socrates runs today." The other kind modifies the very composition of the predicate with the subject, as in the example, "That Socrates run is possible." The former determines how or when running is in Socrates; the latter determines the kind of conjunction there is between running and Socrates. The former, which affects the actuality of the verb, does not make a modal enunciation. Only the modes that affect the composition make a modal enunciation, the reason being that the composition, as the form of the whole, contains the whole enunciation.

3.   This kind of mode, properly speaking, is fourfold: possible, impossible, necessary, and contingent. True and false are not included because, strictly speaking, they do not seem to modify the composition even though they fall upon the composition itself, as is evident in "That Socrates runs is true," and "That man is four-footed is false." For something is said to be modified in the proper sense of the term when it is caused to be *in a certain way*, not when it comes to be according to its substance. Now, when a composition is said to be true it is not proposed that it is *in a certain way*, but that it is. To say, "That Socrates runs is true," for example, is to say that the composition of running with Socrates *is*. The case is similar when it is false, for what is said is that it is not; for example, to say, "That Socrates runs is false" is to say that the composition of running with Socrates *is not*. On the other hand, when the composition is said to be possible or contingent, we are not saying that it is but that it is in a certain way. For example, when we say, "That Socrates run is possible," we do not make the composition of running with Socrates substantial, but we qualify it, asserting that it is possible.

Consequently, Aristotle in proposing the modes, does not mention the true and false at all, although later on he infers the true and the not true, and assigns the reason for it where he does this.

4.   Since the modal enunciation contains two compositions, one between the parts of what is said, the other between what is said and the mode, it must be understood that it is the former composition that is modified, i.e., the composition between the parts of what is said, not the composition between what is said and the mode. This can be seen in an example. In the modal enunciation, "That Socrates be white is possible," there are two parts: one, "That Socrates be white," the other, "is possible." The first is called the dictum because it is that which is asserted by the indicative, namely, "Socrates is white"; for in saying "Socrates is white" we are simply saying, "That Socrates be white." The second part is called the mode because it is the addition of a restriction.

The first part of the modal enunciation consists of a certain composition of Socrates and white; the second part, opposed to the first, indicates a composition from the composition of dictum and mode.[98] Again, the first part, although it has all the properties of an enunciation —subject, predicate, copula, and composition—is, in its entirety, the subject of the modal enunciation; the second part, the mode, is the predicate. In a modal enunciation, therefore, the composition of the dictum is subjected and modified; for when we say, "That Socrates be white is possible," it does not signify the kind of conjunction of possibility there is with the dictum "That Socrates be white," but it implies the kind of composition there is of the parts of the dictum among themselves, i.e., of white with Socrates, namely, that it is a possible composition. The modal enunciation, therefore, does not say that something is present in or not present in a subject, but rather, it enunciates a mode of the dictum. Nor properly speaking does it compose according to what is signified, since it is not a composition of the composition; rather, it adds a mode to the composition of the things. Hence the modal enunciation is simply an enunciation in which the dictum is modified.

5.   Because the modal enunciation has everything duplicated, it must not on that account be thought to be many. It enunciates one mode of only one composition, although there are many parts of that composition. The many concurring for the composition of the dictum are like the many that concur to make one subject, of which it was said above that it does not impede the unity of the enunciation.[99] The enunciation, "The house is white," is also a case in point, for it is not multiple, although a house is built of many parts.

6.   Modal enunciations are rightly treated after the absolute enunciation, for parts are naturally prior to the whole, and knowledge of the

[98] A modal enunciation can be expressed in different ways grammatically, i.e., by an adverb, an adjective, or a verb, e.g., "Socrates runs contingently," or "That Socrates run is contingent," or "Socrates may run." Logically, however, it makes no difference what part of speech is used to express the mode, for the meaning is the same and hence as far as logic is concerned the above enunciations are identical.

In the Latin text of Cajetan the second mode of expression is used, which has the advantage of putting the dictum first, as the subject, and the mode second, as the predicate. Hence "the first part" here refers to

the subject of the modal enunciation, the dictum, whether it is stated first or second grammatically.

It should be noted that Aristotle's wording is both abbreviated and in reverse. When he speaks of "possible to be" and "possible not to be," etc., "possible" and "not possible," which are placed first, are the modes and "to be" and "not to be," which are placed second, are the dictums. Thus there are four possible combinations: possible to be, possible not to be, not possible to be, and not possible not to be, and so with the other modes, i.e., the contingent, necessary, and impossible.

[99] See 20b 15; Cajetan, Lesson V, n. 1.

whole depends on knowledge of the parts. Moreover, a special discussion of them was necessary because the modal enunciation has its own peculiar difficulties.

Aristotle indicates in his text many of the things we have taken up here: the order of modal enunciations, when he says, *Having determined these things,* etc.; what and how many modes there are when he expresses and lists them; the variation of the same mode by affirmation and negation when he says, *the possible* and *not possible, contingent* and *not contingent;* the necessity of treating them, when he adds, *for they have many difficulties of their own.*[100]

7.   Then he investigates the opposition of modal enunciations, where he says, *Let us grant that of those things that are combined,*[101] *contradictories are those opposed to each other by being related in a certain way according to "to be" and "not to be,"* etc. First, he presents the question and in so doing gives arguments for the parts; secondly, he determines the truth, where he says, *For it follows from what we have said, either that the same thing is asserted and denied at once of the same subject,* etc.

The question with respect to the opposition of modals is this: Is a contradiction made in modal enunciations by a negation added to the verb of the dictum, which expresses what is; or is it not, but rather by a negation added to the mode which qualifies? Aristotle first argues for the affirmative part, that the negation must be added to the verb; then he argues for the negative part, that the negation must not be added to the verb, where he says, *However it seems that the same thing is possible to be and possible not to be,* etc.

8.   His first argument is this. If of combined things, contradictions are those related according to "to be" and "not to be" (as is clear inductively in substantive enunciations with a second determinant, in those with a third determinant, and in adjectival enunciations) and all contradictions must be obtained in this way, the contradictory of "possible to be" will be "possible not to be," and not, "not possible to be." Consequently, the negation must be added to the verb to get opposition in modal enunciations.

The consequence is clear, for when we say "possible to be" and "possible not to be" the negation falls on "to be." Accordingly, he says, *Let us grant that of those things that are combined, i.e., of complex things,*[102] *contradictions are those opposed to each other which are disposed according to "to be" and "not to be,"*[103] i.e., in one of which "to be" is affirmed and in the other denied.

21a34

21a38

21b19

21b12

21a38

---

[100] *Supra,* note 97.
[101] *Supra,* note 95.

[102] *Supra,* note 95.
[103] The Greek here is, ". . . αὗται

9.   He goes on to give an induction, beginning with an enunciation having a second determinant. The negation of "Man is," is, "Man is not," in which the verb is negated. The negation of "Man is," is not, "Nonman is," for this is not the negative but the affirmative of the infinite subject, which is true at the same time as the first enunciation, "Man is."

10.   He continues the induction with substantive enunciations having a third determinant. The negation of the enunciation "Man is white" is "Man is not white," in which the verb is negated. The negation is not "Man is nonwhite," for this is not the negative, but the affirmative of the infinite predicate.

Now it might be thought that the affirmatives of the finite and infinite predicates are contradictories since they cannot be verified of the same thing because of their opposed predicates. To obviate this error, Aristotle interposes an argument proving that these two are not contradictories. The nature of contradictories, he reasons, is such that either the assertion, i.e., the affirmation, or the negation, is verified of anything, for between contradictories no middle is possible. Now the two enunciations, that something "is white man" and "is nonwhite man" are per se contradictories. Therefore, they are of such a nature that one of them is verified of anything. For example, it is false to say "is white man" of wood; hence "is nonwhite man" will be true to say of it, namely of wood, i.e., "Wood is nonwhite man." This is manifestly false, for wood is neither white man nor nonwhite man. Consequently, there is not a contradiction in the case in which each is at once false of the same subject. Therefore, contradiction is effected when the negation is added to the verb.

11.   He continues his induction with enunciations having an adjective verb: *Now if the case is as we have stated it,* i.e., contradiction is taken as said above, *then in enunciations in which "to be" is not the determining word added* (explicitly), *that which is said in place of "to be" will effect the same thing* with respect to the opposition obtained (i.e., the adjective verb that occupies the place of "to be," inasmuch as the truth of "to be" is included in it, effects the function of the copula). For example, the negation of the enunciation "Man walks" is not, "Non-man walks" (for this is the affirmative of the infinite subject) but "Man is

ἀλλήλαις ἀντίκεινται αἱ ἀντιφάσεις, ὅσαι κατὰ τὸ εἶναι καὶ μὴ εἶναι τάττονται. . . ." Moerbeke has ". . . illae sunt sibi invicem oppositae contradictiones, quaecunque secundum esse et non esse disponuntur," Cajetan's is the same except for the

"quaecunque" for which he has substituted "quae." The present translation of this is, ". . . contradictories are those opposed to each other by being related in a certain way according to 'to be' and 'not to be.'"

not walking." In this case, as in that of the substantive verb, the negation must be added to the verb, for there is no difference between using the adjective verb, as in "Man walks," and using the substantive verb, as in "Man is walking."

12.   Then he posits the second part of the induction: *And if this is always the case,* i.e., that contradiction must be gotten by adding the negation to "to be," we must conclude that the negation of the enunciation that asserts "possible to be" is "possible not to be," and not, "not possible to be." The consequent of the conclusion is evident, for in "possible not to be" the negation is added to the verb, in "not possible to be," it is not.

At the beginning of this argument, Aristotle said, *Of those things that are combined,*[104] i.e., complex things, the contradictions are effected according to "to be" and "not to be." He said this in reference to the difference between complex and incomplex things, for opposition in the latter is not made by the negation expressing "not to be," but by adding the negative to the incomplex thing itself, as in "man" and "non-man," "reads" and "nonreads."

13.   When he says, *However, it seems that the same thing is possible*   21b12
to be and possible not to be, etc., he argues for the negative part of the question, namely, to get a contradiction in modals the negation should not be added to the verb. His reasoning is the following: It is impossible for two contradictories to be true at once of the same subject; but "possible to be" and "possible not to be" are verified at once of the same thing; therefore, these are not contradictories. Consequently, contradiction of the modals is not obtained by negation of the verb.

In this reasoning, the minor is posited first, with its proof; secondly, the major; finally, the conclusion. The minor is: *However, it seems that the same thing is possible to be and possible not to be.* For instance, everything that has the possibility of being divided also has the possibility of not being divided, and that which has the possibility of walking also has the possibility of not walking. The proof of this minor is that *everything that is possible in this way* (as are possible to walk and to be divided) *is not always in act;* for he who is able to walk is not always actually walking, nor is that which can be divided always divided. *And so the negation* of the possible *will also be inherent in it,* i.e., therefore not only is the affirmation possible but also the negation.

Notice that since the possible is manifold, as will be said further on, Aristotle explicitly adds "in this way" when he assumes here that *that which is possible is not always in act.* For it is not true to say of every possible that it is not always in act, but only of some, namely, those

---
[104] *Supra,* note 95.

that are possible in the way in which to walk and to be divided are possible.

Note also that "possible in this way" has two conditions: that it is able to be in act, and that it is not always in act. It follows necessarily, then, that it is true to say of it simultaneously that it is both possible to be and possible not to be. From the fact that it can be in act it follows that it is possible to be; from the fact that it is not always in act it follows that it is possible not to be, for that which not always is, is able not to be. Aristotle, then, rightly infers from these two: *and so the negation* of the possible *will also be inherent in it;* and not just the affirmation, *for that which could walk could also not walk and that which could be seen not be seen.*

The major is: *But it is impossible that contradictions in respect to the same thing be true.*[105] The final conclusion inferred is: *Therefore, the negation of "possible to be" is not, "possible not to be"* because they are true at once of the same thing.

In relation to this part of the text, be careful not to suppose that possible as it is a mode, is always to be taken for possible to either of two alternatives, for this will be shown to be false later on. If you consider the matter carefully you will see that it was enough for his intention to give as an instance one modal contained under the modals of the possible in order to show that contradiction in modals is not obtained by negation of the verb.

14.   Aristotle establishes the truth with respect to this difficulty
21b19   where he says, *For it follows from what we have said, either that the same thing is asserted and denied at once of the same subject,* etc. Since he is investigating two things, i.e., whether contradiction of modals is made by the negation of the verb or not; and, whether it is not rather by negation of the mode, he first determines the truth in relation to the first question, namely, that contradiction of modals is not made by negation of the verb; then he determines the truth in relation to the second, namely, that contradiction of modals is made by negation of the mode,
21b23   where he says, *Therefore, the negation of "possible to be" is "not possible to be,"* etc.[106]

Hence he says that because of the foresaid reasoning one of these two follows: first, that *either the same thing,* i.e., one and the same thing is said, i.e., *is asserted and denied at once of the same subject,* i.e., either two contradictories are verified at once of the same thing, as the first argument concluded; or secondly, that *assertions and denials* of modals, which are opposed contradictorily *are not made by the addi-*

[105] The Greek text has, "τὰς ἀντικειμένας φάσεις," i.e., "opposed asser- tions," instead of "contradictions."
[106] At the beginning of the next lesson.

tion of "to be" or *"not to be,"* i.e., contradiction of modals is not made by the negation of the verb, as the second argument concluded. *If the former alternative is impossible,* namely, that two contradictories can be true of the same thing at once, *the latter,* that contradiction of modals is not made according to negation of the verb, *must obtain,* for impossible things must always be avoided. His mode of speaking here indicates that there is some obstacle to each alternative. But since in the first the obstacle is an impossibility that cannot be accepted, while in the second the only obstacle is that the negation must fall upon the copula of the enunciation if a negative enunciation is to be formed, and this can be done otherwise than by denying the verb of the dictum, as will be shown later on, then the second alternative must be chosen, i.e., that the contradiction of modals is not made according to negation of the verb, and the first alternative is to be rejected.

In Contradictions of Modal Propositions the Negation Must Be Added to the Modes, Not to the Verb

21b 23   Therefore, the negation of "possible to be" is "not possible to be." The reasoning is the same in regard to "contingent to be," for its negation is "not contingent to be." So, too, in the others, that is, the necessary and the impossible.

21b 26   For just as "to be" and "not to be" are the determining additions in the former [i.e., absolute enunciations] and the things subjected are "white" and "man," so here "to be" is as the subject and "is possible" and "is contingent" are determining additions; and just as "to be" and "not to be" determine the true [and the false] in the former,[107] in like manner these determine the true [and the false] in regard to what is possible and not possible.

21b 33   The negation, then, of "possible not to be" is "not possible not to be."[108] Wherefore "possible to be" and "possible not to be" would appear to be consequent to each other; for the same thing is "possible to be" and "possible not to be," since these are not contradictory to each other. But "possible to be" and "not possible to be" are never true at once of the same subject, for they are opposed. Nor are "possible not to be" and "not possible not to be" ever true at once of the same subject.

The case is the same with respect to the necessary. The negation of "necessary to be" is not, "necessary not to be" but, "not necessary to be"; and the negation of "necessary not to be," "not necessary not to be."

Likewise, the negation of "impossible to be" is not, "impossible not to be" but, "not impossible to be"; and of "impossible not to be," "not impossible not to be."

22a 8   And universally, as has been said, "to be" and "not to be" must be posited as the subject, and those that produce affirmation and negation [i.e., possible, not possible, contingent, not contingent, etc.] must be joined to "to be" and "not to be." And these are the words that are to be considered opposed:

possible	—	not possible		necessary	—	not necessary
contingent	—	not contingent		true	—	not true
impossible	—	not impossible				

---

[107] In manuscripts βΔΣa there is the addition of "καὶ τὸ Ψεῦδος" after "ἀληθές."

[108] There are various differences in this portion of the text as follows: ἀπόφασις + οὐ τὸ οὐ δυνατὸν εἶναι

1.   Aristotle now determines where the negation must be placed in order to obtain contradiction in modals. He first determines the truth summarily; secondly, he presents the argument for the truth of the position, which is also the answer to the reasoning induced for the opposite position, where he says, *For just as "to be" and "not to be" are the de-*   21b26 *termining additions in the former, and the things subjected are "white" and "man,"* etc.; thirdly, he makes this truth evident in all the modals, where he says, *The negation, then, of "possible not to be" is "not possible*   21b33 *not to be,"* etc.; fourthly, he arrives at a universal rule where he says, *And universally, as has been said, "to be" and "not to be" must be posited*   22a8 *as the subject,* etc.

Since the negation must be added either to the verb or to the mode and it was shown above in virtue of an argument from division that it is not to be added to the verb, he concludes: *Therefore, the nega-*   21b23 *tion of "possible to be" is "not possible to be"; * that is, the mode is negated. The reasoning is the same with respect to enunciations of the contingent, for the negation of "contingent to be" is "not contingent to be." And the judgment is the same in the others, i.e., the necessary and the impossible.

2.   When he says, *For just as "to be" and "not to be" are the deter-*   21b26 *mining additions in the former, and the things subjected are "white" and "man,"* etc., he gives the argument for the truth of his position. To obtain contradiction among any enunciations the negation must be applied to the determining addition, i.e., to the word that joins the predicate with the subject; but in modals the determining additions are the modes; therefore, to get a contradiction in modals, the negation must be added to the mode.

The major of the argument is subsumed; the minor is stated in Aristotle's wording by a further similitude to absolute enunciations. In absolute enunciations the determining additions, i.e., the predications, are "to be" and "not to be," i.e., the verb signifying "to be" or "not to be" (for the verb is always a sign of those things that are predicated of another). The things subjected to the determining additions, i.e., to which "to be" and "not to be" are applied, are "white," in "White is," or "man," in "Man is." This happens in modals in the same way but in a manner appropriate to them. *"To be" is as the subject,* i.e., the dictum signifying "to be" or "not to be" holds the place of the subject; *"is possible" and "is contingent,"* i.e., the modes, are the predicates. And just as

ἀλλὰ (Δ) α#, alt. δυνατὸν + εἶναι (μη εἶν [Δ]), ἀλλ' οὐ τὸ δυνατὸν (ΔΣ). The Oxford Greek text incorporates none of these variations. If incorporated the text would read:

"The negation, then, of 'possible not to be' is not 'not possible to be' but 'not possible not to be' and the negation of 'possible to be' is not 'possible not to be' but 'not possible to be.'"

in absolute enunciations we determine truth or falsity with "to be" and "not to be," so in modals with the modes. He makes this point when he says, *determining additions,* i.e., these modes effect truth just as "to be" and "not to be" determine truth and falsity in the others.

3.　　Thus the response to the argument for the opposite position, which he gave first, is evident. That argument concluded that the negation should be added to the verb as it is in absolute enunciations. But since the modal enunciates a mode of a dictum—as the absolute enunciation enunciates "to be" or "not to be" such, for instance, "to be white" of a subject—the mode holds the same place here that the verb does there. Consequently, the negation falls upon the same thing proportionally here and there, for the proportion of mode to dictum is the same as the proportion of verb to subject.

Again, since truth and falsity follow upon affirmation and negation, the affirmation and negation of an enunciation and its truth and falsity must be controlled by the same thing. In absolute enunciations truth and falsity follow upon "to be" or "not to be," hence in the modals they follow upon the mode; for that modal is true which modifies the dictum as the composition of the dictum permits, just as that absolute enunciation is true which signifies that something is as it is. Therefore, negation is added here to the mode just as it is added there to the verb, since the power of each is the same with respect to the truth and falsity of an enunciation.

Notice that he calls the modes "determining additions," i.e., predications—as "to be" is in absolute enunciations—understanding by the mode the whole predicate of the modal enunciation, for example, "is possible." As a sign of this he expresses the modes themselves verbally when he says, *"is possible" and "is contingent" are determining additions.* For "is contingent" and "is possible" comprise the whole predicate of the modal enunciation.

21b33　4.　　When he says, *The negation, then, of "possible not to be" is* [not, "not possible to be" but] *"not possible not to be,"* etc., he makes this truth evident in all the modals, i.e., the possible, the necessary, and the impossible (the contingent being convertible with the possible). And since any mode makes two modal affirmatives, one having an affirmed dictum and the other having a negated dictum, he shows what the negation of each affirmation is in each mode. First he takes those of the possible. The negation of the first affirmative of the possible (the one with an affirmed dictum), i.e., "possible to be," was assigned as "not possible to be." Hence, going on to the remaining affirmative of the possible he says, *The negation, then, of "possible not to be"* [wherein the dictum is negated] is, *"not possible not to be."* Then he

[200]

proves this. The contradictory of "possible not to be" is either "possible to be" or "not possible not to be." But the former, i.e., "possible to be," is not the contradictory of "possible not to be," for they can be at once true. Hence they are also thought to follow upon each other, for, as was said above, the same thing is possible to be and not to be. Consequently, just as "possible not to be" follows upon "possible to be," so conversely "possible to be" follows upon "possible not to be." But the contradictory of "possible to be," which cannot be true at the same time, is "not possible to be," for these, as has been said, are opposed. Therefore, the negation of "possible not to be" is, "not possible not to be," for these are never at once true or false.

Note that he says, *Wherefore "possible to be" and "possible not to be" would appear to be consequent to each other,* and not that they do follow upon each other, for it is not true that they follow upon each other universally, but only particularly (as will be said later); this is the reason they appear to follow upon each other simply.

Then he manifests the same thing in the modals of the necessary, and first in the affirmative with an affirmed dictum: *The case is the same with respect to the necessary. The negation of "necessary to be" is not, "necessary not to be"* (in which the mode is not negated) *but, "not necessary to be."* Next he adds the affirmative of the necessary with a negated dictum: *and the negation of "necessary not to be" is "not necessary not to be."*

Next, he takes up the impossible, keeping the same order. *The negation of "impossible to be" is not, "impossible not to be" but, "not impossible to be,"* in which the mode is negated. The negation of the other affirmative, "impossible not to be" is "not impossible not to be." The negation, therefore, is always added to the mode.

5.   Then he says, *And universally, as has been said, "to be" and "not to be" must be posited as the subject, and those that produce affirmation and negation must be joined to "to be" and "not to be,"* etc. Here he concludes with the universal rule. As has been said, the dictums denoting "to be" and "not to be" must be posited in the modals as subjects, and the one making this an affirmation and negation, i.e., the opposition of contradiction, must be added only to the selfsame mode, not to diverse modes, for the selfsame mode which was previously affirmed must be denied if there is to be a contradiction.[109] He gives examples of how

[109] Notice that Cajetan is not saying precisely what Aristotle says on this point. Aristotle says that " 'to be' and 'not to be' must be posited as the subject" and then that "those that produce an affirmation and negation must be joined to 'to be' and 'not to be,' " i.e., possible and not possible, etc. Cajetan says that "to be" and "not to be" must be added

[201]

this is to be done when he adds, *And these are the words that are to be considered opposed,* i.e., affirmations and negations in modals, possible —not possible, contingent—not contingent.

Moreover, when he said elsewhere but in another way that the negation must be applied only to the mode, he did not exclude the copula of the mode, but the copula of the dictum. For it is unique to modals that the same opposition is made by adding a negation to the mode and to its verb. The contradictory of "is possible to be," for instance, is not only "is not possible to be," but also "not is possible to be."[110] There are two reasons, however, for his mentioning the mode rather than the verb: first, for the reason we have just given, namely, so as to imply that the negation placed after the verb of the mode, the mode having been put first, accomplishes the same thing as if it were placed before the modal verb; and secondly, because the modal enunciation is never without a mode; hence the negation can always be put on the mode. However, it cannot always be put on the verb of a mode, for the modal enunciation may lack the verb of a mode as for example in "Socrates runs necessarily," in which case the negation can always be adapted to the verb.

In adding "true" and "not true" at the end he implies that besides the four modes mentioned previously there are others that also determine the composition of the enunciation, for example, "true" and "not true," "false" and "not false"; nevertheless he did not posit these among the modes first given because, as was shown, they do not properly modify.

to the modes. Cf. note 98 for the difference in Aristotle's and Cajetan's wording of modals.

[110] The contradictory of "possibilis est esse" is not only "non possible est esse" but "possible non est esse." These have been translated so as to correspond to the previous translations of such phrases. In the next sentence, however, in which the reasons are given for these two ways of expressing the contradictories of "possible to be," the Latin rendering of these should be kept in mind since Cajetan's remarks depend upon the order of the words in Latin.

The Logical Consequents of the Modals

22a 14 Logical sequences result from modals ordered thus. From "possible to be" follows "contingent to be" and the latter is convertible with the former; "not impossible to be" and "not necessary to be" also follow from "possible to be." From "possible not to be" follows "contingent not to be," "not necessary not to be," and "not impossible not to be." From "not possible to be" and "not contingent to be" follows "necessary not to be" and "impossible to be." From "not possible not to be" and "not contingent not to be" follows "necessary to be" and "impossible not to be." Let us consider these with the help of a table.

22a24

possible to be	not possible to be
contingent to be	not contingent to be
not impossible to be	impossible to be
not necessary to be	necessary not to be
possible not to be	not possible not to be
contingent not to be	not contingent not to be
not impossible not to be	impossible not to be
not necessary not to be	necessary to be

22a 32 Now the impossible and the not impossible follow contradictorily upon the contingent and the possible and the not contingent and the not possible, but inversely. The negation of "impossible to be" follows upon "possible to be" and the affirmation of the former follows upon the negation of the latter, i.e., "impossible to be" follows upon "not possible to be"; for "impossible to be" is an affirmation, "not impossible to be" a negation.

22a 38 Now we must consider how enunciations predicating necessity are related to these. It is evident that the case here is not the same, for the contraries follow, but their contradictories are separated.

22a 39 For the negation of "necessary not to be" is not "not necessary to be," since both may be true of the same subject, for the necessary not to be is not necessary to be.

22b 3 Now the reason why enunciations predicating necessity do not follow in the same way as the others is that the impossible expresses contrarily the same thing as the necessary. For if it is impossible that this be, it is necessary, not that it be, but necessary that it not be; and if it is impossible that it not be, it is necessary that it be. So, if the impossible and not impossible follow in like manner from the possible and not possible, the necessary and not necessary follow contrarily,[111] since the necessary and the impossible signify the same thing,[112] but as has been said, inversely.

22b 10   Or is it impossible to arrange the contradictions of enunciations predicating necessity in this way? For what is necessary to be, is possible to be (for if not, the negation will follow, since it is necessary either to affirm or deny; and if it is not possible to be, it is impossible to be; therefore, that which is necessary to be is impossible to be, which is absurd). But from "possible to be" "not impossible to be" follows, and from this, "not necessary to be"; and thus what is necessary to be is not necessary to be, which is absurd.

22b 17   But in fact neither "necessary to be" nor "necessary not to be" follow upon "possible to be"; for "to be possible" admits of two possibilities, whereas if either "necessary to be" or "necessary not to be" is true both possibilities will no longer be true. For a thing is at once possible to be and not to be, but if it is necessary to be or not to be, the two alternatives will not be possible. It remains, therefore, that "not necessary not to be" follows upon "possible to be";

22b 23   for this is true also with respect to "necessary to be." For "not necessary not to be" is the contradictory of what follows upon "not possible to be," for "not possible to be" is followed by "impossible to be" and by "necessary not to be," and the negation of this is "not necessary not to be."

22b 26   Thus, these contradictions also follow in the way indicated, and nothing impossible follows when they are thus arranged.

---

1.   Having established the opposition of modals, Aristotle now intends to determine their consequents. He first presents the true doctrine; then, he raises a difficulty where he says, *But it may be questioned whether "possible to be" follows upon "necessary to be,"* etc.[113] In presenting the true doctrine, he first posits the consequents of the opposition of modals according to the opinion of others; secondly, he determines the truth by examining and correcting their opinion, where he says, *Now the impossible and the not impossible follow contradictorily upon the contingent and the possible and the not contingent and the not possible, but inversely,* etc.

22b29

22a32

[111] That is, the impossible and not impossible have "to be" as subjects, whereas the necessary and not necessary have "not to be" and "to be" as subjects respectively.

[112] There is a variation in the texts here: βΔΣa have ἐπεὶ οὐ, so that the phrase would read, ". . . since

the necessary and the impossible do *not* signify the same thing, but as has been said, inversely" (italics added). It would seem more consonant with what Aristotle has said (22b 3) to omit the "not" as the Oxford Greek does.

[113] 22b 29; Cajetan, Lesson XI.

[204]

2.   Before we consider these consequents according to the opinion
of others, we must first note that since any mode makes two affirmations
and there are two negations opposed to these, there will be four enunci·
ations according to any one mode, two affirmatives and two negatives.
And since there are four modes, there will be sixteen modals. Among
these sixteen, anyone of each mode, from wherever you begin, has only
one of each mode following upon it. Hence, to assign the consequents
of the modals, we have to take one from each mode and arrange them
among themselves to form an order of consequents.

3.   The modals were ordered in this way by the ancients. They disposed them in four orders placing together in each order those that were
consequent to each other. Aristotle speaks of this order when he says,
Logical consequents follow according to the order in the table below,
which is the way in which the ancients posited them.[114]

Henceforth, however, to avoid confusion let us call the affirmative of dictum and mode in any one mode, *the simple affirmative,* as it is
by Averroes, among others; affirmative of mode and negative of dictum,
the declined affirmative; negative of mode and not of dictum, *the simple*
negative; negative of both mode and dictum, *the declined negative.*
Hence, simplicity of mode designates affirmation or negation, and so,
too, does declination of dictum.

The ancients said, then, that simple affirmation of the contingent,
i.e., "contingent to be" follows upon simple affirmation of the possible,
i.e., "possible to be" (for the contingent is converted with the possible);
the simple negative of the impossible also follows upon this, i.e., "not
impossible to be"; and the simple negative of the necessary, i.e., "not
necessary to be." This is the first order of modal consequents.

In the second order they said that the declined negatives of the
necessary and impossible, i.e., "not necessary not to be" and "not impossible not to be," follow upon the declined affirmative of the possible
and the contingent, i.e., "possible not to be" and "contingent not to be."

In the third order, according to them, the declined affirmative
of the necessary, i.e., "necessary not to be," and the simple affirmative of
of the impossible, i.e., "impossible to be," follow upon the simple negatives of the possible and the contingent, i.e., "not possible to be" and
"not contingent to be."

Finally, in the fourth order, the simple affirmative of the necessary, i.e., "necessary to be," and the declined affirmative of the impossible, i.e., "impossible not to be," follow upon the declined negatives of

[114] This is Cajetan's summary of the
    text from 22a 14 to 22a 31.

the possible and the contingent, i.e., "not possible not to be" and "not contingent not to be."

4.   To make this ordering more evident, let us consider it with the help of the following table.

CONSEQUENTS OF MODAL ENUNCIATIONS IN THE FOUR
ORDERS POSITED AND ORDERED BY THE ANCIENTS[115]

FIRST ORDER	THIRD ORDER
It is possible to be	It is not possible to be
It is contingent to be	It is not contingent to be
It is not impossible to be	It is impossible to be
It is not necessary to be	It is necessary not to be

SECOND ORDER	FOURTH ORDER
It is possible not to be	It is not possible not to be
It is contingent not to be	It is not contingent not to be
It is not impossible not to be	It is impossible not to be
It is not necessary not to be	It is necessary to be

22a32   5.   When he says, *Now the impossible and the not impossible follow contradictorily upon the contingent and the possible and the not contingent and the not possible, but inversely,* etc., he determines the truth by examining the foresaid opinion. First, he examines the consequents of enunciations predicating impossibility; secondly, those predi-
22a38   cating necessity, where he says, *Now we must consider how enunciations predicating necessity are related to these,* etc.

From the opinion advanced, then, he concludes with approval that the impossible and the not impossible follow upon the contingent and the possible and the not contingent and the not possible, contradictorily, i.e., the contradictories of the impossible follow upon the contradictories of the possible and the contingent, *but inversely,* i.e., not so that affirmation follows upon affirmation and negation upon negation, but inversely, i.e., negation follows upon affirmation and affirmation upon negation.

He explains this when he says, *The negation of "impossible to be" follows upon "possible to be,"* i.e., the negation of the impossible, i.e., "not impossible to be," follows upon the affirmation of the possible, and the affirmation of the impossible follows upon the negation of the possible. For the affirmation, "impossible to be" follows upon the negation, "not possible to be." In the latter the mode is negated, in the for-

[115] The position of Cajetan's second and third orders in the diagram have been changed to correspond to the way in which Aristotle has arranged them, i.e., enunciations that are contradictories are placed opposite to each other, those in the third order to those in the first and those in the fourth order to those in the second; the numbering of the orders remains the same.

[206]

mer it is not. Therefore, the ancients were right in saying that in any order, the consequences of enunciations predicating impossibility are as follows: from affirmation of the possible, negation of the impossible is inferred; and from negation of the possible, affirmation of the impossible is inferred. This is apparent in the diagram.

6.   When he says, *Now we must consider how enunciations predi-* 22a38
cating necessity are related to these, etc., he proposes an examination of the consequents of enunciations predicating necessity in order to determine the truth about them. First he examines what was said by the ancients; secondly, he determines the truth, where he says, *But in fact* 22b17
neither "necessary to be" nor "necessary not to be" follow upon "possible to be," etc. In his examination of the ancients, Aristotle makes four points. First, he shows what was well said by the ancients and what was badly said.

It must be noted in regard to this that, as we have said, there are four enunciations predicating necessity, which differ among themselves in quantity and quality, and hence they make up a diagram of opposition in the manner of the absolute enunciations. Two of them are contrary to each other, and two are contradictory to these contraries, as is clear in the diagram below.

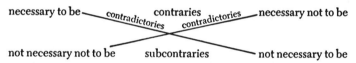

Now the ancients correctly inferred the universal contraries from the possibles, contingents, and impossibles, but incorrectly inferred their contradictories, namely, particulars. This is the reason Aristotle says that it remains to be considered how enunciations predicating necessity are related consequentially to the possible and not possible. From what Aristotle says, it is clear that those predicating necessity do not follow upon the possibles in the same way as those predicating impossibility follow upon the possibles, for all of the enunciations predicating impossibility were correctly inferred by the ancients, but those predicating necessity were not. Two of them, the contraries, "necessary to be" and "necessary not to be," follow, i.e., correct consequents were deduced by the ancients in the third and fourth orders; the remaining two, "not necessary not to be" and "not necessary to be," which are contradictories of the contraries, are outside of the consequents of these, i.e., in the second and first orders. Hence, the ancients represented everything correctly in the third and fourth orders, but in the first and second they erred, not with respect to all things, but only with respect to enunciations predicating necessity.

[207]

7.　　Secondly, he says, *For the negation of "necessary not to be"* is *not "not necessary to be," since both may be true of the same subject*, etc. Here he replies to a tacit objection. This reply could be used to defend the consequent of the enunciation of the necessary made by the ancients in the first order. The tacit objection is this: "not possible to be" and "necessary not to be" follow convertibly in the third order which has already been shown to be correct; therefore, "possible to be" and "not necessary to be" ought to follow upon each other in the first order. The consequent holds; for the contradictories of two that convertibly follow upon each other, mutually follow upon each other; but those two follow upon each other convertibly in the third order and these two in the first order are their contradictories; therefore, those of the first order, i.e., "possible to be" and "not necessary to be," mutually follow upon each other.

　　　　Aristotle replies here to this objection by destroying what was assumed in the minor, i.e., that the necessary of the first order and the necessary of the third order are contradictories. He says, *For the negation of "necessary not to be"* (which is in the third order) *is not "not necessary to be"* (which has been placed in the first order). He also gives the reason: it is possible for both to be true at once of the same subject, which is repugnant to contradictories. For the same thing which is necessary not to be, is not necessary to be; for example, it is necessary that man not be wood and it is not necessary that man be wood. Notice, as will be clear later, that these two which the ancients posited in the first and third orders, are subalterns and therefore are at once true, whereas they should be contradictories; hence the ancients were in error.

8.　　Boethius and Averroes read both this and the preceding part of the text, not reprovingly, but as explanatorily joined together. They say Aristotle explains the quality of the above table with respect to the consequents of enunciations predicating necessity after he has explained in what way those predicating impossibility are related. What Aristotle is saying, then, is that those of the necessary do not follow those of the possible in the same way as those of the impossible follow upon the possible. For contradictories of the impossible follow upon contradictories of the possible, although inversely; but contradictories of the necessary are not said to follow the contradictories of the possible, but rather the contraries of the necessary follow upon them. It is not the contraries among themselves that follow, but contraries in this way: the negation of the necessary is said to follow upon the affirmation of the possible; but what follows on the negation of this possible is not the affirmation of the necessary contradictory to that negative of the necessary following upon the possible, but the contrary of such an affirmation of the necessary. That this is the case is evident in the first and third orders. The sources are negation and affirmation of the possible, and the extremes are "not necessary to be" and "necessary not to be." But these are not contradictories, for the negation of "necessary not to be" is not "not necessary to be," for it is possible for them to be at once true of the same thing. "Necessary not to be" is the contrary of the contradictory of "not necessary to be," which contradictory is "necessary to be."

In my judgment, however, the first exposition should be accepted and this portion of the text taken as a reproof of the ancients, because the contraries seem to be explained in a forced way by others, whereas our introduction is more in accord with what follows in the next part of the text; in addition, it agrees with Albert's interpretation.

9.   Thirdly, he says, *Now the reason why enunciations predicating* 22b3 *necessity do not follow in the same way as the others,* etc. Here Aristotle shows why enunciations predicating impossibility and necessity do not follow in a similar way upon those predicating possibility. This was the error made by the ancients in both the first and second orders, for in the first order they posited the simple negative of the impossible, and in a similar way the simple negative of the necessary, and in the second order their declined negatives, the reason being that they inferred those predicating impossibility and necessity in a similar way. The cause of this error, then, and *the reason why* enunciations predicating necessity *do not follow* the possible *in the same way,* i.e., in a similar mode, *as the others,* i.e., as the impossibles, is that *the impossible expresses the same meaning as the necessary,* i.e., is equivalent to the necessary, *contrarily,*[116] i.e., taken in a contrary mode, and not in the same mode. For if something is impossible to be, we do not infer, therefore it is necessary to be, but it is necessary not to be. Since, therefore, the impossible and necessary mutually follow each other when their dictums are taken in a contrary mode—and not when their dictums are taken in a similar mode—it follows that the impossible and necessary are not related in the same way to the possible, but in a contrary way. For the negated dictum of the necessary follows upon that possible which follows the affirmed dictum of the impossible, and contrarily. Why this is so will be explained later. Therefore, the ancients erred when they located similar enunciations of the impossible and necessary in the first and in the second orders.

116 The Greek here is, ". . . ὅτι ἐναντίως τὸ ἀδύνατον τῷ ἀναγκαίῳ ἀποδίδοται, τὸ αὐτὸ δυνάμενον." Moerbeke's Latin is, ". . . quoniam contrarie, impossibile esse, necessario redditur idem valens."

[209]

22a38 10.   Hence it appears that our exposition is more in conformity with Aristotle. For he introduced this text to manifest these words: *It is evident that the case here is not the same,* etc. By taking this meaning, then, these words are made clear through the cause. Moreover, it is evident that here the cause is given of a true dissimilitude between necessaries and impossibles in following the possibles, and not of a dissimilitude falsely held by the ancients, for from a true cause only the truth is concluded. Therefore in reproving the ancients it must be understood that a true dissimilitude between the necessary and impossible in following the possible, which they did not heed, has been proposed, and now has been made manifest. It will be clear from what will be said later that the dissimilitude posited by the ancients between the necessary and impossible is falsely posited, for it will be shown that contradictories of the necessary follow contradictories of the possible inversely, and that in this they do not differ from enunciations predicating impossibility. They do differ, however, in the way we have indicated, i.e., the dictum of the possibles and of the impossibles following on them is similar, but the dictum of the possibles and of the necessaries following on them is contrary, as will be seen clearly later.

22b10 11.   Fourthly, when he says, *Or is it impossible to arrange the contradictions of enunciations predicating necessity in this way?* he manifests another point he had proposed, namely, that contradictories of enunciations predicating necessity were badly placed according to consequence by the ancients when they ordered them thus: the contradictory negation to "necessary to be," i.e., "not necessary to be," in the first order, and the contradictory negation to "necessary not to be," i.e., "not necessary not to be," in the second.

Aristotle only proves that this mode of consequence is incorrect in the first order, for when this is known the mistake in the second order is readily seen. He does this by an argument leading to an impossibility. "Possible to be" follows upon "necessary to be"; otherwise "not possible to be" would follow, which it manifestly implies. "Not impossible to be" follows upon "possible to be" as is evident, and, according to the ancients, in the first order, "not necessary to be" follows upon "not impossible to be." Therefore, from first to last, "not necessary to be" follows upon "necessary to be," which is inadmissible because there is an obvious implication of contradiction. Therefore, it is erroneous to say that "not necessary to be" follows in the first order.

He says, then, that in fact it is impossible to posit contradictions of the necessary according to consequence as the ancients posited them, i.e.,[117] in the first order the contradictory negation of "necessary to be,"

---

[117] Cajetan is returning here to Aristotle's text (22b 10), which is

i.e., "not necessary to be" and in the second the contradictory negation of "necessary not to be," i.e., "not necessary not to be." For "possible to be" follows upon "necessary to be"; if not, i.e., if you deny this consequence, the negation of the possible follows upon "necessary to be," since the possible must either be asserted of the necessary or denied, the reason being that of anything there is a true affirmation or a true negation. Therefore, if you say that "possible to be" does not follow upon "necessary to be," but "not possible to be" does follow, then, since the latter is equivalent to the former, i.e., "not possible to be" to "impossible to be," "impossible to be" follows upon "necessary to be" and the same thing will be "necessary to be" and "impossible to be," which cannot be admitted. Consequently, the first inference was good, i.e., "It is necessary to be, therefore it is possible to be."

But again, "possible to be" follows upon "not impossible to be," as is evident in the first order, and according to the ancients, "not necessary to be" follows upon "not impossible to be" in the same first order. Therefore, from first to last we arrive at this: "not necessary to be" follows upon "necessary to be," which is unlikely, not to say impossible.

12.   There is a doubt about this, for in I *Priorum,* it is said that the not necessary follows upon the possible,[118] while here the opposite is said.

The possible, however, is taken in two ways: commonly, and thus it is superior to the necessary and the contingent to either of two alternatives, as is the case with animal in relation to man and cow; taken in this way, the not necessary does not follow upon the possible, just as not-man does not follow upon animal. In another way the possible is taken for one part of the possible commonly, i.e., for the possible or contingent to either of two alternatives, namely, for what can be and not be. The not necessary follows upon the possible taken in this way, for what can be and not be is not necessary to be, and likewise is not necessary not to be.

In the *Prior Analytics,* then, Aristotle is speaking of the possible in particular; here of the possible commonly.

13.   When he says, *But in fact neither "necessary to be" nor "neces-*   22b17
sary not to be" follow upon "possible to be," etc., he determines the truth. First he determines which enunciation of the necessary follows upon the possible; secondly, he orders the consequents of all of the modals, where he says, *Thus, these contradictions also follow in the*   22b26
way indicated, etc.

worded as a question in the Greek but not in the Latin; nor is the "in   fact" (*certe*) in the Greek text.
[118] *Prior Anal.* I, 13, 32a 28 and 32b 15.

Aristotle has reproved the ancients in two ways; on the basis of these two he now proves which enunciation of the necessary follows upon the possible. What he intends to show is that "not necessary not to be" follows upon "possible to be." The first argument is taken from a locus of division. "Not necessary to be" does not follow upon "possible to be" (as has been proved), but neither does "necessary to be" nor "necessary not to be." Therefore, "not necessary not to be" follows upon "possible to be," since there are no more enunciations of the necessary.

He first proposes the remaining two members that are to be excluded from this common division: *But in fact neither "necessary to be" nor "necessary not to be" follow upon "possible to be."* Then he proves this: no formal consequent diminishes its antecedent, for if it did, the opposite of the consequent would stand with the antecedent; but both of these, namely, "necessary to be" and "necessary not to be," diminish "possible to be"; therefore, etc.

The major is therefore implied and he gives the proof of the minor when he says that "possible to be" admits of two possibilities, namely, "to be" and "not to be"; but of these, namely, "necessary to be" and "necessary not to be" (whichever should be true), these two, "to be" and "not to be," will not be true at the same time in potency. He explains the first point thus: when I say "possible to be" it is at once possible to be and not to be. With respect to the second, he adds: if you should say, "necessary to be" or "necessary not to be," both do not remain, i.e., possible to be and not to be do not remain, for if a thing is necessary to be, possibility not to be is excluded, and if it is necessary not to be, possibility to be is removed. Both of these, then, diminish the antecedent, possible to be, for it is extended to "to be" and "not to be," etc.

Thirdly, he concludes: it remains, therefore, that "not necessary not to be" accompanies "possible to be," and consequently will have to be placed in the first order.

14. A difficulty arises at this point with respect to his saying that the necessary does not follow upon the possible, since he has also said that the not necessary does not follow upon it.[119] For the necessary and the not necessary are opposed contradictorily, and since of anything there is a true affirmation or negation, it seems impossible to avoid the conclusion that either the necessary or the not necessary follows upon the possible; and since the necessary does not follow, the not necessary must follow, as the ancients said. Furthermore, the difficulty is augmented by the fact that Aristotle just used such a mode of argumenta-

[119] Cf. 22a 39.

tion when, to prove that the possible follows upon the necessary, he said, *for if not, the negation will follow;* for it is necessary either to affirm 22b11 or deny.

15. In order to resolve this, we must recall the relationship between the possible and the necessary, namely, that the possible is superior to the necessary. Now the superior potentially contains its own inferior and the opposite of it in such a way that neither of them is actually appropriated by the superior, but each is possible to it; as in the case of man and not-man in relation to animal. We must also consider that the proportion of the superior as related to the affirmation and negation of one inferior is the same (which is the proportion of some subject to the affirmative and negative of a future contingent), for it is had by neither of the two, and the potency to either is kept. Accordingly, as in future contingents neither the affirmation nor the negation is determinately true, but under disjunction one is necessarily true (as was concluded at the end of the first book),[120] so neither the affirmation nor negation of the inferior follows upon the affirmation or negation of the superior determinately, but under disjunction one follows necessarily. This, for instance, is not valid: "It is animal, therefore it is man," nor is "therefore it is not man" valid, but, "therefore it is man or it is not man."

Since, then, the possible is superior to the necessary, Aristotle has correctly determined that neither part of the contradiction of the necessary determinately follows upon the possible. However, he has not said that under disjunction neither follows; for this would be opposed to the first principle, that of anything there is a true or false affirmation.

The response to what was added, beginning with "Furthermore, the difficulty is augmented," etc., is based upon the same point. Since the necessary is inferior to the possible, and the inferior does not include its superior in potency but in act, the superior must follow determinately upon the inferior; otherwise the contradiction of it would follow determinately. Hence, because of the dissimilar relationship between the necessary and the possible and not possible on the one hand, and between the possible and the necessary and not necessary on the other, the movement of the earlier argument to one part of the contradiction determinately was quite right, and the movement here to neither determinately was quite right.

16. There is another slight difficulty, for it seems that Aristotle takes the possible in a different way in the preceding text and in this. There he takes it commonly as it follows upon the necessary; here he seems to

120 18b 17; St. Thomas, Lesson XII, nn. 12 ff.

take it specifically for the possible that is indifferent to alternatives, since he says that the possible is at once possible to be and not to be.

But in fact Aristotle has used the possible uniformly. Nor are his words at variance, for it is also true to say of the possible as common that it admits of both possibilities, i.e., of "to be" and "not to be"; first, because whatever is verified of its inferior is verified also of its superior, although not in the same mode; secondly, because the possible as common determines neither part of the contradiction to itself and consequently admits of either happening, although it does not affirm a potency to each part, as does the possible to either of two alternatives.

17.   The second grounds for proving the same thing corresponds to the tacit objection of the ancients he excluded above: *For this,* he says, *is true also with respect to "necessary to be,"* etc. It should be noted here that Aristotle subsumes under the major cited as a proof for the position of the ancients (namely, contradictories of consequences convertibly following each other mutually follow upon each other) this minor: but the contradictories of those following upon each other convertibly in the third order (i.e., of "not possible to be" and "necessary not to be") are "possible to be" and "not necessary not to be" (for they are opposed to them by negation of mode); therefore, these two (i.e., "possible to be" and "not necessary not to be") follow upon each other and are to be placed in the first order.

22b23   Hence, with respect to the basis of the above argument, he says, *For this,* i.e., what has been said, *is true,* i.e., is shown to be true, *also with respect to "necessary not to be,"* i.e., of the opposite of "not necessary not to be," i.e., "necessary not to be." Or, *For this,* namely, "not necessary not to be," *is true,* namely, is the true contradictory of "necessary not to be."[121] He gives the minor when he says, *For "not nec-*

---

[121] The Greek here is, ". . . τοῦτο γὰρ ἀληθὲς καὶ κατὰ τοῦ ἀναγκαῖον εἶναι." Moerbeke's Latin is, "Haec enim vero est, et de necesse esse." Cajetan has, "Hoc enim verum est, et de necesse *non* esse" (italics added). He gives as an alternative to the above, "Hoc enim verum est, contradictorium illius de necesse *non* esse." There are no Greek manuscripts with the οὐ (non) before εἶναι (esse). The use of γὰρ (for) at the beginning of this phrase and at the beginning of the next sentence in which the point is made that "not necessary not to be" is the contradictory of "necessary not to be" might

lead one to think that Cajetan's reading and interpretation (i.e., with a "not") is the correct one. On the other hand, the phrase in question is the last part of Aristotle's concluding sentence in the Greek. The sentence reads, "It remains, therefore, that 'not necessary not to be' follows upon 'possible to be'; *for this is true also with respect to 'necessary to be'*" (italics added). If there is no οὐ (non) in this latter phrase, and it is attached to the whole preceding argument as a part of the conclusion, then what Aristotle seems to be saying is that just as "not necessary not to be" follows

[214]

essary not to be" is the contradictory of what follows upon *"not possible to be."*

Then he states this explicitly: for "not possible to be," which is the source of the third order is followed by this impossible, namely, "impossible to be," and by this one of the necessary, namely, "necessary not to be," of which the negation or contradictory is "not necessary not to be." And since, other things being equal, the mode is negated, and, "possible to be" is (it is understood) the contradictory of "not possible to be," therefore, these two mutually follow upon each other, namely, "possible to be" and "not necessary not to be," as contradictories of the two mutually following upon each other.

18.   When he says, *Thus, these contradictions also follow in the way*   22b26
indicated, etc., he orders all of the consequents of modals according to his own opinion. He says, then, that these contradictions, namely, of the necessary, follow those of the possible, according to the foresaid and approved mode of those of the impossible. For just as contradictories of the impossible follow upon contradictories of the possible, although inversely, so contradictories of the necessary follow contradictories of the possible inversely. In the latter, however, as has been said, there is a dissimilarity in that the dictum of the contradictories of the possible and impossible is similar, but the dictum of the contradictories of the possible and necessary is contrary. This can be seen in the following table.

CONSEQUENTS OF MODAL ENUNCIATIONS POSITED AND ORDERED BY ARISTOTLE ACCORDING TO FOUR ORDERS

First Order	Third Order
It is possible to be	It is not possible to be
It is contingent to be	It is not contingent to be
It is not impossible to be	It is impossible to be
It is not necessary not to be	It is necessary not to be
Second Order	**Fourth Order**
It is possible not to be	It is not possible not to be
It is contingent not to be	It is not contingent not to be
It is not impossible not to be	It is impossible not to be
It is not necessary to be	It is necessary to be

Here you see that there is no difference between Aristotle and the ancients except in the first two orders with respect to those of the necessary. The ancients inverted the position of these, placing the necessary that should have been placed in the first order in the second order, and the one that should have been in the second in the first.

upon "possible to be," so "necessary to be" follows upon "not possible not to be," i.e., there is an inverse parallel between the two.

Notice, too, that he has ordered them in such a way that the contradictories of those following upon each other convertibly, always follow each other, for each one in the first order is the contradictory of each one in the third order, and similarly, each of the fourth order the contradictory of each in the second. This the ancients did not observe.

LESSON XI

Whether "Possible To Be" Follows Upon "Necessary To Be"

22b 29   But it may be questioned whether "possible to be" follows upon "necessary to be." Yet if not, the contradictory, "not possible to be," would have to follow; or if someone should say that this is not the contradictory, then "possible not to be." But both of these are false in regard to that which is necessary to be.

22b 33   On the other hand, it seems possible for the same thing to be cut and not to be cut, and to be and not to be, and thus it would follow that what is necessary to be is possible not to be, which is false.

22b 36   It is evident by now that not every possibility of being or walking is one that admits of opposites. There are those of which this is not true. First of all, this is not true of potentialities which are not according to reason, as fire, which has an irrational potentiality, the power to heat. Potentialities that are in conjunction with reason are capable of more than one and of contraries; but not all irrational potentialities are capable of contraries; as has been said, fire does not have the potentiality to heat and not to heat, nor does anything that always acts have this potentiality; however, even some of the irrational potencies are simultaneously capable of opposites. We have spoken of this in order to show that not every potentiality is a potentiality to opposites, not even all those that are called potentialities according to the same notion.

---

1.   Now that he has explained the consequents of modals, Aristotle raises a question about one of the points that has already been determined, namely, that the possible follows upon the necessary. He first raises the question and then settles it where he says, *It is evident by now*   22b36 *that not every possibility of being or walking is one that admits of opposites,* etc. Secondly, he establishes another order of the same consequents from the determination of the present question, where he says *Indeed the necessary and not necessary may well be the principle of all*   23a18 *that is or is not,* etc.[122]

First, then, he raises the question: *But it may be questioned*   22b29 *whether "possible to be" follows upon "necessary to be."* Secondly, he argues to the affirmative part: *Yet if not, the contradictory, "not possible to be," would have to follow,* as was deduced earlier, for either the affirmation or the negation is true of anything. And if someone should say

---

[122] 23a 18; Cajetan, Lesson XII, n. 7.

"not possible to be" is not the contradictory of "possible to be," because he wants to avoid the conclusion by saying that neither of these follows upon "necessary to be," this may be conceded, although what he says is false. But then he will have to say that the contradictory of "possible to be" is "possible not to be," for the contradictory of "possible to be" has to be either "not possible to be" or "possible not to be." But if he says this, he will fall into another error, for it is false to say it is not possible to be of that which is necessary to be, and it is false to say it is possible not to be. Consequently, neither follows upon it, for no enunciation follows upon an enunciation whose truth it destroys. Therefore, "possible to be" follows upon "necessary to be."

22b33   2.   Thirdly, he argues to the negative part where he says, *On the other hand, it seems possible for the same thing to be cut and not to be cut,* etc. His argument is as follows: If "possible to be" follows upon "necessary to be," then, since "possible not to be" follows upon the possible (through conversion to the opposite quality, as is said in I *Priorum*,[123] for the same thing is possible to be and not to be), from first to last it will follow that the necessary is possible not to be, which is clearly false.

In this argument, Aristotle supplies a hypothesis opposed to the position that possible to be follows upon necessary to be: *On the other hand, it seems possible for the same thing to be cut and not to be cut,* for instance a garment, *and to be and not to be,* for instance a house. Therefore, from first to last, necessary to be will be possible not to be. But this is false. Therefore, the hypothesis that the possible follows upon the necessary is false.

22b36   3.   When he says, *It is evident by now that not every possibility of being or walking,* etc., he answers the question he proposed. First, he manifests the truth simply, then applies it to the question where he says,
23a15   "*So it is not true to say the latter possible of what is necessary simply,* etc.[124]

First, then, he proposes the truth he is going to explain: *It is*
22b36   *evident by now that not every possibility of being or walking,* i.e., of operating; that is, not everything possible according to first or second act admits of opposites, i.e., has access to opposites; there are some possibles of which it is not true to say that they are capable of opposites.

Then, since the possible arises from potency, he manifests how potency is related to opposites; for it will be clear from this how the possible is related to opposites. First he manifests this in potencies having the same notion; secondly, in those that are called potencies equi-

---

[123] *Prior Anal.* I, 13, 32a 31 ff.   [124] 23a 15; Cajetan, Lesson XII, n. 5.

vocally where he says, *But some are called potentialities equivocally,*
etc.[125] With respect to the way in which potencies of the same specific
notion are related to opposites, he does three things. First of all he
manifests how an irrational potency is related to opposites; an irrational
potency, he says, is not a potency that is capable of opposites.

4.   It must be noted in this connection that active potency, since it
is the principle by which we act on something else, is divided into rational and irrational potency, as is said in IX *Metaphysicae.*[126] Rational
potency operates in connection with reason and choice; for example, the
art of medicine by which the physician, knowing and willing what is
expedient in healing an illness, applies a remedy. Irrational potency
operates according to its own natural disposition, not according to reason
and liberty; for example, the heat of fire is an irrational potency, because it heats, not as it knows and wills, but as its nature requires.

In the *Metaphysics,* a twofold difference between these potencies
is assigned which is relevant here. The first is that an irrational
active potency is not capable of two opposites, but is determined to
one opposite, whether "opposite" is taken contradictorily or contrarily; e.g., heat cannot heat and not heat, which are opposed contradictorily; nor can it heat and cool, which are contraries, but is determined to heating. Understand this per se, for heat can cool accidentally,
either by destroying the matter of heat, namely, the humid, or through
alternation of the contrary. It also has the potentiality not to heat accidentally, if that which can be heated is lacking. A rational potency,
on the other hand, is capable of opposites, both contradictorily and contrarily; for by the art of medicine the physician can employ a remedy
and not employ it, which are contradictories, and employ healing and
harmful remedies, which are contraries.

The second difference is that an irrational active potency necessarily operates when a subject is present and impediments are withdrawn; for heat necessarily heats when a subject that can be heated is
present, and nothing impedes it. A rational potency, however, does not
necessarily operate when a subject is present; e.g., when a sick man is
present the physician is not forced to employ a remedy.

5.   The reasons for these differences are given in the *Metaphysics,*
but let us return to the text. Explaining how an irrational potency is
related to opposites, he says, *First of all, this is not true,* i.e., it is not true
to say that there is a potency to opposites *in those which are not according to reason,* i.e., whose power is through irrational potencies; *as fire
which is calefactive,* i.e., capable of heating, *has this power,* i.e., this

[125] 23a 6; Cajetan, Lesson XII, n. 1.   [126] *Metaph.* Θ, 2, 1046a 36 ff.

irrational potentiality,[127] since it is not able to cool, nor is it in its power to heat and not to heat.

Note that he speaks here of a first kind. This is in relation to a second genus of the possible which he will speak of later, in which there is not a potency to opposites either.[128]

6.   Secondly, he shows how a rational potency is related to op-
22b39 posites, i.e., it is capable of opposites: *Therefore potentialities that are in conjunction with reason,* i.e., rational potencies, *are capable of contraries,* not only of two, but even of many; for example, a physician by the art of medicine can employ many pairs of contraries and he can abstain from doing or not doing many things.

He begins with "therefore" so as to imply that this follows from what has been said.[129] The argument would be: properties of opposites are opposites; an irrational potency, because it is irrational, does not extend itself to opposites; therefore a rational potency, because it is rational, has access to opposites.

7.   Thirdly, he explains what he has said about irrational potencies. He will assign the reason for doing this later. He makes the point that what he has said about irrational potentiality, i.e., that it is not capable of opposites, is not true universally, but particularly.

It should be noted here that irrational potency is divided into active potency, which is the principle of acting, and passive potency, which is the principle of being acted upon; e.g., potency to heat is divided into potentiality to heat and potentiality to be heated.

Now it is true that active irrational potencies are not capable of opposites, as was explained. This is not true, however, of passive potencies, for what can be heated can also be cooled, because the matter is the same, i.e., the passive potency of contraries, as is said in II *De caelo et mundo.*[130] It can also not be heated, since the subject of privation and of form is the same, as is said in I *Physic.*[131]

23a2   Therefore, in explaining about irrational potencies, he says, *But not all irrational potentialities* should be understood to be excluded from the capacity of opposites. Those like the potentiality of fire to heat are to be excluded (for it is evident that fire cannot not heat), and uni-

---

[127] The Greek for the quotation is: ". . . οἷον τὸ πῦρ θερμαντικὸν καὶ ἔχει δύναμιν ἄλογον." The Latin of Moerbeke is: ". . . ut ignis calefactibilis est, et habet vim irrationalem." Cajetan has "calefactivus" for "calefactibilis."

[128] *Infra,* Cajetan, Lesson XII, n. 4.

[129] Actually Aristotle does not begin this sentence with "therefore." He uses οὖν, which simply indicates a continuation of what he is saying. The Latin text has "igitur."

[130] *DeCaelo et Mundo* II, 7, 286a 23 ff.

[131] *Phys.* I, 7, 189b 32 ff.

versally, whatever others are potencies of such a kind that they always act, i.e., the ones that of themselves cannot not act, but are necessitated by their form always to act. All active irrational potencies are of this kind, as we have explained. There are others, however, of such a condition that even though they are irrational potencies (i.e., passive) are simultaneously capable of certain opposites; for example, air can be heated and cooled.

"Simultaneously" modifies "are capable" and not "opposites." What he means is that the thing simultaneously has a passive potency to each opposite, and not that it has a passive potency to have both opposites simultaneously, for it is impossible to have opposites at one and the same time. Hence it is customary and correct to say that in these there is simultaneity of potency, not potency of simultaneity. Therefore, irrational potency is excluded from the capacity of opposites, not completely, but according to its part, namely, according to active potencies.

8. Because it might seem superfluous to have added the differences between active and passive irrational potencies, since enough had already been said to show that not every potency is of opposites, Aristotle gives the reason for this. It was not only to make it known that not every potency is of opposites, speaking of potency most commonly, but also that not all that are called potencies according to the same species are capable of opposites. For all irrational potencies are included under one species of irrational potency, and yet not all are capable of opposites, but only the passive potencies. It was not superfluous, therefore, to point out the difference between passive and active irrational potencies, since this was necessary in order to show that not all potencies of the same species are capable of opposites.

"This" in the phrase "this has been said" could designate each difference, the one between rational and irrational potencies, and the one between active and passive irrational potencies. The meaning is, then, that we have said this to show that not every potentiality which is said according to the same notion of physical power—namely, because it can be in something as rational and irrational—not even every potentiality which is contained under the same species, as active and passive under the species irrational, is capable of opposites.

The Explanation of Potencies that Are Called Such Equivocally and the Determination, Through the Notion of the Impossible, of the Possible that Follows Upon the Necessary

23a 6   But some are called potentialities equivocally, for "possible" has more than one meaning. On the one hand, it is that which is true of a thing because it is in act, as walking is possible to someone because he is actually walking, and, in general, possible is said of that which is possible to be because it is already actualized. On the other hand, possible is said of that which can be actualized, as walking is possible to someone because he could walk.

23a 11   This latter potentiality is only in that which is movable, but the former is also in the immovable. Now it is true to say, both of that which is walking already and is actual, and of that which could walk, that it is not impossible that it walk or be.

23 a15   So it is not true to say the latter possible [i.e., the possible which could be] of what is necessary simply, but it is true to say the former of it. Therefore, since the universal follows upon the part,[132] possible to be follows upon that which necessarily is, though not every kind of possible does.

23a 18   Indeed the necessary and not necessary may well be the principle of all that is or is not and the others must be regarded as consequent to these.

23a 21   It is evident, then, from what has been said that that which necessarily is, actually is; and, if eternal things are prior, that actuality is prior to potentiality.

23a 23   Some things are actualities without potentiality, namely, the primary substances. Others are actualities with potentiality—those that are prior in nature, but posterior in time. And some never are actualities but are only potentialities.

---

1.   Aristotle now proposes to show in what way potencies that are called equivocal are related to opposites. He first explains the nature of this kind of potency, and then gives the difference and agreement
23a11 between these and the foresaid, where he says, *This latter potentiality*

132 That is, the universal follows upon   therefore man is.
the subjective part, e.g., Socrates is,

is only in that which is movable, but the former is also in the immovable, etc.

In V and IX *Metaphysicae*,[133] Aristotle divides potency into those that are called potencies for the same reason, and those that have the name potency for another reason than the aforesaid potencies. The latter are named "potencies" equivocally. Under the first member are included all active and passive, rational and irrational potencies, for whatever are said to be possible through the active or passive potency they have, are potencies for the same reason, i.e., because there is in them the originative force of something active or passive.

Mathematical and logical potencies are included under the second member of this division. That by which a line can lead to a square we call a mathematical potency, for a line constitutes a square when protracted back to itself. That by which two terms can be joined in an enunciation without contradiction is a logical potency. Logical potency also comprises that which is called "potency" because it is. The latter [mathematical and logical potencies] are named from the former equivocally because they predicate no active or passive capacity; and what is said to be possible in these ways is not termed possible in virtue of having the capacity to do or undergo as in the first case. Hence, since the potencies related to opposites are active or passive, the ones that are called potentialities equivocally are not related to opposites.

These, then, are the potencies he speaks of when he says *But*   23a6 *some are called potentialities equivocally,* and therefore they are not related to opposites.

2.   To clarify the kind of potency that is called equivocal, he gives the usual division of the possible through which this is known. "Possible," he says, is not said in one way, but in two. Something is said to be possible because it is true as in act, i.e., inasmuch as it actually is; for example, it is possible to walk when one is already walking, and in general, i.e., universally, that is said to be possible which is possible to be because it is already in act. Something is said to be possible in the second way, not because it actually is, but because it is about to act, i.e., because it can act; for instance, it is possible for someone to walk because he is about to walk.

Notice here that by this two-membered division of the possible he makes the division of potency posited above evident a posteriori, for the possible is named from potency. Under the first member of the possible he signifies potencies equivocally; under the second, potencies univocally, i.e., active and passive potencies. He means to show, then,

---

133 *Metaph.* Δ, 12, 1019a 15 ff.; and Θ,
     1, 1046a 4 ff.

that since possible is said in two ways, potentiality is also twofold. He explains equivocal potentialities in terms of only one member, namely, those that are called possible because they are, since this was sufficient for his purpose.

23a11   3.   When he says, *This latter potentiality is only in that which is movable, but the former is also in the immovable*, etc., he specifies the difference between each potency. This last potency, he says, [possible because it can be] which is called physical potency, is only in things that are movable; but the former is in movable and immovable things. The possible that is named from the potency which can act, but is not yet acting, cannot be found without the mutability of that which is said to be possible in this way. For if that which can act now and is not acting, should act, it is necessary that it be changed from rest to operation. On the other hand, that which is called possible because it is, requires no mutability in that which is said to be possible in this way, for to be in act, which is the basis of such a possibility, is found in necessary things, in immutable things, and in mobile things. Therefore, the possible which is called logical, is more common than the one we customarily call physical.

4.   Then he shows that there is a correspondence between these possibles when he adds that not impossible to be is true of both of these potentialities and possibles, e.g., to walk is not impossible for that which is already walking in act, i.e., acting, and it is not impossible for that which could now walk; that is, they agree in that not impossible is verified of both—of either what is said to be possible from the fact that it is in act or of what is said to be possible from the fact that it could be. Consequently, the necessary is verified as possible, for possible follows upon not impossible.

The possible that is already in act is the second genus of the possible in which access is not found to both opposites, of which Aris-
22b38   totle spoke when he said, *First of all this is not true of the potentialities which are not according to reason*, etc. For that which is said to be possible because it is already in act is already determined, since it is supposed as being in act. Therefore, not every possible is the possible of alternatives, whether we speak of the physical possible or the logical.

23a15   5.   When he says, *So it is not true to say the latter possible of what is necessary simply*, etc., he applies the truth he has determined to what has been proposed. First, by way of a conclusion from what has been said, he shows the relationship of each possible to the necessary. So, he says, it is not true to say and predicate this possible, namely physical, which is only in mobile things, of the necessary simply, because what

[224]

is necessary simply cannot be otherwise. The physical possible, however, can be thus and otherwise, as has been said.

He adds "simply" because the necessary is manifold. There is the necessary for well-being and there is also the necessary from supposition, but it is not our business to treat these, only to indicate them. In order, then, to avoid the modes of the necessary that do not have the notion of the necessary perfectly and in every way, he adds "simply." Now the physical possible is not verified of this kind of necessary [i.e., of the necessary simply], but it is true to enunciate the logical possible, the one found in immovable things, of the necessary, since it takes away nothing of the necessity.

The argument introduced for the negative part of this question[134] is destroyed by this. The error in that argument was the inference—by way of conversion into the opposite quality—of the possible to both alternatives from the necessary.

6.   Then he replies to the question formally. He states that the affirmative part of the question must be held, namely, that the possible follows upon the necessary. Next, he assigns the cause. The whole universal follows constructively upon its subjective part; but the necessary is a subjective part of the possible, because the possible is divided into logical and physical and under the logical is comprehended the necessary; therefore, the possible follows upon the necessary. Hence he says, *Therefore, since the universal follows upon the part,* i.e., since the whole 23a16 universal follows upon its subjective part, to be possible to be, i.e., possible, as the whole universal, follows upon that which necessarily is, i.e., necessary, as a subjective part. He adds: *though not every kind of possible does,* i.e., not every species of the possible follows; just as animal follows upon man, but not in every way, i.e., it does not follow upon man according to all its subjective parts, for it is not valid to say, "He is a man, therefore he is an irrational animal."

By this proof of the validity of the affirmative part, Aristotle has explicitly destroyed the reasoning adduced for the negative part, which, as is evident, erred according to the fallacy of the consequent in inferring the possible from the necessary by descending to one species of the possible.

7.   When he says, *Indeed the necessary and not necessary may well* 23a18 *be the principle of all that is or is not,* etc., he disposes the same consequences of modals in another arrangement, placing the necessary before all the other modes. First he proposes the order of modals and then assigns the cause of the order where he says, *It is evident, then,* 23a21

---

[134] Aristotle's argument is at 22b 33 of
the preceding lesson, Cajetan, n. 2.

from what has been said that that which necessarily is, actually is, etc.

Indeed, he says, *the necessary and not necessary may well be the principle of the "to be" or "not to be" of all modal enunciations,*[135] i.e., the necessary and not necessary is the principle of affirmatives or negatives. And the others, i.e., the possible, contingent, and impossible to be must be considered as consequent to these, i.e., to the necessary and not necessary.

THE CONSEQUENTS OF MODAL ENUNCIATIONS ACCORDING TO THE FOUR ORDERS, POSITED AND DISPOSED BY ARISTOTLE IN ANOTHER APPROPRIATE ARRANGEMENT

First Order	Third Order
It is necessary to be	It is not necessary to be
It is not possible not to be	It is possible not to be
It is not contingent not to be	It is contingent not to be
It is impossible not to be	It is not impossible not to be

Second Order	Fourth Order
It is necessary not to be	It is not necessary not to be
It is not possible to be	It is possible to be
It is not contingent to be	It is contingent to be
It is impossible to be	It is not impossible to be

Nothing is changed here except the enunciations predicating necessity. They have been allotted the first place, whereas in the former table they were placed last.

When he says "may well be," it is not because he is in any doubt, but because he is proposing this here without a determinate proof.

23a21   8.   When he says, *It is evident, then, from what has been said that that which necessarily is, actually is,* etc., he gives the cause of this order. First he gives the reason for placing the necessary before the possible: the sempiternal is prior to the temporal; but "necessary" signifies sempiternal (because it signifies "to be in act," excluding all mutability and consequently temporality, which is not imaginable without movement), and the possible signifies temporality (since it does not exclude the possibility of being and not being); therefore, the necessary is rightly placed before the possible.

He proposes the minor of this argument when he says, *It is evident, then, from what has been said* in treating the necessary, that that which necessarily is, is totally in act, since it excludes all mutability and

---

[135] The Greek text has, ". . . πάντων ἤ εἶναι ἤ μὴ εἶναι. . . ." Moerbeke's Latin is, ". . . omnium vel esse, vel non esse. . . ." Cajetan has, ". . . *omnium enunciationum modalium* vel esse vel non esse . . ." (italics added). Cajetan interprets the πάντων (*omnium*) as limited to modal enunciations.

potency to the opposite—for if it could be changed into the opposite in any way, then it would not be necessary. Next he gives the major, which is in the mode of an antecedent conditional: *and if eternal things are prior to temporal,* etc. Finally, he posits the conclusion: those that are wholly in act in every way, namely necessary, are prior to the potential, i.e., to possibles, which do not have being in act wholly although they are compatible with it.

9. Then he says, *Some things are actualities without potentiality,* 23a23 *namely, the primary substances,* etc. Here he assigns the cause of the whole order established among modals. The grades of the universe are threefold. Some things are in act without potentiality, i.e., not combined with potency. These are the primary substances—not those we have called "first" in the present work because they principally and especially sustain—but those that are first because they are the causes of all things, namely, the Intelligences. In others, act is accompanied with possibility, as is the case with all mobile things, which, according to what they have of act, are prior in nature to themselves according to what they have of potency, although the contrary is the case in regard to the order of time. According to what they have of potency they are prior in time to themselves according to what they have of act. For example, according to time, Socrates first was able to be a philosopher, then he actually was a philosopher. In Socrates therefore, potency precedes act according to the order of time. The converse is the case, however, in the order of nature, perfection, and dignity, for when he actually was a philosopher, Socrates was regarded as prior according to dignity, i.e., more worthy and more perfect than when he was potentially a philosopher. Hence, when we consider each order, i.e., nature and time, in one and the same thing, the order of potency and act is reversed.

Others never are in act but are only in potency, e.g., motion, time, the infinite division of magnitude, and the infinite augmentation of number. These, as is said in IX *Metaphysicae*,[136] never terminate in act, for it is repugnant to their nature. None of them is ever such that something of it is not expected, and consequently they can only be in potency. These, however, must be treated in another place.

10. This has been said so that once the order of the universe has been seen it should appear that we were imitating it in our present ordering. The necessary, which signifies "to be in act" without potentiality or mutability, has been placed first, in imitation of the first grade of the universe. We have put the possible and contingent, both of which signify act with possibility, in second place in conformity with the second grade

[136] *Metaph.* Θ, 6, 1048b 9-17.

of the universe. The possible has been placed before the contingent because the possible relates to act whereas the contingent, as the force of the name suggests, relates to the defect of a cause—which pertains to potency, for defect follows upon potency. The order of these is similar to the order in the second part of the universe, where act is prior to potency according to nature, though not according to time.

We have reserved the last place for the impossible because it signifies what never will be, just as the last part of the universe is said to be that which is never in act. Thus, a beautifully proportioned order is established when the divine is observed.

11. Since the consequents of modals, i.e., those placed under each other, are their equivalents in meaning, and these are produced by the varying position of the negation changing the quality or quantity or both, a few things must be said about their quality and quantity to complete our knowledge of them.

The nature of the whole arises from the parts, and therefore we should note the following things about the parts of the modal enunciation. The subject of the modal enunciation asserts to be or not to be, and is a singular dictum, and contains in itself the subject of the dictum. The predicate of a modal enunciation, namely, the mode, is the total predicate (since it explicitly or implicitly contains the verb, which is always a sign of something predicated of another, for which reason Aristotle says that the mode is a determining addition) and contains in itself distributive force according to the parts of time. The necessary and impossible distribute in all time either simply or in a limited way; the possible and contingent distribute according to some time commonly.

12. As a consequence of these five conditions there is a twofold quality and a threefold quantity in any modal. The twofold quality results from the fact that both the subject and the predicate of a modal have a verb in them. One of these is called the quality of the dictum, the other the quality of the mode. This is why it was said above that there is an enunciation which is affirmative of mode and not of dictum, and conversely.[137]

Of the threefold quantity of a modal enunciation, one arises from the fact that the subject of the modal contains in it the subject of the dictum. This is called the quantity of the subject of the dictum, and is distinguished into universal, particular, and singular, as in the case of the quantity of an absolute enunciation. For we can say: "That 'Socrates,' 'some man,' 'every man,'" or "'no man,' run is possible."

The second quantity is that of the dictum, which arises from the

[137] Cf. Cajetan, Lesson X, n. 3.

fact that the subject of one modal is one dictum. This is a unique singularity, for every dictum of a modal is the singular of that universal, i.e., dictum. "That man be white is possible" means "This dictum, 'that man be white,' is possible." "This dictum" is singular in quantity, just as "this man" is. Hence, every modal is singular with respect to dictum, although with respect to the subject of the dictum it is universal or particular.

The third quantity is that of the mode, or modal quantity, which arises from the fact that the predicate of the modal, i.e., the mode, has distributive force. This is distinguished into universal and particular.

13.   Now, there are two things about modal enunciations that must be carefully noted. The first—which is peculiar to modals—is that the predicate quantifies the modal proposition simply, as it also qualifies it simply. For just as the modal enunciation in which the mode is affirmed is affirmative simply, and negative when the mode is negated, so the modal enunciation in which the mode is universal is universal simply and particular in which the mode is particular. The reason for this is that the modal follows the nature of the mode.

The second thing to be noted (which is the cause of the first) is that the predicate of a modal, i.e., the mode, not only has the relationship of a predicate to its subject (i.e., to "to be" and "not to be"), but also has the relationship to the subject, of a distributive syncategorematic term, which has the effect of distributing the subject, not according to the quantity of its subjective parts, but according to the quantity of the parts of its time. And rightly so, for just as the proper quantity of the subject of an absolute enunciation varies according to the division or lack of division of its subject (since the subject is a name which signifies in the mode of substance, whose quantity is from the division of the continuous, and therefore the quantifying sign distributes according to the subjective parts), so, because the proper quantity of the subject of a modal enunciation is time (since the subject is a verb, which signifies in the mode of movement, whose proper quantity is time), the quantifying mode distributes the subject, i.e., "to be" or "not to be" according to the parts of time. Hence, we arrive at the subtle point that the quantity of the modal is the quantity of the proper subject of the modal enunciation, namely, of "to be" or "not to be." Therefore, a modal enunciation is universal simply when the proper subject is distributed throughout all time, either simply, as in "That man is an animal is necessary or impossible," or taken in a limited way, as in "That man is running today," or "while he is running, is necessary or impossible."

A modal enunciation is particular in which "to be" or "not to be" is distributed, not throughout all time, but commonly throughout some time, as in "That man is an animal is possible or contingent."

[229]

This modal quantity is therefore also a property of its subject (in that, universally, quantity comes from the matter) but is derived from the mode, not insofar as it is a predicate (because, as such, it is understood formally), but insofar as it performs a syncategorematic function, which it has in virtue of the fact that it is properly a mode.

14.   Therefore, with respect to their proper quantity, some modals are universal affirmatives, i.e., those of the necessary because they distribute "to be" to all time. Others are universal negatives, i.e., those of the impossible because they distribute "to be" to no time. Still others are particular affirmatives, i.e., those signifying the possible and contingent, for both of these distribute "to be" to some time. Finally, there are particular negatives, i.e., those of the not necessary and not impossible, for they distribute "not to be" to some time. This is similar to the diversity in absolute enunciations from the use of "every," "no," "some," "not all," and "not none."

Now, since this quantity belongs to modals insofar as they are modals, as has been said, and since Aristotle is now considering them in this particular respect, the modal enunciations that are equivalent, i.e., their consequents, are ordered by the different location of the negation, as is the case with absolute enunciations that are equivalent. A negative placed before the mode makes an enunciation equivalent to its contradictory; placed after the mode, i.e., with the verb of the dictum, makes it equivalent to its contrary; placed before and after the mode makes it equivalent to its subaltern, as you can see in the last table of consequents given by Aristotle. In that table of oppositions, you see all the mutual consequents, according to one of the three rules for making enunciations equivalent. Consequently, the whole first order of equivalent enunciations is contrary to the second, contradictory to the third, and the fourth is subalternated to it.

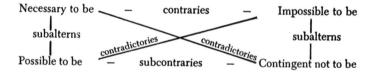

TABLE OF OPPOSITION OF
EQUIPOLLENT MODALS[138]

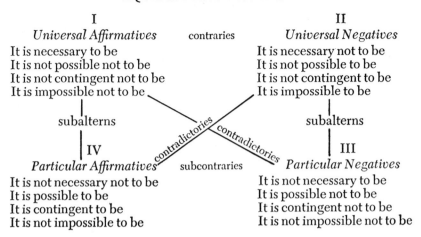

I		II
Universal Affirmatives	contraries	*Universal Negatives*
It is necessary to be		It is necessary not to be
It is not possible not to be		It is not possible to be
It is not contingent not to be		It is not contingent to be
It is impossible not to be		It is impossible to be

subalterns   subalterns

contradictories   contradictories

IV		III
Particular Affirmatives	subcontraries	*Particular Negatives*
It is not necessary not to be		It is not necessary to be
It is possible to be		It is possible not to be
It is contingent to be		It is contingent not to be
It is not impossible to be		It is not impossible not to be

---

[138] This table is not Cajetan's but is a full arrangement of the orders of modal enunciations as developed in this lesson.

[231]

Lesson XIII

Contrariety of Opinions in the Mind Is Constituted by an Opposition of the True and the False

23a 27   There is a question as to whether the contrary of an affirmation is a negation, or whether the contrary of an affirmation is another affirmation; and in the case of speech whether the one saying that no man is just is contrary to the one saying that every man is just, or is the one saying that every man is unjust contrary to the one saying that every man is just. For example, which of these are contraries: "Callias is just," "Callias is not just," "Callias is unjust"?

23a 32   For if those things that are in vocal sound are determined by those in the intellect, and if in the intellect that opinion is contrary which is about a contrary, for instance, the contrary of "Every man is just" is "Every man is unjust," the case must be the same with respect to spoken affirmations. But if in the intellect the contrary opinion is not one which is about a contrary, then in speech the affirmation will not be contrary to the affirmation, but the negation will be. We must therefore consider which false opinion is contrary to a true opinion, whether it is a negation of the true opinion or the opinion affirming a contrary.

What I mean is this: there is a true opinion of that which is good, that it is good, and a false opinion, that it is not good, and another kind, that it is evil; of the latter two which one is contrary to the true opinion; and if they are one and the same, which one is the contrary?

23b 2   It is false, of course, to suppose that opinions are to be defined as contrary because they are about contraries; for the opinion of that which is good, that it is good, and of that which is evil, that it is evil, are probably the same, and, whether they are many or one are true. Yet good and evil are contraries. However, opinions are not contraries because they are about contraries; rather, they are contrary because they are related contrarily.

23b 7   Now if there is the opinion of that which is good, that it is good, and the opinion that it is not good, and there are other opinions that something that does not belong and could not possibly belong to the good belongs to the good, none of the latter should be posited as the contrary, neither those purporting that what does not belong to the good belongs to it nor those purporting that what belongs to the good does not belong to it, for the opinions that that belongs which does not belong and the opinions that that does not belong which does, are infinite.

1.   Now that he has treated the enunciation as it is diversified by an addition made to the terms and by an addition made to its composition (which is the division of the text made by St. Thomas at the beginning of the second book), Aristotle takes up another question about oppositions of enunciations. This question concerns the oppositions that result from something added to the simple enunciation. First he asks the question; secondly, he shows that this question depends upon another, which must be treated first, where he says, *For if those* 23a32 *things that are in vocal sound are determined by those in the intellect,* etc.; third, he settles the latter question where he says, *It is false, of* 23b2 *course, to suppose that opinions are to be defined as contrary because they are about contraries,* etc.; finally, he replies to the first question where he says, *If, therefore, this is the case with respect to opinion, and* 24b1 *affirmations and negations in vocal sound are signs of those in the soul,* etc.[139]

The first question he raises is this: is the contrary of an affirmative enunciation the negation of the same predicate or the affirmation of a contrary or privative predicate? Hence he says, *There is a question* 23a27 *as to whether the contrary of an affirmation is the contradictory negation,*[140] and universally, whether affirmative speech is contrary to negative speech. For instance, is affirmative speech which says "Every man is just," contrary to negative speech which says "No man is just," or to the affirmative of the privative predicate, "Every man is unjust"? And similarly, is the affirmation "Callias is just" contrary to the contradictory negation, "Callias is not just" or is it contrary to "Callias is unjust," the affirmative of the privative predicate?

2.   Since this question has not been discussed by others, we must begin by noting that there are two things in an enunciation, namely, the enunciation itself, i.e., the signification, and the mode of enunciating or signifying. Hence, a twofold opposition can be made between enunciations, one by reason of the enunciation itself, the other by reason of the mode of enunciating.

If we consider the modes of enunciating, we find two species of opposition among enunciations, namely, contrariety and contradiction. This point was made earlier when opposed enunciations were divided into contraries and contradictories. There is contradiction by reason of mode of enunciating when the same thing is predicated of the same subject in a contradictory mode; so that just as one of a pair of contradic-

---

[139] 24b1; Cajetan, Lesson XIV, n. 17.
[140] The Greek here is, "πότερον δὲ ἐναντία ἐστὶν ἡ κατάφασις τῇ ἀποφάσει. . . ." Moerbeke's Latin is,

"Utrum autem contraria est affirmatio negationi. . . ." Cajetan has, "Utrum contraria est affirmatio negationi contradictoriae. . . ."

tories posits nothing but only destroys the other, so one enunciation asserts nothing, but only destroys what the other was enunciating. All enunciations that are called contradictories are of this kind; e.g., "Every man is just," "Not every man is just"; "Socrates is just," "Socrates is not just." It follows from this that they cannot be at once true or false, just as two contradictories cannot be at once.

There is contrariety between enunciations by reason of mode of enunciating when the same thing is predicated of the same subject in a contrary mode of enunciating; so that just as one of a pair of contraries posits matter common to itself and to the other which is at the extreme distance under that genus—as is evident for instance in white and black—so one enunciation posits a subject common to itself and its opposite at the extreme distance under that predicate. All the enunciations in the diagram that are called contrary are of this kind, for example, "Every man is just," "No man is just." These make the subject "man" distant to the greatest degree possible under justice, one enunciating justice to be in man, not in any way, but universally, the other enunciating justice to be absent from man, not in any way, but universally. For no distance can be greater than the distance between the total number of things having something and none of the total number of things having that thing. It follows that contrary enunciations cannot be at once true, just as contraries cannot be in the same thing at once. They can, however, be false at the same time, just as it is possible that contraries not be in the same thing at the same time.

If we consider the enunciation itself (viz., its signification) according to only one species of opposition, we will find in the whole range of enunciations an opposition of contrariety, i.e., an opposition according to truth and falsity. The reason for this is that the significations of two enunciations are positive, and accordingly cannot be opposed either contradictorily or privatively because the other extreme of both of these oppositions is formally non-being. And since significations are not opposed relatively, as is evident, the only way they can be opposed is contrarily.

3.　　The contrariety spoken of here consists in this: of two enunciations one is not compatible with the other either in truth or falsity—presupposing always the conditions for contraries, that they are about the same thing and at once. It can be shown that such opposition is contrariety from the nature of the conceptions of the soul when composing and dividing, each of which is an enunciation. Adequate conceptions of the soul are opposed to inadequate conceptions only contrarily, and inadequate conceptions, if each cancels the other, are also called contraries. It is from this that St. Thomas proves, in part I, ques-

[234]

tion XVII, that the true and false are contrarily opposed.[141] Therefore, as in the conceptions of the soul, so in enunciations, adequate significations are contrarily opposed to inadequate, i.e., true to false; and the inadequate, i.e., the false, are also contrarily opposed among themselves if it happens that they are not compatible, supposing always the conditions for contraries.

There is, therefore, in enunciations a twofold contrariety, one by reason of mode, the other by reason of signification, and only one contradiction, that by reason of mode. To avoid confusion, let us call the first contrariety modal and the second formal. We may call contradiction modal—not to avoid confusion since it is unique—but for propriety of expression.

Formal contrariety is found between all contradictory enunciations, since one contradictory always excludes the other. It is also found between all modally contrary enunciations in regard to truth, since they cannot be at once true. However it is not found between the latter in regard to falsity, since they can be at once false.

4.   Aristotle in this question is speaking of the contrariety of enunciations that extends to contraries modally and to contradictories. This is evident from what he says in the beginning and at the end of the question. In the beginning, he proposes both contradictories when he says, *an affirmation . . . to a negation,* etc.; and contraries modally, when he says, *and in the case of speech whether the one saying . . . is opposed to the one saying . . .*etc. It is evident, too, from the examples immediately added. At the end, he explicitly divides what he has concluded to be contrary to a true universal affirmative, into the modally contrary universal negative and the contradictory. It is clear at once that this division would be false unless it comprised the contrary formally.

Since he takes contrariety in this way the question must be understood with respect to formal contrariety of enunciations. This is a very subtle question and one that has to be treated and has not been thus far.

The question, therefore, is this: whether the formal contrary of the true affirmative is the false negative of the same predicate or the false affirmative of the privative predicate, i.e., of the contrary. The meaning of the question is now clear, and it is evident why he does not ask about any other oppositions of enunciations—no other opposition is found in them formally. It is also evident that he is taking contrariety properly and strictly, notwithstanding the fact that such contrariety is found among contradictories modally and contraries modally.

St. Thomas has already pointed out that this question arises

---

[141] *Sum. Theol.* I, q. 17, a. 4.

from the fact that something is added to the simple enunciation, for as far as simple enunciations are concerned, i.e., those with only a second determinant, there is no occasion for the question. When, however, something is added, namely a predicate, to the simple enunciation, i.e., to the subject and the substantive verb, the question arises as to whether what ought to be added in contrary enunciations is the selfsame predicate with a negation added to the verb or a contrary, i.e., privative, predicate without a negation added to the verb.

23a32   5.   When Aristotle says, *For if those things that are in vocal sound are determined by those in the intellect,* etc.; he shows where we have to begin in order to settle this question. First he shows that the question depends on another question, namely, whether a true opinion (i.e., a conception of the soul in the second operation of the intellect) is contrary to a false negative opinion of the same predicate, or to a false affirmative of the contrary, i.e., privative, predicate. Then he gives the reason why the former question depends on this. Vocal enunciations follow upon mental as adequate effects upon proper causes and as the signified upon adequate signs. So, in this the nature of each is similar.

23a32   He begins, then, with the reason for this dependence: *For if those things that are in vocal sound are determined by those in the intellect* (as was said in the beginning of the first book)[142] and if in the soul, those opinions are contrary which affirm contrary predicates about the same subject, (for example, the mental enunciations, "Every man is just, "Every man is unjust"), then in affirmations that are in vocal sound, the case must be the same. The contraries will be two affirmatives about the same subject with contrary predicates. But if in the soul this is not the case, i.e., that opinions with contrary predicates constitute contrariety in mental enunciations, then the contrary of a vocal affirmation will not be a vocal affirmation with a contrary predicate. Rather, the contrary of an affirmation will be the negation of the same predicate.

     6.   The first question, then, depends on this question as an effect upon its cause. For this reason, and by way of a conclusion to what he has just been saying, he adds the second question, which must be treated first so that once the cause is known the effect will be known:

23a38   *We must therefore consider to which false opinion the true opinion is contrary, whether it is to the false negation or to the false affirmation that it is to be judged contrary.*[143] Then in order to propose the question

---

[142] Cf. 16a 3.

[143] The Greek is, "ὥστε σκεπτέον ποία δόξα ἀληθὴς ψευδεῖ δόξῃ ἐναντία, πότερον ἡ τῆς ἀποφάσεως ἢ ἡ τὸ ἐναντίον εἶνα ιδοξάζονσα." Moer-

beke's Latin reads, "Quare considerandum est quae opinio vera opinioni falsae contraria est, utrum negationis, an ea, quae contrarium esse opinatur." Cajetan has, "Quare con-

by examples he says: what I mean is this; there are three opinions of a good, for instance, of life. One is a true opinion, that it is good, for instance, that life is good. The other is a false negative, that it is not good, for instance, that life is not good. Still another, likewise false, is the affirmative of the contrary, that it is evil, for instance, that life is evil. The question is, then, which of these false opinions is contrary to the true one.

7.　　Then he adds, the question, *and if there is one, is either one the contrary.*[144]

This passage can be read in three ways. It can be read inquiringly so that it is a part of the question, and then the meaning is: which of these false opinions is contrary to the true opinion, and, is there one of these by which the contrary to the true one is effected? For since one is contrary to one other, as is said in X *Metaphysicae*,[145] in asking which of these is the contrary we are also asking whether one of them is the contrary.

This can also be read adversatively, and then the meaning is: which of these is the contrary, given that we know it is not both but one by which the contrariety is effected?

This can be read in a third way by dividing the first clause, "and if it is one" from the second clause, "is either one the contrary." The first part is then read assertively, the second inquiringly, and the meaning is: which of these two false opinions is contrary to the true opinion if the two false opinions differ as to consequence, and also if both are one, i.e., united to each other indivisibly?

Boethius explains this passage in the last way. He says that Aristotle adds these words because of immediate contraries in which the contrary does not differ from the privative. For the difference between mediate and immediate contraries is that in the former the contrary is not inferred from the privative. For example, this is not valid: "A colored body is not white, therefore it is black"—for it could be red. In immediate contraries, on the other hand, it is valid to infer the contrary from the privative; e.g., "An animal is not healthy, therefore it is ill," "A number is not even, therefore it is odd." Therefore, Aristotle

siderandum est, opinio vero cui opinioni falsae contraria est: utrum negationi falsae an certe ei affirmationi falsae, quae contrarium esse opinatur."

144 The Greek for this is, ". . . καὶ εἰ ἔστι μία, κατὰ ποτέραν ἐναντία." Moerbeke's Latin is, ". . . si est una, secundum quamnan contraria est." Cajetan has "quam" for "quamnan." According to the first interpretation of this phrase the translation would have to be: "and if there is one is either one the contrary," i.e., with no comma after "one."

145 *Metaph.* I, 1055a 19.

intends to show here that when we ask which of these false opinions, i.e., negative and affirmative contraries, is contrary to the true affirmative, we are asking universally whether these two false opinions follow each other indivisibly or not.

23b2   8.   When he says, *It is false, of course, to suppose that opinions are to be defined as contrary because they are about contraries,* etc., he proceeds with the second question. First he shows that contrariety of opinions is not determined by the contrariety of the matter involved, but rather by the opposition of true and false; secondly, he shows that there is not contrariety of opinions in just any opposites according to
23b7   truth and falsity, where he says, *Now if there is the opinion of that which is good, that it is good, and the opinion that it is not good,* etc.; third, he determines that contrariety of opinions is concerned with the per se first opposites according to truth and falsity, for three reasons,
23b13   where he says, *Rather, those opinions in which there is fallacy must be posited as contrary to true opinions,* etc.;[146] finally, he shows that
24a3   this determination is true of all, where he says, *It is evident that it will make no difference if we posit the affirmation universally, for the universal negation will be the contrary,* etc.[147]

Aristotle says, then, proposing the conclusion he intends to prove, that it is false to suppose that opinions are to be defined or determined as contrary because they are about contrary objects. He gives two arguments for this. Contrary opinions are not the same opinion; but opinions about contraries are probably the same opinion; therefore, opinions are not contrary from the fact that they are about contraries. And, contrary opinions are not simultaneously true; but opinions about contraries, whether many or one, are sometimes true simultaneously; therefore, opinions are not contraries because they are about contraries.

Having supposed the majors of these arguments, he posits a manifestation of each minor at the same time. In relation to the first argument, he says, *for the opinion of that which is good, that it is good, and of that which is evil, that it is evil are probably the same.* In relation to the second argument he adds: *and, whether many or one, are true.* He uses "probably," an adverb expressing doubt and disjunction, because this is not the place to determine whether the opinion of contraries is the same opinion, and, because in some way the opinion is the same and in some way not. In the case of habitual opinion, the opinion of contraries is the same, but in the case of an actual opinion it is not. One mental composition is actually made in conceiving that a good is good and another in conceiving that an evil is evil, although we know

[146] 23 b 15; Cajetan, Lesson XIV, n. 2.   [147] 24a 3; Cajetan, Lesson XIV, n. 16.

both by the same habit, the former per se and first, the latter secondarily, as is said in IX *Metaphysicae*.[148]

Then he adds that good and evil—which are used for the manifestation of the minor—are contraries even when the contrariety is taken strictly in moral matters; and so in using this our exposition is apposite.

Finally, he draws the conclusion: however, opinions are not contraries because they are about contraries, but rather because they are contraries, i.e., opinions are to be considered as contrary from the fact that they enunciate contrarily, adverbially, i.e., in a contrary mode, i.e., they enunciate truly and falsely. Thus the first argument is clear.

9.   When he says, *Now, if there is the opinion of that which is good,*   23b7
that it is good, and the opinion that it is not good, etc., he takes up the second point. Since he has just said that contrariety of opinions is taken according to their opposition of truth and falsity, he goes on to show that not just any opposites according to truth and falsity are contraries. This is his argument. Four opinions can be held about a good, for instance justice: that justice is good, that it is not good, that it is avoidable, that it is not desirable. Of these, the first is true, the rest false. The three false ones are diverse. The first denies the same predicate the true one affirmed; the second affirms something which does not belong to the good; the third denies what belongs to the good, but something other than the true one affirmed. Now if all opinions opposed as to truth and falsity are contraries, then not only are there many contraries to one true opinion, but an infinite number. But this is impossible, for one is contrary to one other. The consequence holds because infinite false opinions about one thing, similar to those cited, can be imagined; such opinions would affirm of it what does not belong to it and deny what is joined to it in some way. Both kinds are indeterminate and without number. We can think, for instance, that justice is a quantity, that it is a relation, that it is this and that; and likewise we can think that it is not a quality, is not desirable, is not a habit.

Hence, from what was said above in proposing the question,[149] Aristotle infers a plurality of false opinions opposed to one true opinion: *Now if there is the opinion of that which is good,* for instance jus-   23b7
tice, *that it is good,* and there is a false opinion denying the same thing, namely, *that it is not good,* and besides these a third opinion, false also, affirming that some other thing belongs to justice that does not belong and cannot belong to it (for instance, that justice is avoidable, that it is illicit) and a fourth opinion, also false, that denies something other than the true opinion affirms, something, however, which does belong to justice (for instance, that it is not a quality, that it is

---

[148] *Metaph.* Θ, 4, 1051a 4.   [149] Cf. nn. 6 and 7 of this lesson.

not a virtue), none of these other false enunciations are to be posited as the contrary of the true opinion. To explain what he is designating by "of these others," he adds, *neither those purporting that what is not, is,*[150] as opinions of the third order do, *nor those purporting that what is, is not,* as opinions of the fourth order signify. Then he adds the reason these cannot be posited as the contrary of the true opinion: *for both the opinions that that is which is not, and that which is not, is, are infinite,* as was shown above. Therefore, not just any opinions opposed according to truth and falsity are contraries. Thus the second argument is clear.

---

[150] Cajetan uses "esse quod non est" and "non esse quod est" in this and the following phrase quoted; Aristotle has "ὑπάρχειν τὸ μὴ ὑπάρχον" and "μὴ ὑπάρχειν τὸ ὑπάρχον."

The Opposition of True and False that Constitutes Contrariety of Opinions Is Opposition According to Affirmation and Negation of the Same Predicate of the Same Subject

23b 13   Rather, those opinions in which there is fallacy must be posited as contrary to true opinions. Now the things from which fallacies arise are the things from which generations arise; but generations are from opposites, therefore also fallacies.

23b 15   Now if that which is good is both good and not evil, the former per se, the latter accidentally (for it is accidental to that which is good not to be evil), and the true opinion which is a per se opinion of a thing is more true, then the false opinion which is a per se opinion is also more false. But the opinion that that which is good is not good is a false opinion about what belongs per se to a good and the opinion that it is evil, a false opinion concerning what belongs to it accidentally. Therefore the opinion of the negation of the good will be more false than the opinion affirming a contrary. Now the one who holds the contrary opinion about each thing is most mistaken; for contraries are those that differ most with respect to the same thing. If, then, of two opinions one is the contrary, but the opinion of the negation[151] is more contrary, it is evident that it must be the contrary. The opinion that that which is good is evil, however, is implicative; for probably along with this opinion one must understand that the good is not good.

23b 27   Further, if this necessarily holds in a similar way in all other cases, it would seem that what we have said is correct; for the opposition of contradiction either holds everywhere or nowhere. Now in the case where there is no contrary, that opinion is false which is the opposite of the true opinion; for instance, he who thinks man is not man thinks falsely. If then these are contraries, the others in which there is contradiction are also contraries.

23b 33   Again, the opinions of that which is good, that it is good, and of that which is not good, that it is not good, are parallel; so also are the opinions of that which is good, that it is not good, and of that which is not good, that it is good. What, then, would be the contrary of a true opinion that that which is not good is not good? It is not the opinion saying that it is evil. This might be at the same time true and a true opinion is never con-

---

[151] That is, the contradictory.

trary to a true opinion; for some things that are not good are evil and therefore it is possible for both opinions to be true. Nor is the opinion that it is not evil the contrary, for this too might be true, since something could be at one and the same time not good and not evil. It remains, therefore, that the contrary of an opinion that that which is not good is not good, is the false opinion that that which is not good is good; for the former is true. Therefore, also, the opinion that that which is good is not good is contrary to the opinion that that which is good is good.

24a 3   It is evident that it will make no difference if we posit the affirmation universally, for the universal negation will be the contrary. For instance, the contrary of the opinion that everything that is good is good, is that nothing that is good is good. For the opinion that that which is good is good, if the good is taken universally, is the same as the opinion that whatever is good is good; and this is no different from the opinion that everything that is good is good. And the same is the case with respect to the not good.

24b 1   If, therefore, this is the case with respect to opinion, and affirmations and negations in vocal sound are signs of those in the soul, it is evident that the contrary of the affirmation is the negation of the same subject universally. For example, the contrary of the enunciation "Everything good is good" is "Nothing good is good," or of "Every man is good," "No man is good." The contradictories, on the other hand, are "Not everything good is good," and "Not every man is good."

24b 6   It is evident, too, that true cannot be contrary to true, either in opinion or in contradiction. For contraries are about opposites, and while it is possible for the same thing to be said truly about contraries,[152] it is not possible for contraries to belong at once to the same subject.

---

1.   Aristotle has just completed a subtle investigation in which he has shown that contrariety of matter does not constitute contrariety of opinion, nor does just any kind of opposition of true and false, but some opposition of true and false does. Now he intends to determine what kind of opposition of true and false it is that constitutes contrariety of opinions, for this will answer the question directly.

He maintains that only opposition of opinions according to affirmation and negation of the same thing of the same thing, etc., constitutes their contrariety. Accordingly, as the response to the question, he intends to prove the following conclusion: opinions opposed ac-

[152] E.g., number said of odd and even;
color of black and white, etc.

cording to affirmation and negation of the same thing of the same thing are contraries; and consequently, opinions opposed according to affirmation of contrary predicates of the same subject are not contraries, for if these were contraries, the true affirmative would have two contraries, which is impossible, since one is contrary to one other.

2.	Aristotle uses three arguments to prove this conclusion.[153] The first one is as follows: Those opinions in which there is fallacy first are contraries. Opinions opposed according to affirmation and negation of the same predicate of the same subject are those in which there is fallacy first. Therefore, these are contraries.

The sense of the major is this: Opinions which first in the order of nature are the limits of fallacy, i.e., of deception or error, are contraries; for when someone is deceived or errs, there are two limits, the one from which he turns away and the one toward which he turns.

In the text the major of the argument is posited first: *Rather,* 23b13 *those opinions in which there is fallacy must be posited as contrary to true opinions.* By uniting this part of the text adversatively with what was said previously, Aristotle implies that not just any of the number of opinions enumerated are contraries, but those in which there is fallacy first in the manner we have explained. Then he gives this proof of the minor: those things from which generations are and from which fallacies are, are the same proportionally; generations are from opposites according to affirmation and negation; therefore fallacies, too, are from opposites according to affirmation and negation (which was assumed in the minor). Hence he posits the major of this prosyllogism: *Now the* 23b13 *things from which fallacies arise,* namely, limits, *are the things from which generations arise*—proportionally however. Under it he posits the minor: but generations are *from opposites,* i.e., according to affirmation and negation. Finally, he concludes, *therefore also fallacies,* i.e., they are from opposites according to affirmation and negation of the same thing of the same thing.

3.	This proof will be more evident from the following: Knowledge and fallacy, or error, bring about the same thing in the intellect's progression as generation and corruption do in nature's progression. For just as natural perfections are acquired by generations and perish by corruptions, so intellectual perfections are acquired by knowledge and lost by errors or deceptions. Accordingly, just as generation and corruption are between affirmation and negation as proper terms, as is said in V *Physicae,*[154] so both to know something and to be deceived about it is between affirmation and negation as proper terms. Conse-

---

[153] The second argument begins in n.	[154] *Phys.* V, 1, 224b 35.
14, the third in n. 15.

quently, what one who knows attains first in the second operation of the intellect is affirmation of the truth, and what he rejects per se and first is the negation of it. In like manner, what he who is deceived loses per se and first is affirmation of the truth, and acquires first is negation of the truth. Therefore Aristotle is correct in maintaining that the terms between which there is generation first and between which there is fallacy first are the same, because with respect to both, the terms are affirmation and negation.

4.   When he says, *Now, if that which is good is both good and not evil, the former per se, the latter accidentally,* etc., he intends to prove the major of the principal argument. He has already shown that the opinions in which there is fallacy first are affirmation and negation, and therefore in place of the major to be proved (i.e., opinions in which there is fallacy first are contraries) he uses his conclusion—which has already been shown to be equivalent—that opinions opposed according to affirmation and negation of the same thing are contraries. Thus with his customary brevity he at once proves the major, responds directly to the question, and applies it to what he has proposed.

In place of the major, then, he proves the conclusion principally intended, i.e., that opinions opposed according to affirmation and negation of the same thing are contraries, and not those opposed according to affirmation of contraries about the same thing. His argument is as follows: A true opinion and the opinion that is more false in respect to it are contrary opinions, but opinions opposed according to affirmation and negation are the true opinion and the opinion that is more false in respect to it; therefore, opinions opposed according to affirmation and negation are contraries. The major is proved thus: those things that are most distant in respect to the same thing are contraries; but the true and the more false are most distant in respect to the same thing, as is clear. The proof of the minor is that the opposite according to negation of the same thing of the same thing is per se false in relation to the true affirmation of it. But a per se false opinion is more false than any other, since each thing that is per se such is more such than anything that is such by reason of something else.

5.   Accordingly, returning to the opinions already given in proposing the question so as to show his intention more clearly by example, he begins with the proof of the minor. There are four opinions, of which two are true, "A good is good," "A good is not evil"; two are false, "A good is not good" and "A good is evil." It is evident that the first is true by reason of itself, the second accidentally, i.e., by reason of another, for not to be evil is added to that which is good. Hence, "A good is not evil" is true because a good is good, and not contrarily. There-

[244]

fore, the first of these opinions, which is per se true, is more true than the second, for in each genus that which per se is true is more true. The two false opinions are to be judged in the same way. The more false is the one that is per se false. The first of them, the negative, "A good is not good," in relation to the affirmative, "A good is good," is per se false, not false by reason of another. The second, the affirmative of the contrary, "A good is evil," in relation to the same opinion, is false accidentally, i.e., by reason of another (for "A good is evil" is not immediately falsified by the true opinion, "A good is good," but mediately through the other false opinion "A good is not good"). Therefore, the negation of the same thing is more false in respect to a true affirmation than the affirmation of a contrary. This was assumed in the minor.

6.   As was pointed out above, Aristotle returns to the opinions already posited, and infers the first two true opinions: *Now if that* 23b15 *which is good is both good and not evil,* and if what the first opinion says is true per se, i.e., by reason of itself, and what the second opinion says is true accidentally (since it is accidental to it, i.e., added to it, that is, to the good, not to be evil), and if in each order that which is per se true is more true, then that which is per se false is more false, since, as has been shown, the true also is of this nature, namely, that the more true is that which per se is true.

Therefore, of the two false opinions proposed in the question, namely, "A good is not good," and "A good is evil," the one saying that what is good is not good, namely, the negative, is an opinion positing what is per se false, i.e., by reason of itself it contains falsity in it. The other false opinion, the one saying it is evil, namely, the affirmative contrary in respect to it, i.e., in respect to the affirmation saying that a good is good, is false accidentally, i.e., by reason of another.

Then he gives the minor: *Therefore, the opinion of the negation of the good will be more false than the opinion affirming a contrary.* Next, he posits the major, *the one who holds the contrary judgment about each thing is most mistaken,* i.e., in relation to the true judgment the contrary is more false. This was assumed in the major. He gives as the proof of this, *for contraries are those that differ most* 23b22 *with respect to the same thing,* for nothing differs more from a true opinion than the more false opinion in respect to it.

7.   Finally, he directly approaches the question. *If* (for "since"), *then, of two opinions* (namely, false opinions—the negation of the same thing and the affirmation of a contrary), one is the contrary of the true affirmation, and, the contradictory opinion, i.e., the negation of the same thing of the same thing, is more contrary according to falsity, i.e., is more false, it is evident that the false opinion of negation will be

[245]

contrary to the true affirmation, and conversely. The opinion saying that what is good is evil, i.e., the affirmation of a contrary, is not the contrary but implies it, i.e., it implies in itself the opinion contrary to the true opinion, i.e., "A good is not good." The reason for this is that the one conceiving the affirmation of a contrary must conceive that the same thing of which he affirms the contrary, is not good. If, for example, someone conceives that life is evil, he must conceive that life is not good, for the former necessarily follows upon the latter and not conversely. Hence, affirmation of a contrary is said to be implicative, but negation of the same thing of the same thing is not implicative. This concludes the first argument.

8.   The general rule about the contrariety of opinions that Aristotle has given here (namely, that contrary opinions are those opposed according to affirmation and negation of the same thing of the same thing) is accurate both in itself and in the propositions assumed for its proof. Many questions may arise, however, as a consequence of this doctrine and its proof. First of all, all philosophers hold that opposition according to affirmation and negation constitutes contradiction, not contrariety. How, then, can Aristotle maintain that opinions opposed in this way are contraries? The difficulty is augmented by the fact that he has said that those opinions in which there is fallacy first are contraries, yet he adds that they are opposed as the terms of generation are, which he establishes to be opposed contradictorily. In addition, there is a difficulty as to the way in which the assertion of St. Thomas, which we used above, is true, namely, that no two opinions are opposed contradictorily,[155] since here it is explicitly said that some are opposed according to affirmation and negation.

The second question involves his assumption that the contrary of each true opinion is per se false. This does not seem to be true, for according to what was determined previously, the contrary of the true opinion "Socrates is white" is "Socrates is not white." But this is not per se false, for the opposed affirmation is true accidentally, and hence its negation is false accidentally. Falsity is accidental to such an enunciation because, being in contingent matter, it can be changed into a true one.

A third difficulty arises from the fact that Aristotle says the contradictory opinion is *more* contrary. He seems to be proposing, according to this, that both the opinion of the negation and of a contrary are contrary to a true affirmation. Consequently, he is either positing two opinions contrary to one or he is not taking contrariety strictly,

[155] Cajetan, Lesson XIII, n. 3.

although we showed above that he was taking contrariety properly and strictly.[156]

9.   In order to answer all of the difficulties in regard to the first argument it must be noted that opinions, or intellectual conceptions in the second operation, can be taken in three ways: (1) according to what they are absolutely; (2) according to the things they represent absolutely, (3) according to the things they represent, as they are in opinions. We will omit the first since it does not belong to the present consideration. If they are taken in the second way, i.e., according to the things represented, there can be opposition of contradiction, of privation, and of contrariety among them. The mental enunciation "Socrates sees," according to what it represents, is opposed contradictorily to "Socrates does not see"; privatively to "Socrates is blind"; contrarily to "Socrates is purblind." Aristotle points out the reason for this in the *Postpredicamenta*:[157] not only is blindness privation of sight but to be blind is also a privation of to be seeing, and so of others.

Opinions taken in the third way, i.e., as the things represented through opinions are in the opinions, have no opposition except contrariety; for opposites as they are in opinions, whether represented contradictorily or privatively or contrarily, only admit of the opposition that can be found between two real beings, for opinions are real beings. The rule is that whatever belongs to something according to the being which it has in another, belongs to it according to the mode and nature of that in which it is, and not according to what its own nature would require. Now, between real beings only contrariety is found formally. (I am omitting here the consideration of relative opposition.) Therefore, opinions taken in this mode, if they are opposed, represent contrariety, although not all are contraries properly. Only those differing most in respect to truth and falsity about the same thing are contraries properly. Now Aristotle proved that these are judgments affirming and denying the same thing of the same thing. Therefore, these are the true contraries. The rest are called contraries by reduction to these.

10.   From this the answer to the objections is clear. We grant that affirmation and negation in themselves constitute contradiction. In actual judgments,[158] affirmation and negation cause contrariety between opinions because of the extreme distance they posit between real beings, namely, true opinion and false opinion in respect to the same thing. And these two stand at the same time: those in which there is fallacy first are opposed as the terms of generation are and yet they are

---

[156] Cf. Cajetan, Lesson XIII, n. 4.
[157] *Categ.*, 10, 12a 35 ff.

[158] That is, opinions actually existing in the mind.

contraries by the use of the foresaid distinction—for they are opposed contradictorily as terms of generation according to the things represented, but they are contraries insofar as they have in themselves those contradictories and hence differ most.

It is also evident that there is no disagreement between Aristotle and St. Thomas, for we have shown that it is true that some opinions are opposed according to affirmation and negation if we consider the things represented, as is said here.

11.   It will be noted, however, by those of you who are more penetrating and advanced in your thinking, that between opposite opinions there is something of true motion when a change is made from the affirmed to the affirmed; but according to the order of representation there is a certain similitude to generation and corruption so long as the change is bounded by affirmation and negation. Consequently, fallacy or error may be regarded in different ways. Sometimes it has the aspect of both movement and change. This is the case when someone changes his opinion from a true one to one that is per se false, or conversely. Sometimes change alone is imitated. This happens when someone arrives at a false opinion apart from a former true opinion. Sometimes, however, there is movement in every respect. This is the case when reason passes from the true affirmation to the false affirmation of a contrary about the same thing.[159]

However, since the first root of being in error is the opposition of affirmation and negation, Aristotle is correct in saying that those in which there is fallacy first are opposed as are the terms of generation.

12.   With respect to the second question, I say that there is an equivocation of the term "per se false" and "per se true" in the objection. Opinion, as well as enunciation, can be called per se true or false in two ways. It can be called per se true in itself. This is the case in respect to all opinions and enunciations that are in accordance with the modes of perseity enumerated in I *Posteriorum*.[160] Similarly, they can be said to be per se false according to the same modes. An example of this would be "Man is not an animal." Per se true or false is not taken in this mode in the rule about contrariety of opinions and enunciations, as the objection concludes. For if this were needed for contrariety of opinions there could not be contrary opinions in contingent matter, which is false.

Secondly, an opinion or enunciation can be said to be per se true or false in respect to its opposite: per se true with respect to its opposite false opinion, and per se false with respect to its opposite

[159] Cf. *Phys.* V for the difference between movement and change.   [160] *Post. Anal.* I, 4, 73a 34-73b 15.

true opinion. Accordingly, to say that an opinion is per se true in respect to its opposite is to say that on its own account and not on account of another it is verified by the falsity of its opposite. Similarly, to say that an opinion is per se false in respect to its opposite means that on its own account and not on account of another it is falsified by the truth of the opposite. For example, the opinion that is per se false in respect to the true opinion "Socrates is running" is not, "Socrates is sitting," since the falsity of the latter does not immediately follow from the former, but mediately from the false opinion, "Socrates is not running." It is the latter opinion that is per se false in relation to "Socrates is running," since it is falsified on its own account by the truth of the opinion "Socrates is running," and not through an intermediary. Similarly, the per se true opinion in respect to the false opinion "Socrates is four-footed" is not, "Socrates is two-footed," for the truth of the latter does not by itself make the former false; rather, it is through "Socrates is not four-footed" as a medium, which is per se true in respect to "Socrates is four-footed"; for "Socrates is not four-footed" is verified on its own account by the falsity of "Socrates is four-footed," as is evident.

We are using "per se true" and "per se false" in this second mode in propounding the rule concerning contrariety of opinions and enunciations. Thus the rule that the true opinion and the per se false opinion in relation to it and the false opinion and the per se true in relation to it are contraries, is universally true in all matter. Consequently, the response to the objection is clear, for it results from taking "per se true" and "per se false" in the first mode.

13.   The answer to the third difficulty is the following. Since there is no other opposition but contrariety between opinions pertaining to each other, Aristotle (since he chose to use limited terms) has been forced to say that one is more contrary than another, which implies that both have opposition of contrariety in respect to a true opinion. However, he determines immediately that only one of them, the negative opinion, is contrary to a true affirmation, when he adds, *it is evident* 23b25 *that it must be the contrary.*

What he says, then, is that each, i.e., both negation of the same thing and affirmation of a contrary, is contrary to a true affirmation, and that only one of them, i.e., the negation, is contrary. Both of these statements are true, for both contrarieties are caused by an opposition contrary to the affirmation, as was said, but not uniformly. The opinion of negation is contrary first and per se, the opinion of affirmation of a contrary, secondarily and accidentally, i.e., through another, namely, by reason of the negative opinion, as has already been shown. There is a parallel to this in natural things: both black and red are contrary to

[249]

white, the former first, the latter reductively, i.e., inasmuch as red is reduced to black in a motion from white to red, as is said in V *Physicorum*.[161]

However, the second statement, i.e., that only one of them, the negation, is contrary, is true simply, for the most distant extremes of one extent are contraries absolutely. Now there are only two extremes of one distance and since between opinions pertaining to each other true affirmation is at one extreme, the remaining extreme must be granted to only one false opinion, i.e., to the one that is most distant from the true opinion. This has been proved to be the negative opinion. Only this one, then, is contrary to that absolutely speaking. Other opposites are contrary by reason of this one, as was said of those in between.

Therefore, Aristotle has not posited many opinions contrary to one, nor used contrariety in a broad sense, both of which were maintained by the objector.

23b27   14.   When Aristotle says, *Further, if this necessarily holds in a similar way in all other cases, it would seem that what we have said is correct*, etc., he gives the second argument to prove that the negation of the same thing is contrary to the affirmation, and not the affirmation of a contrary. If opinions are necessarily related in a similar way, i.e., in the same way, in other matter, that is, in such a way that affirmation and negation of the same thing are contraries in other matter, it would seem that what we have said about the opinions of that which is good and that which is evil is correct, i.e., that the contrary of the affirmation of that which is good is not the affirmation of evil but the negation of good. He proves this consequence when he adds: *for the opposition of contradiction either holds everywhere or nowhere*, i.e., in every matter one part of a contradiction must be judged contrary to its affirmation—or never, i.e., in no matter. For if there is a general art which deals with contrary opinions, contrary opinions must be taken everywhere and in every matter in one and the same mode. Consequently, if in any matter, negation of the same thing of the same thing is the contrary of the affirmation, then in all matter negation of the same thing of the same thing will be the contrary of the affirmation.

Since he intends in his proof to conclude from the position of the antecedent, Aristotle affirms the antecedent through its cause: in matter in which there is not a contrary, such as substance and quantity, which have no contraries, as is said in the *Predicamenta*,[162] the one contradictorily opposed to the true opinion is per se false. For example, he who thinks that man, for instance Socrates, is not man, is per se mis-

---

[161] *Phys.* V, 5, 229b 15 ff.   [162] *Categ.* 5, 3b 24 ff.; 6, 5b 10 ff.; 6, 5b 40 ff.

taken with regard to one who thinks that Socrates is man. Then he affirms the antecedent formally and concludes directly from the position of the antecedent to the position of the consequent. *If then these,* namely, affirmation and negation in matter which lacks a contrary, are contraries, all other contradictions must be judged to be contraries.

15.   Then he says, *Again, the opinions of that which is good, that* 23b33
it is good and of that which is not good, that it is not good, are parallel.
This begins the third argument to prove the same thing.

The two opinions of that which is good, that it is good, and that it is not good, are related in the same way as the two opinions of that which is not good, that it is not good and that it is good; i.e., the opposition of contradiction is kept in both. The first opinion of each combination is true, the second false. Hence with respect to the first true opinions of each combination he proposes this major: *Again, the opinions of that which is good, that it is good, and of that which is not good, that it is not good, are parallel.* With respect to the second false judgment of each combination he adds: *so also are the opinions of that which is good, that it is not good, and of that which is not good, that it is good.* This is the major. But the contrary of the true opinion of that which is not good, namely, the true opinion "That which is not good is not good," is not, "That which is not good is evil," nor "That which is not good is not evil," which have a contrary predicate, but the opinion that that which is not good is good, which is its contradictory. Therefore, the contrary of the true opinion of that which is good, namely, the true opinion "That which is good is good," will also be its contradictory, "That which is good is not good," and not the affirmation of the contrary "That which is good is evil." Hence he adds the minor which we have already stated: *What, then, would be the contrary of the true opinion asserting that that which is not good is not good?* The contrary of it is not the opinion which asserts the contrary predicate affirmatively, "That which is not good is evil," because these two are sometimes at once true. But a true opinion is never contrary to a true opinion. That these two are sometimes at once true is evident from the fact that some things that are not good are evil. Take injustice; it is something not good, and it is evil. Therefore, contraries would be true at one and the same time, which is impossible. But neither is the contrary of the above true opinion the one asserting the contrary predicate negatively, "That which is not good is not evil," and for the same reason. These will also be true at the same time. For example, a chimera is something not good, and it is true to say of it simultaneously that it is not good and that it is not evil.

There remains the third part of the minor: the contrary of the

[251]

true opinion that that which is not good is not good is the opinion that it is good, which is the contradictory of it. Then he concludes as he intended: the opinion that a good is not good is contrary to the opinion that a good is good, i.e., its contradictory. Therefore, it must be judged that contradictions are contraries in every matter.

24a3 16.   He then says, *It is evident that it will make no difference if we posit the affirmation universally,* etc. Here he shows that the truth he has determined is extended to opinions of every quantity. The case has already been stated in respect to indefinites, particulars, and singulars. On this point their status is alike, for indefinites and particulars, unless they stand for the same thing, as is the case in singulars, are not opposed by way of affirmation and negation, since they are at once true. Therefore he turns his attention to those of universal quantity. It is evident, he says, that it will make no difference with respect to the proposed question if we posit the affirmations universally, for the contrary of the universal affirmative is the universal negative, and not the universal affirmation of a contrary. For example, the contrary of the opinion that everything that is good is good is the opinion that nothing that is good (i.e., no good) is good. He manifests this by the nominal definition of universal affirmative: for the opinion that that which is good is good, if the good is universal, i.e., the universal opinion "Every good is good," is the same, i.e., is equivalent to the opinion that whatever is good is good. Consequently, its negation is the contrary I have stated, "Nothing which is good is good," i.e., "No good is good."

The case is similar with respect to the not good. The universal negation of the not good is opposed to the universal affirmation of the not good, as we have stated with respect to the good.

24b1 17.   Then he says, *If, therefore, this is the case with respect to opinion, and affirmations and negations in vocal sound are signs of those in the soul,* etc. With this he returns to the question first advanced, to reply to it, for he has now completed the second on which the first depends.[163] He first replies to the question, then manifests a point in 24b6 the solution of a preceding difficulty where he says, *It is evident, too, that true cannot be contrary to true, either in opinion or in contradiction,* etc.

First, then, he replies directly to the question: If, therefore, contrariety is such in the case of opinions, and affirmations and negations in vocal sound are signs of affirmations and negations in the soul, *it is evident that the contrary of the affirmation,* i.e., of the affirmative, enunciation, *is the negation of the same subject.* In other

163 Cf. Cajetan, **Lesson** XIII, nn. 1 and
    5.

[252]

words, the negative enunciation of the same predicate of the same subject will be the contrary, and not the affirmative enunciation of a contrary. Thus the response to the first question—whether the contrary of the affirmative enunciation is its negative or the contrary affirmative—is clear. The answer is that the negative is the contrary.

Next, he divides negation as it is contrary to affirmation, i.e., into the universal negation, and the contradictory: *The universal*, i.e., negation, is contrary to the affirmation, etc. In order to state this division by way of example he relates one enunciation to one enunciation: the contrary of the universal affirmative enunciation "Every good is good" or "Every man is good," is the universal negative "No good is good" or "No man is good." Again, relating one to one, he says that the contradictory negation contrary to the universal affirmation is "Not every man is good" or "Not everything good is good." Thus he posits both members of the division and makes the division evident.

18.   A difficulty arises at this point which we cannot disregard. If the contrary of the universal affirmative is a twofold negation, namely, the universal and the contradictory, either there are two contraries to one affirmation or Aristotle is using contrariety in a broad sense, although we showed that this was not the case apropos of an earlier passage of the text. The difficulty is augmented by the fact that Aristotle said in the passage immediately preceding that it makes no difference if we take the universal negation as contrary to the universal affirmation, i.e., as one of its negations. Hence, the conclusion cannot be avoided that in the mode in which Aristotle speaks of contrariety here, there are two contrary negations to the universal affirmative.

19.   To clear up this difficulty we must note that it is one thing to speak of the contrariety there is between the negation of some universal affirmative in relation to the affirmation of a contrary, and another to speak of that same universal negative in relation to the negation contradictory to the same affirmative. For example, the four enunciations of which we are now speaking are the universal affirmative, the contradictory, the universal negative, and the universal affirmation of a contrary: "Every man is just," "Not every man is just," "No man is just," "Every man is unjust." Notice that although all the rest are contrary to the first in some way, there is a great difference between the contrariety of each to the first. The last one, the affirmation of a contrary, is contrary to the first by reason of the preceding universal negation, for it is false, not per se but by reason of that negation, i.e., it is implicative, as Aristotle has already proved.[164] The third, the universal negation, is not

164 Cf. Cajetan, Lesson XIII, nn. 4 ff.,
   especially n. 7.

per se contrary to the first either. It is contrary by reason of the second, the contradictory negation, and for the same reason, i.e., it is not per se false in respect to the truth of the affirmation but is implicative, for it contains the contradictory negation "Not every man is just," by means of which it is made false in respect to the truth of the affirmation. The reason for this is that the falsity of the contradictory negation is prior absolutely to the falsity of the universal negation, for the whole is more composite and posterior as compared to its parts. There is, therefore, an order among these three false enunciations. Only the contradictory negation is simply contrary to the true affirmation, for it is per se false simply in respect to the affirmation; the affirmative of the contrary is per accidens contrary, since it is per accidens false; the universal negation, which is a medium partaking of the nature of each extreme, is per se contrary and per se false as related to the affirmation of a contrary, but is per accidens false and per accidens contrary as related to the contradictory negation; just as red in a motion from red to black takes the place of white, and in a motion from red to white takes the place of black, as is said in V *Physicorum*.[165]

Therefore, it is one thing to speak of the universal negation in relation to affirmation of a contrary and another to speak of it in relation to the contradictory negation. If we are speaking of it in the first way, the universal negation is per se contrary and per se false; if in the second, it is not per se false or contrary to the affirmation.

20.   Since Aristotle is now treating the question as to which is the contrary of a true affirmation, affirmation of a contrary or the negation, and not the question as to which of the negations is contrary to a true affirmation—as is clear in the whole progression of the question—his answer is that both negations are contrary to the true affirmation without distinction, and that affirmation of a contrary is not. His intention is to manifest the diversity between the negation, and the affirmation of a contrary, inasmuch as they are contrary to a true affirmation. He does not intend to say that both negations are contrary simply, for this is not the difficulty in question here, but the former is.

With respect to his saying that it makes no difference if we posit the universal negation, the same point applies, for in regard to showing that affirmation of a contrary is not contrary to a true affirmation, which is the question at issue here, it makes no difference which negation is posited. It would make a great deal of difference, however, if we wished to discuss which negation was contrary to a true affirmation.

It is evident, then, that Aristotle's discussion of the true contrariety of enunciations is very subtle, for he has posited one to one con-

[165] *Phys.* V, 5, 229b 15 ff.

traries in every matter and quantity, and affirmed that contradictions are contraries simply.

21.   When he says, *It is evident, too, that true cannot be contrary to*   24b6
true, either in opinion or in contradiction, etc., he returns to a statement he has already made in order to prove it.[166] *It is evident,* too, from what has been said, *that true cannot be contrary to true, either in opinion or in contradiction,* i.e., in vocal enunciation. He gives as the cause of this that contraries are opposites about the same thing; consequently, true enunciations and opinions about diverse things cannot be contraries. However, it is possible for all true enunciations and opinions about the same thing to be verified at the same time, inasmuch as the things signified or represented by them belong to the same thing at the same time; otherwise they are not true. Consequently, not all true enunciations and opinions about the same thing are contraries, for it is not possible for contraries to be in the same thing at the same time. Therefore, no true opinion or enunciation, whether it is about the same thing or is about another is contrary to another.

---

[166] The statement Cajetan refers to, that a true opinion is never contrary to a true opinion, is made in this lesson, at 23b 37.

INDEX

On the name "contradiction," 75

On the indefinite negative, 92

On simple enunciation with a third element, 133-35

On extent of power of enunciation, 134

On diagram of indefinite enunciations, 141

Simple negative enunciation follows upon infinite affirmative enunciation, but not conversely, 154

ANALOGY

Differentiated from univocity, 64

ANDRONICUS

Holds *On Interpretation* not to be a work of Aristotle, 26

ANIMALS

Manifest their conceptions through certain vocal sounds, 24

Use unlettered sounds, 40

Are moved to act by a kind of natural instinct, 112

APPETIBLE

See GOOD

ARISTOTLE (other works cited)

Categories, 61, 78, 247, 250

I Prior Analytics, 134, 153, 211, 218

I Posterior Analytics, 149, 248

II Topics, 172

On Sophistical Refutations, 76

I Physics, 33, 93, 220

II Physics, 115

III Physics, 93

IV Physics, 117

V Physics, 243, 250, 254

VI Physics, 48

II On the Heavens, 220

On Prophesying by Dreams, 116

I On the Soul, 26

II On the Soul, 21, 32, 38

III On the Soul, 17, 26, 28, 30, 31, 32, 33, 58, 79, 115, 117

On the Generation of Animals, 21

II On Generation and Corruption, 106

IV Metaphysics, 28, 33, 127

V Metaphysics, 115, 223

VI Metaphysics, 33, 61, 114

VII Metaphysics, 66, 78, 79

VIII Metaphysics, 66

IX Metaphysics, 118, 219, 223, 227, 239

X Metaphysics, 182, 237

XII Metaphysics, 32

II Nicomachean Ethics, 25

III Nicomachean Ethics, 110, 120

VI Nicomachean Ethics, 32

VII Nicomachean Ethtics, 116

I Politics, 25

ARTIFICIAL THINGS

In what genus they are and how defined, 38

How they are true and false, 32

ASPASIUS

Objects to definition of speech by Aristotle, 55

AVERROES

On divided predication as inferred from conjoined predication, 185

On terminology to use in modal enunciation, 205

On consequents following upon opposition of modals, 208

B

BEING *(ens)*

Convertible with truth, 31, 33

Convertible with one, 64

Source and origin of *esse*, 51-52

Not properly said equivocally, but according to prior and posterior, 52

Not the genus of substance and accident, 65

Every being by participation is divine, 116-17

All being and all differences of being flow from divine will as from a cause, 118-19

Is either per se or accidental, 114

[257]

How accidental being is reduced to what is per se, 115

Accidental being is not one, 116

Accidental being can be grasped by intellect as one, 116

Signifies nothing other than that which is, 52

Does not signify existence principally, 52

How nonbeing is called being, 127

BEING (esse)

In what can be or not be, not being is prior to being, 22

To be or not to be in present time is to be or not to be in act and simply; in past or future, relatively, 34-35, 53

What is in the present has being in itself, 107

Impossible for the same thing to be and not to be, 122

Divine being comprehends everything which in any way is, 117

The verb to be or not to be expresses a judgment of intellect, 34

The verb to be is a sign of predication, 131

The verb to be is a word, not an enunciation, 70

By itself, is not significative of truth or falsity, 51

Signifies existence, but as such does not signify that something is, 52

In enunciation, signifies not only being of the subject but also that the predicate is in it, 74

When it signifies existence of subject it is predicated according to itself, 131

When it signifies the conjunction between the predicate and subject, the enunciation is called of the third element, 131-32

BODY

A corporeal force can act of itself only in a corporeal thing, 115

Celestial body in relation to intellect, will, and sense, 115-16

BOETHIUS

Defines interpretation, 17

Explains how passions of the soul are the same for all, 28

Infinite name can be said of being and nonbeing, 41

Examines part of definition of verb, 47

On the unity and plurality of enunciation, 68

Maintains Aristotle simultaneously defines and divides simple enunciation, 72

Summarizes opinions on nature of possible and necessary, 113

Refers to Porphyry on simple enunciation of third element, 135

Explanation of diagram of indefinite and universal enunciations, 141

On enunciations having an adjective verb, 147

Simple negation follows upon infinite affirmation, but not conversely, 154

On dialectical interrogation, 167

On divided predication as inferred from conjoined predication, 185

On consequents following upon opposition of modals, 208

On which false opinion is contrary to a true one, 237

C

CASES OF NAMES

Why so called, 42

Are not names absolutely, 43

Even with is added, do not make an enunciation, 42, 128

CASES OF VERBS

Excluded from definition of verb, 49

Signify with time and thus included under verbs, 128

What they are, 49

Signify past and future, 128

CATEGOREMATIC TERMS

Contrasted with syncategorematic terms, 149

CAUSE

Divided into per se and accidental, 115

Divided into necessary and contingent, 118-19

Every created cause falls under order of necessity or contingency, 119

Not every cause is such that its effect cannot be impeded, 114

See EFFECT, FUTURE

CHOICE

Follows upon deliberation, 119

Is not about what is necessary, 120

COGNITION (Knowledge)

Requires a likeness of the thing in sense or in intellect, 27

Nothing is knowable except as in act, 118

Intellectual cognition abstracts from here and now; sense cognition regards only the here and now, 24

Human cognition falls under order of time per se or accidentally, 117

How God knows things in time, 118

Divine cognition is infallible, 117

COMPOSITION

How related to intellect and to reality, 31

Belongs to second operation of intellect, 17, 31

Cannot be understood without extremes of composition, 51-52, 66

In composition, mind necessarily includes time, 117

CONCEPTIONS

In what sense called passions of the soul, 25, 28

Prior in order of nature to words, 27, 30

Similitudes of things, 27, 31-32

Sufficient alone if man were a solitary animal, 24

First conceptions of intellect, which incomplex words signify, are the same for all, 27-28

CONJUNCTIONS

Are not called interpretations, 17

Are not principal parts of speech but connectors, 21

Are not names or verbs, 52

CONSEQUENCES-CONSEQUENTS

In relation to enunciations with infinite subjects, 157

Following upon opposition of modals according to ancient opinion, 205

Diagram of consequents predicating necessity, 206

Following upon opposition of modals according to Aristotle, 215

Following upon opposition of modals with the necessary first, 226

CONTINGENT

What the contingent is, 113

Three kinds of, 105

Concerns order of cause to effect, 118

Its root in things done by man is deliberation, 112-14, 119

CONTRADICTION

In broad sense, signifies any opposition of affirmation and negation, 98

Properly speaking is absolute opposition of affirmation and negation, 75-76

Consists only in the removal of affirmation by negation, 90-91

Contradictories are not at once true, 92, 97, 122

Contradictories are not at once false, 97, 123

One contradictory necessarily true, the other false, 92, 98, 103

Is opposition between universal and particular enunciations, 90, 103

Singular affirmative enunciation always contradicted by singular negative, 91-92, 103

Indefinite enunciations as enunciations not contradictory, 92-93, 103

Of predicates in an enunciation, 181

Is effected when negation is added to verb, 194

Formal contrariety found in contradictories, 235-36

See OPPOSITION OF ENUNCIATIONS

CONTRARIES

Are farthest apart from each other, 84

Mutually remove each other, 85, 91

Opinions about contraries are not contrary, 85-86

See CONTRARIETY, OPPOSITION

CONTRARIETY

An opposition between universal affirmative and universal negative enunciations, 84, 86, 90-91

Admits a middle, namely particular enunciations, 91

Both contraries cannot at once be true, 91

Contradictories of contraries can be verified at once, 91

Both contraries can be at once false, 98

Indefinite enunciations are not contraries, 84-85

Indefinite enunciations can have contrariety on the part of what is signified, 86

Particular enunciations are not contraries, 86

Formal and modal, 234

Mediate and immediate, 237

See OPPOSITION OF ENUNCIATIONS

D

DEFINITION

Is a kind of speech, but not enunciative without verb, 65

Is something one, 66, 69

Genus and difference are its parts, 99

Why definitions are called positions, 20

Why a definition is called a limit, 37-38

DELIBERATION (COUNSEL)

Is not of what is necessary but of what is contingent, 110

Beings without deliberation do not have dominion over their acts, 112

Is about what is related to an end, 110, 120

Is the root of contingency in human acts, 112, 119-20

DEMONSTRATION

Presupposes definition and concludes from it, 20

Absolute truth required in it, 21

In demonstrative science, the mind is led to assent to the truth from what is proper to the thing, 62

DENOMINATION

Made from the form which gives species to the thing, 66

DEPRECATIVE

A species of perfect speech, 61

What it expresses, 61

DETERMINANT

When second determinant can be inferred from third and when not, 183, 186

DICTUM

Distinguished from a mode, 191

DIFFERENCE

A part of definition, 99

Taken from form, 66

Differences dividing a genus do not fall in definition of it, 72

DIODORUS

Defines necessary, possible and impossible, 113

DIVISION

Closer to parts than to whole, 22

Made by resolution to what is simple, 31

How it belongs to second operation of intellect, 17, 31

As second operation of mind, must include time, 117

E

EFFECT

Not everything which comes to be has a cause, 114-15

Must be proportionately referred to its cause, 115

As accidental, has accidental cause, 115

As accidental, cannot be reduced to per se cause by a natural power, 115-16

How every effect depends on divine will, 118-19

When cause posited, not necessary that effect follow, 114-15

See CAUSE, FATE, PROVIDENCE

ENUNCIATION

Speech in which there is true and false, 61

As a sign, 61

Same as interpretation, 17-18

Can be made from name and verb alone, 21

Name and verb are its integral parts, 21, 37

Speech is its formal principle, 54

Analogous division into simple and composite, 63-64, 70-71, 81

Definition of it by nature of its parts, 70-71

Basis for its unity, 69, 98-100

What does not prevent its unity, 67, 69, 98, 126

How enunciations can be many, 67-69

Division into affirmative and negative, 21-22, 64-65, 71-72, 80-83, 129

Division by reason of finite and infinite subject, 129

Division of those having second and third element into opposites, 131

Division according to present, past, and future, 102

How present and past enunciations are true, 103, 132-34

Whether future singular enunciations are true, 103-4, 109-20

Division into necessary, impossible, possible, and contingent, 102-3

Contradictory enunciations in contingent matter, 108, 123

True and false enunciations explained, 74, 104, 107-8, 111

Varied in four ways, 74

Division into categorical and hypothetical, 21, 66

Three kinds of absolute *(de inesse)* enunciation, 143-44

Divided into three orders, 144-45

With an adjective verb, 147

How enunciations with infinite subjects are to be understood, 157

With transposed names and verbs, 158

Distinguished into its signification and mode of enunciating, 233

A twofold transmutation, positional and formal, 161

Four modes of multiple enunciation, 165

How unity of enunciation is realized with accidental predicates, 171-78

Diagram of equivalent enunciations, 153

See NAME, VERB, SPEECH, SUBJECT, PREDICATE, AFFIRMATION, NEGATION, UNIVERSAL ENUNCIATION, PARTICULAR ENUNCIATION, INDEFINITE ENUNCIATION, SINGULAR ENUNCIATION, MODAL ENUNCIATION

ERROR

How related to movement and change, 248

ETERNITY

Is wholly simultaneous existence, 118

EVERY

What *every* signifies, 82

Does not signify universal itself, but mode of universality, 85, 148

F

FALSITY

See TRUTH

FATE

Signifies a cause determined to one, inferring necessity in natural things, 114

FORM

Why Aristotle calls form something divine, 33

Difference is taken from form, 66

From form and matter something one comes to be, 66-67

Nothing mediates between form and matter, 67

As communicable to many matters, 79

FORTUITOUS

How reduced to order of divine providence, 116

FUTURE

Is that which will be present, 49, 128

Is extrinsic to the present, 75-76

Is in a certain way in its cause, 107

Is in its cause in three ways, 107

Man as a principle of future things, 112

See COGNITION, ENUNCIATION

G

GENUS

Taken from matter, 66

Differences dividing a genus do not fall in its definition, 72

GOD

See ETERNITY, COGNITION, BEING, INTELLECT, PROVIDENCE, WILL

GOOD

Some good desirable for itself, other good because of an end, 119

Whatever is good falls under divine will, 117

H

HERMINUS

Exposition of enunciations with a third element, 131

Explanation of diagram of indefinite and universal enunciations, 141

I

IDEA

Subsists only in the intellect, 25

IMAGINATION

Called *passive intellect* by Aristotle, 26

IMPERATIVE

A species of perfect speech, 61

IMPOSSIBLE

Defined, 113

Absolute and by supposition, 122

Impossible not to take place means *necessarily to take place*, 107, 122

INDEFINITE ENUNCIATION

What it is, 83, 86

Not to be taken as universal negative, 92-93

Diagrams of, 133, 136, 140

INDIVIDUAL, VAGUE

What it is, 83

INFINITE NAME

Not a name absolutely speaking, 41-42, 127

Signifies something one in a certain way, 127

Not truly a negation, 156

Signifies neither a determinate nature or person, 41

Can be said equally of being and nonbeing, 41

Imposed from a negation, 41

INSTRUMENT

Is that by which an agent operates, 58

Must be defined by its end, its use, 60

INTELLECT

Twofold operation of human intellect, 17, 30-31, 50, 60

Proper object of human intellect is what a thing is, 79

Forms certain intentions, 80

Does not know singulars, 116

Is instituted by man, 25, 39, 40

Differs from sounds signifying naturally, 39

Signifies without time, 46

No part of it signifies separated from whole, 39-40, 55, 57

Distinguished from speech, 39

A part of a composite name does not really signify, 40

Is a word, not an enunciation, 57, 70

Material part of speech, 45

Is affirmation or negation in potency, 57

Does not imply composition, 66

Can be posited on part of subject and predicate, 45

Signifies simple concept, 40, 55, 78

Composite names signify simple concepts, 34

Immediately signifies conceptions, 25, 78

What name signifies is definition, 28

Signifies substance of a thing, 37

Signifies accidental form as concrete in subject, 38

Signifies something per se existent, 45, 50

Every name signifies determinate nature or person, 41

One thing is signified by many names, 41

That from which name is imposed differs from what name signifies, 40

How assimilated to simple understanding with respect to truth, 34, 70

With addition of verb becomes true or false, 34, 42, 70

How when said alone, verb still understood, 34, 70

Divided into simple and composite, 39-40

Divided into finite and infinite, 126

Finite name is prior to infinite, 129

Universal and singular name, 78-79

Singular name signifies in two ways, 79

How singular name is equivocal, 79-80

Equivocal name signifies many, 51

How one name may be imposed on many from which one thing is not constituted, 164

NECESSITY (NECESSARY)

Defined, 113

That everything be by necessity is unlikely, 106-7

Absolute and by supposition, 122

In relation to contradiction, 122-23

Necessary to be and *impossible not to be* signify the same, 107, 122

Why the necessary is placed before the possible, 226

NEGATION

Defined by Aristotle, 72

Contains division, 22

Why called division, 31

Signifies *not to be* or *not to belong*, 22, 64, 71-72, 74

Not an integral part of enunciation, but a species, 21, 65, 72, 81

Divides enunciation equally with affirmation, 22, 65

According to proper notion, is posterior to affirmation, 22, 64-65, 128

Posterior to affirmation for three reasons, 64

Adds something to affirmation, 55, 64, 128

Is true or false, 74, 108

What one negation is, 98-99

Opposed per se to affirmation, 75

How a negative enunciation is realized, 128

In relation to infinite verbs, 48-49, 128

Never added to sign of universality or particularity, 148

How simple negation follows upon infinite affirmation, 154

Varying position of negation varies

quantity in universal enunciations, not in singular enunciations, 155

Infinite names and verbs not truly negations, 156

In relation to enunciations with transposed names and verbs, 160

See CONTRADICTION, CONTRARIETY, ENUNCIATION, OPPOSITION

NO

What *no* signifies, 82-83
As a syncategorematic term, 150

NOMINATIVE

S٦id principally in relation to name, 42

NOUN

See NAME

NUMBER

Is multitude measured by one, 65

O

ONE

Being and one are convertible, 64, 127

Divided into simple and composite, 71

One by composition is one from many, 69

Divided into one simply and one according to reason, 127

One made from many in three ways, 99

OPINION

Opinions not defined as contrary because they are about contrary objects, 238

Opposition of opinions according to affirmation and negation of same thing of same thing constitutes contrariety, 244, 252

False negative opinions are contrary to true affirmative opinions and conversely, 245

Taken in two ways: as representing things absolutely and as in opinions, 247

Called per se true or false in two ways, 248

No true opinion can be contrary to another true opinion, 255

OPPOSITES

What are not opposed can be together, 69

Must be about the same thing, 76

Taken in two ways, formally and denominatively, 182

OPPOSITION

Defined, 75-76, 96-97

Requisite conditions for, 75-76

Contrary vs. contradictory, 97-98

Subcontrary not strictly opposition, 90

Whether indefinite enunciations are opposed, 92, 97-98

Between singular enunciations, 97

Every affirmation has a negation opposed to it, 75, 127

Only one negation is opposed to one affirmation, 96-97

With respect to enunciations of a second or third element, 131

Truth and falsity of opposites, 98, 123-24

When subject is equivocal, 100

As modes of enunciating, two kinds among enunciations, contradictory and contrary, 233

By reason of signification, only opposition of contrariety in enunciations, 234

OPPOSITION OF MODAL ENUNCIATIONS

Whether made by negation added to verb of dictum, 193-95

Whether made by negation not added to verb of dictum, 195-96

Must be made by negation the mode, 199

Consequents following upon opposition of modal enunciations according to ancients, 205-6

Diagram of consequents predicating necessity, 207

Consequents following upon opposi-

[265]

tion of modal enunciations according to Aristotle, 215

Consequents following upon opposition of modal enunciations with the necessary placed first, 225-26

Diagram of opposition of equipollent modal enunciations, 231

OPTATIVE

Reduced to deprecative speech, 61

P

PART

Its meaning, 57

No part separated has form of whole, 39

How related to whole, 56

Division of whole into subjective, defining, and integral parts, 99

PARTICIPLE

Comprehended under verb, 21

Signifies substance as subjected to motion, 39

Signifies with time, 21, 39, 45

Can be posited on part of predicate and subject, 44

PARTICULAR ENUNCIATION

What it is, 82-83

What is required for its truth, 93

How equivalent in a certain way to indefinite enunciation, 129

PASSION

From impression of something acting, 24

Implies motion, 39

Verb signifies action and passion, 39

With its privation is in time, 48

In the instant, there is no action or passion, 49

Can be extended to all reception, 26

PAST

Said with respect to present, 49, 128

Is extrinsic to present, 75, 129

PERI HEREMENEIAS

How understood as On Interpretation, 17

Treats name and verb as parts of enunciation, 20

Ordered principally to demonstrate, 21

PER SE

Per se predicates opposed to accidental, 173

Referred to three things in relation to "predicated per se," 184-85

PHANTASM

Requires corporeal passion, 26

PHILO

On defining necessary, impossible, possible, and contingent, 113

PLATO

On relation of names to things, 41

On speech as natural, 58

Opinion on universal existing apart from mind, 79

Maintains species of things per se subsistent, 79, 80, 82

Did not distinguish privation from matter, 93

On the accidental as more ordered to nonbeing, 114

PLURALITY

How opposed to unity, 67

The plural (multiple) enunciation, 164-66

POETS

How they move listeners and induce assent, 62

PORPHYRY

On relation of writing to vocal sound, 26

On sameness of concepts for all, 28

Explanation of "if you were to say 'is' alone," etc., 51

Holds definition of speech applies to simple speech, 55

On definition of simple enunciation, 72

Dialectical question offers an option in answering, 168

See INTERROGATIVE

R

REASON

See INTELLECT

REST

Measured by time, 48

RHETORICIANS

How they move listeners and induce assent, 62

S

SCIENCE

Every science begins with treatment of principles, 20, 37

See DEMONSTRATION

SENSE

Does not compose or divide, 32

Sense powers accidentally subject to extrinsic influences, 115

SIGN

Division into natural and by institution, 27, 40

Natural sign is a likeness of the thing, 27

A natural sign is not made a sign, 40

Special signs designed for attributing to a universal universally or particularly, 82

Universal and particular; affirmative and negative, 82-83

Universal and particular signs belong more to the subject, 86-87

Many things can be signified under what is common, 69

SINGULAR

What is proper to it and what it shares with others, 78-79

Two modes of, 79

Something attributed to and denied of in three ways, 81

How something is predicated of singular, 83

Singular, contingent events, 103-4

Is called first substance, 78

SINGULAR ENUNCIATION

What it is, 80

Not diversified by singularity or universality of predicate, 83

Not all differences reflected in singular enunciations, 129

In singular enunciation, singular negation and infinite affirmation of of same subject are of same truth, 155

In singular enunciation, the varying position of the negation does not vary the quantity, 155

SOUNDS

Are not names, but names have sounds, 40-41

See VOCAL SOUNDS

SPECIES

Equally dividing a genus are simultaneous according to nature, 22

If separated in existence would be individual, 79

SPEECH (*Oratio*)

Defined, 54-55

Vocal sound not properly its genus, 22

As conventionally significant, 58-59

Signifies composite conception, 40

Some parts of it are significant separately, 40, 55-56

Its parts do not signify affirmation and negation in act, 57

Some speech is composed from names, some from verbs, 45

Only name and verb are principal parts, 21

All parts are referred principally to perfect speech, 56

Only enunciative speech properly called interpretation, 18

Is prior to enunciation, 22

Is genus of enunciation, 21, 65

Divided into perfect and imperfect, 56-61

Imperfect speech does not signify true and false, 61

Only perfect speech brings intellect to rest, 50

Five species of perfect speech, 61

Division into simple and composite, 56

STOICS

Teach nominatives to be cases, 42

Define necessary, possible, and impossible, 113

Hold all things to happen necessarily because of fate, 114

Hold many concurrent causes reduce to one per se cause, 114

SUBCONTRARY OPPOSITION

Subcontraries can be at once true in contingent matter, 152

See OPPOSITION

SUBJECT

Of enunciation signifies as that in which something inheres, 47

Is a material or integral part of enunciation, 37

Compared to predicate is a material part of enunciation, 67, 81, 86

Is a name or something in place of a name, 78, 127

Two kinds of multiple subjects, accidental and per se, 173

See ENUNCIATION, PREDICATE

SUBSTANCE

Considered in itself, not measured by time, 39

Aristotle holds second substances are only in first substances, 78

Is not univocal in being with accident, 65

SYLLABLES

As parts of names and verbs are not per se significant, 57

SYNCATEGOREMATIC TERMS

Signify only a relation of one thing to another, 55

Contrasted with categorematic terms, 149

T

THEOPHRASTUS

On enunciations with infinite predicate, 133

THING (Res)

Exists naturally and same for all men, 27

Related to intellect in two ways, 32

Related to divine intellect, 33

As signified by names, divided into universal and singular, 78

See INTELLECT

TIME

Three ways of considering, 39

To be measured by time is proper to motion, 46

Divided into present, past, and future, 74-75, 128

Other times said with respect to present, 49, 128

What signifying with time means, 46-47

TRANSMUTATION

Twofold in enunciation: positional and formal, 161

TRUTH

Must be in relation to intellect, 32

What it is to know truth, 33

Some truths are known per se, others not, 119

Divided into truth of things, intellect, vocal sound, and sense, 32-33

Being and truth are convertible, 31, 33

A thing is true in the way it has being, 107

How artificial things are true or false, 32

When thought is true or false, 32-33, 74

In mind as in a subject, 61

Only intellect knows truth, 33

Found in one operation of intellect, not in another, 30

Is found in intellect as composing and dividing, 30-34

First and highest truth is in divine intellect, 32, 34

Truth and falsity in vocal sound as in a sign, 33

Name or verb, said by itself, not true or false, 34

Only enunciative speech signifies true and false, 61

No truth of vocal sound without composition and division, 126

Relation of true ad false enunciation to being and nonbeing, 104, 108

Truth of enunciation is not cause of existence of things, 111

How sense is true, 33

Of modal enunciations and absolute enunciations, 200

U

UNITY

How unity of enunciation is realized with predicates said divisively, 171-78

Unity of name alone does not suffice for unity of enunciation, 99

Unity and multiplicity of enunciations, 164-66

UNIVERSAL

Defined logically, 79

Not something existing outside of the thing, 78

As it can be in many, and as not actually in many, 79

Four ways of attributing something to or denying of universal, 80, 82-83

What is attributed to things according to universal notions, 80-83

How universal is taken universally, 86

See PREDICATE

UNIVERSAL ENUNCIATION

What it is, 82-83

Prior to particular and containing it, 93, 96

Diagrams of, 140, 142

Truth of infinite universal affirmation does not follow from truth of negation of universal affirmative, 154

UNIVERSE

Has threefold grade, 227

V

VERB

Has being in three ways, 25

Definition and explanation of, 45-49

Signifies with time, 39, 46-47, 49, 132

Is always a sign of something predicated of another, 45, 47-48, 66, 126

How different from participle and name, 45

Distinguished from speech, 45

Definition of verb taken commonly, 48

A principle of interpretation rather than interpretation, 18

Is integral part of enunciation, 37

Implies composition, 45, 47-48

A certain formal part of speech, 45

Significant by human institution, 25

Always posited on part of predicate, 45, 47

Signifies something as existing in another, 48

Signifies action or passion, 39, 45-46, 48

Signifies as proceeding from a substance, 46

As such is not true or false, 34, 51

How understood as implicit composition, 34, 70

Substantive verb joined with name always signifies true or false, 42

How understood under name, 49-50

How infinite verb is constituted, 48-49, 128

Infinite verbs not truly negations, 156

See CASES OF VERBS

VOCAL SOUND

Defined, 38

Is something natural, 21-22, 25

Signification of vocal sound pertains to Logic, 24

Not all vocal sounds are significant, 25

Vocal sounds signify by human institution, 27

As sign of conception of intellect, 25, 27-28, 30, 33, 50

Signifies concept immediately, thing mediately, 25

How same for all, how not, 27

Twofold signification of, 55

VOCATIVE

A species of perfect speech, 61

What it expresses, 61

W

WILL

Necessarily adheres to good desirable for its own sake, 119-20

Freely chooses particular good, 119-20

Not the act of a corporeal organ, 115

Will of God as cause of order of things, 118

Will of God comprehends all good, 116

WORD

Aristotle imposes *word (phasis)* to signify parts of enunciation, 70

Simple words can be considered in three ways, 20

Signifies simple understanding, 55

How composite, 58

WRITING

Used to communicate to those distant and future, 24

Signs of spoken words, 26

MARQUETTE UNIVERSITY PRESS
Mediaeval Philosophical Texts in Translation

#1 - Grosseteste: On Light. Trans. by Clare Riedl. $5.95.

#2 - St. Augustine: Against the Academicians. Trans. by Sr. Mary Patricia Garvey, R.S.M. $7.95.

#3 - Pico Della Mirandola: Of Being and Unity. Trans. by Victor M. Hamm. $5.95.

#4 - Francis Suarez: On the Various Kinds of Distinction. Trans. by Cyril Vollert, S.J. $7.95.

#5 - St. Thomas Aquinas: On Spiritual Creatures. Trans. by Mary C. Fitzpatrick. $7.95.

#6 - Meditations of Guigo. Trans. by John J. Jolin, S.J. $7.95.

#7 - Giles of Rome: Theorems on Existence and Essence. Trans. by Michael V. Murray, S.J. $7.95.

#8 - John of St. Thomas: Outlines of Formal Logic. Trans. by Francis C. Wade, S.J. $7.95.

#9 - Hugh of St. Victor: Soliloquy in the Earnest Money of the Soul. Trans. by Kevin Herbert. $7.95.

#10 - St. Thomas Aquinas: On Charity. Trans. by Lottie Kendzierski. $7.95.

#11 - Aristotle On Interpretation: Commentary by St. Thomas and Cajetan. Trans. by Jean T. Oesterle. $7.95.

#12 - Desiderius Erasmus of Rotterdam: On Copia of Words and Ideas. Trans. by Donald B. King and H. David Rix. $7.95.

#13 - Peter of Spain: Tractatus Syncategorematum and Selected Anonymous Treatises. Trans. by Joseph Mullally and Roland Houde. $7.95.

#14 - Cajetan: Commentary on St. Thomas Aquinas' On Being and Essence. Trans. by Lottie Kendzierski and Francis C. Wade, S.J. $14.95.

#15 - Suarez: Disputation VI, On Formal and Universal Unity. Trans. by James F. Ross. $7.95.

#16 - St. Thomas, Siger of Brabant, St. Bonaventure: On The Eternity of the World. Trans. by Cyril Vollert, S.J., Lottie Kendzierski, Paul Byrne. $7.95.

#17 - Geoffrey of Vinsauf: Instruction in the Method and Art of Speaking and Versifying. Trans. by Roger P. Parr. $7.95.

#18 - Liber De Pomo: The Apple or Aristotle's Death. Trans. by Mary Rousseau.

#19 - St. Thomas Aquinas: On the Unity of the Intellect Against the Averroists. Trans. by Beatrice H. Zedler. $7.95.

#20 - The Universal Treatise of Nicholas of Autrecourt. Trans. by Leonard A. Kennedy, C.S.B., Richard E. Arnold, S.J., & Arthur E. Millward, A.M. $7.95.

#21 - Pseudo-Dionysius Aeropagite: The Divine Names and Mystical Theology. Trans. by John D. Jones.

#22 - Matthew of Vendome: Ars Versificatoria (The Art of the Versemaker). Trans. by Roger P. Parr. $9.95.

#23 - Suarez on Individuation, Metaphysical Disputation V: Individual Unity and Its Principle. Trans. by Jorge J.E. Gracia. $24.95.

#24 - Francis Suarez: On the Essence

of the Finite Being as Such, On the Existence of That Essence and Their Distinction. Trans. by Norman J. Wells. $24.95.

#25 - The Book Of Causes (Liber De Causis). Trans. by Dennis Brand. $7.95.

#26 - Giles of Rome: Errores Philosophorum. Trans. by John O.

Reidl. $7.95.

#27 - St. Thomas Aquinas: Questions on the Soul. Trans. by James H. Robb. $24.95.

#28 - William of Auvergne: De Trinitate. Trans. by Roland J. Teske, S.J., & Francis C. Wade, S.J. $19.95

Published by: Marquette University Press, Holthusen Hall, Marquette University, Milwaukee, WI 53233. **Manuscript submissions should be sent to:** Chair, MPTT Editorial Board, Dept. of Philosophy, Coughlin Hall, Marquette University, Milwaukee, WI 53233.